RELIGION IN PUBLIC

Cultural Memory
  in
  the
Present

Hent de Vries, Editor

RELIGION IN PUBLIC
Locke's Political Theology

Elizabeth A. Pritchard

STANFORD UNIVERSITY PRESS
STANFORD, CALIFORNIA

Stanford University Press
Stanford, California

© 2014 by the Board of Trustees of the Leland Stanford Junior University. All rights reserved.

No part of this book may be reproduced or transmitted in any form or by any means, electronic or mechanical, including photocopying and recording, or in any information storage or retrieval system without the prior written permission of Stanford University Press.

Library of Congress Cataloging-in-Publication Data

Pritchard, Elizabeth A. (Elizabeth Ann), author.
  Religion in public : Locke's political theology / Elizabeth A. Pritchard.
    pages cm — (Cultural memory in the present)
  Includes bibliographical references and index.
  ISBN 978-0-8047-8575-4 (cloth : alk. paper)
  ISBN 978-0-8047-8576-1 (pbk. : alk. paper)
    1. Locke, John, 1632–1704—Religion. 2. Political theology. 3. Secularism.
I. Title. II. Series: Cultural memory in the present.
B1298.R4P75 2013
322'.1092—dc23

2013013419

ISBN 978-0-8047-8887-8 (electronic)

Contents

	Acknowledgments	ix
	Introduction	1
1	Fashionable Religion	14
2	Wordish Ways and Ritual Bodies	36
3	Liberal Political Theology	59
4	Force at a Distance	83
5	Secular Family Values	107
6	They're Only Words, But They're Killing Me Softly	133
	Notes	155
	Bibliography	195
	Index	215

Acknowledgments

This book has been a long time in the making. I wish to acknowledge the following people for helping me to place this book in your hands. My colleagues John Holt and Jorunn Buckley gave me the push I needed to get to the next level. Bowdoin College, and specifically the Faculty Development Committee, provided financial support for a year's sabbatical for research. I thank Suzanne Cunningham Dickie and Paul Franco for reading draft proposals. I am very grateful to Elizabeth Castelli and Kathleen Roberts Skerrett for encouraging me to get this material out to publishers. I thank the anonymous reviewers, who provided such detailed reports and generous praise. Tyler Roberts provided just the words I needed to hear for a difficult chapter. Larisa Reznik inspires me to be a better thinker and teacher. Editor Emily-Jane Cohen and assistants Emma S. Harper and Tim Roberts are the epitome of professionalism, timeliness, responsiveness, and grace; Mimi Braverman came through with a quick and thorough copyediting job. Lynn Brettler is a dream of a departmental coordinator. I thank Colin Beckman for bibliographic support. Chick Pritchard and Pam Pritchard celebrated with me and kept tabs all along the way. Props to Dan Pritchard for continually hounding me about this project. My heartfelt gratitude to Cheryl Frodermann for being a consistently dear and supportive friend. A long-overdue thank you to John Hladky for allowing me to carve out time to get this done. Finally, to Jack, Calla, and Madeleine, for sharing with me all the joys and drama of youth.

RELIGION IN PUBLIC

Introduction

Stories of secularization routinely read as enormous cleanup operations. Mixed-up religious and political powers are finally extricated and confined to their respective rooms, possessive spirits are sent packing, liminal and festive orgies are curtailed, and boundaries are installed all around to prevent the indiscriminate mixing that would confound the aspirations of rational actors, nation-states, and capitalist markets. In this book I turn this conventional wisdom on its head and offer a reading of secularization as the promotion of the worldliness of religion. Thus, rather than seeing secularization as requiring the privatization of religion, I argue that secularization is religion placed into circulation. Moreover, I argue that such a project is advocated by John Locke (1632–1704) as part of a political theology.

Locke is frequently summoned to justify readings of the secular as entailing the privatization of religion. His distinction between state and church is linked with those between public and private, and body and soul, and it is widely assumed that Locke simply tucks religion into the second categories of these ready-made pairs. The problem is that these categorical distinctions and their attendant meanings are taken for granted. It is assumed that these are binary oppositions, that they represent well-known and distinct orders, places, or operations, and that they have remained largely unchanged for more than 300 years. In my reading of Locke I do not take these terms as settled but in the process of formation. Rather than confining religion—as though this category, too, was a settled one—to a private, even internal and individual, space of belief, I argue that Locke recasts religion as the basis of the distinction between private and public. Locke's political theology endows humans, as the property of the divine, with an inalienable transcendence that grounds rights, and promotes the conversion of "religion" into persuasions and fashions, suitable for circulation, debate, and judgment in the public sphere.

For his part Locke did not regularly use the distinction between public and private, and they do not easily map onto his distinction between civil and ecclesiastic power or between magistrate and conscience. Locke suggests that private matters are those that have no bearing on others. This suggests that he would regard as public that which has a bearing on others, such as when he insists that the prerogative of the magistrate must be directed to the public good. Although the public is sometimes conflated with the political or with the state, I agree with Charles Taylor that the modern public functions as an independent check on political power. My sense is that Locke is looking to promote a public or civil society distinct from the state. He refers to public meetings or civil assemblies in "cities," "courts," and "markets." He also disagrees with the assumption that civil assemblies are consistently public and open to everyone, whereas religious assemblies are necessarily private.[1] Moreover, Locke is adamant that the highest duty for everyone (including the magistrate) is to attempt to persuade others as to what one regards as religious truth. This indicates that Locke envisions religion, including religious difference and dissent, to be precisely the sort of thing that ought to go public.

Locke never loses sight of the idea that the challenges, risks, and opportunities posed by differences are not merely epistemological—nor, in my view, should we. This point is frequently overlooked. For instance, Lee Ward acknowledges that Locke never asserts the necessity to privatize religion, only the need to transform religion from "self-justifying moral absolutes into probabilistic claims and contestable premises amenable to discursive engagement."[2] This statement does not capture the stakes of Locke's endeavor; moral absolutes may indicate inflexibility, but they are nonetheless the stuff of intellectual and discursive engagement. Ward's analysis reflects a recurring assumption that religious conflict is about competing claims to incommensurable truths. In other words, religious conflict is a matter of debate. But this is not an accurate characterization of Locke's context. At the time of Locke's writing, religion's ability to affiliate bodies across vast spaces or to segregate them despite close quarters was unrivaled. Religion determined which bodies ate together, traded, prayed, married, had sex, and made bodies that would, in turn, belong to the religious body of their parents. If emergent nation-states and their colonial satellites were to succeed at creating sturdy affiliations above, across, or alongside religious bodies, they would have to reconfigure religion's hold on bodies, not pretend that religion and the body would simply part company. In Locke's context, then, religion is not already extricated from the body and its attendant valences of force, infection, sexuality, family, and polity. Thus the challenge was (and still is) to enable divergent bodies and ideas to circulate and even link up without (or at least with a significantly reduced risk of) offense or injury.

If pressed to construe my account of Locke in terms of relevant binaries, then the key ones here are that of body and sign and coercive or punitive power versus persuasive power. Locke certainly looks to dissociate religion and bodies. He argues that true religion is not a weapon pointed at bodies, nor is it instantiated in the wasteful labor of religious ritual. For Locke religion's coin is that of opinion, argument, persuasion, and fashion. Locke's attempt to create some distance between individuals and their religiosities may be seen as an early critique of "identity politics." Yet Locke's reluctance to rely on words and fashions to create linkages between individuals prompts not only a sophisticated reckoning of the valences of power associated with body and communication but also recurrent attempts to enlist the body in order to secure a political order. Given his ongoing negotiation with religion, body, speech, and power, Locke challenges accounts of the secular that portray it as the progressive translation of religion into speech, that is, contestable truth claims. These accounts draw on the binary of body and speech to portray religious individuals as bound up with their religiosity and secular individuals as enjoying a critical and voluntary distance from such obligations. Saba Mahmood draws on this assumption to argue that liberal secularists cannot recognize the *felt* injury of blasphemy.[3] C. John Sommerville describes secularization as the transition from religion as woven into the fabric of life to religion as a conscious set of beliefs or faith; in other words from religion as a manner of being or "culture" or "birthright religion" to religion as something objective, that is, a reasoned faith.⁴ One might shorthand these descriptions of the secular as entailing religion's shift from the body to speech. These authors, however, have not noticed that several early modern writers, including and especially Locke, used this language of shifting from religion as identity or body to religion as speech and "fashion." They have not discussed the theological, political, and economic *motivations* that drove this reconstruction of religion. Nor have they unpacked the debates and anxieties that attended (and continue to attend) these particular shifts. What has to be accounted for are the struggles over religion's secularization, that is, religion being lifted up and away from bodies, families, properties, and polities and reconstructed as speech, text, argument, and even fashion. This book is a partial installment of such an accounting.

I acknowledge that it is unusual to insist on the secular (rather than toleration) as the point of entry into Locke. Yet, on the specific topic of toleration, Locke's arguments are neither innovative nor determinative. Relatedly, Alexandra Walsham has shown that it is a serious misrepresentation to see early modernity as the onset of unmitigated progress toward toleration. Rather, she points to numerous instances as indicating the symbiotic relationship between persecution and toleration.⁵ Moreover, when one invokes "toleration," one conjures either a government policy of neutrality toward religion or a personal virtue of putting up with others with differing tastes and habits. I wish to draw attention to the ways in which Locke's project reflects and advocates transformations in religion, family, and the political. The secular is not something that "happens" only to "religion." Thus I prefer the term *secular* insofar as it indicates the broader scope I spy in Locke's project.⁶

My definition of the secular as worldly may strike readers as simultaneously unremarkable and peculiar. It is, after all, hardly a stretch if one simply consults a thesaurus. Nevertheless, reading the secular as worldly allows me to interrupt the frequent associations of the secular with the irreligious or as the opposite of whatever it is that religion is. Another advantage of reading the secular as worldly is that it avoids the prejudicial connotations of "profane" and disrupts the association of the secular with intellectualist or rationalist preoccupations.⁷ I do not envision the secular as a fall or disenchantment or as a coming to critical consciousness or rationalization. My reading of the secular has little in common with those accounts that portray the secular as a definitive and singular turning point of linear progress toward enlightenment and emancipation.

I agree that the secular is multidimensional, contextual, and thus plural. I also appreciate recent critiques that challenge the notion of secularity as a foregone conclusion or as nebulous processes that are difficult to distinguish from an equally amorphous but no less teleological modernity.[8] At the same time it is undeniable that what Locke (and the related sources I consult) has to say about religion reflects the broader context of early modern England: market expansion, colonialist governance, standardization of monetary policies, and tremendous growth in both population and publishing.

Although Locke uses the word *secular* perhaps only once, he is an advocate of worldliness.[9] He seeks to expand England's capitalist market, to which end he is for relaxing immigration, rewarding large, productive families, and expanding colonization. Locke wants bodies, including the bodies of strangers and foreigners, to come into close contact, trade, produce more bodies, labor to sustain the increasing pool of bodies, and consent to political incorporation. In other words, Locke is for promiscuity, of a sort. After all, he has individual bodies consenting to constitute one large body: the commonwealth of England. Because Locke does not want religion to impede the circulation of bodies, he reconstructs religion. Locke argues that religion is not sedimented in bodies or in recalcitrant wills; nor is it passed along in families, much like inheritable property. He does not, however, reduce it to belief or insist on its inner or private character. Locke does not entomb religion in the mind but places it into *circulation*. In doing so, he retains the character of religion as a variant of communication and force, even as it becomes available for consumption by a broader and more diverse people or public.

Locke is not looking to keep religion out of a preexistent public but to reconfigure religion so as to facilitate the making of modern publics. In such publics assorted speech acts and individuals come together in discursive and physical spaces; affiliations, however fleeting or lasting, range more broadly—yet with a dramatically decreased risk of perceived profanation or pollution, offense or injury. Surely such indiscriminate mixing calls for more effective security measures.[10] But what accounts for this improved security? I suggest that Locke was convinced that it would require more than a strong and "neutral" state. It would require consensus that the purpose of the law is, above all else, to protect all the people in a given polity. Such a consensus does not consist simply in the submission of religion to the rule of law. In Locke's context understandings of divine power had long qualified as law and had long justified the use of force. It would be facile to imagine that religion might be simply privatized, as though it was of no consequence. I suggest, then, that the Lockean secular is no simple disentanglement of the religious and political; rather, it requires that divine power and the relationship between divine and human power be reimagined and made to drive new visceral investments.

In Locke's political theology religion no longer incorporates and sacralizes political bodies. Religion no longer warrants or justifies injury of bodies. Locke envisions members of polities as alternately feeling together (consent) and feeling apart (dissent); accordingly, he seeks to balance affiliation and difference. Locke insists on a theological consensus as the basis for robust and public religious dissensus. Consensus that humans are the inalienable (and thus sacred) property of a benevolent creator God funds the imagination of selves with inviolable recesses—recesses that summon (or indict) political power as articulated in the various instruments of human rights and that serve as prophylaxes against the repeated exposure, indiscriminate mixing, and clamorous debate of modern publics. In other words, Locke's political theology does not privatize religion but rather draws from religion to ground the distinction between private and public. Locke's political theology constructs the difference between what is inalienable and what is alienable. What is inalienable is the property claim the Father God has on each individual; this is the sacred *patrimony* that grounds rights; everything else is, upon consent (and a fair price), up for discussion and up for grabs.

The center of gravity in Locke's religious marketplace is the Father God who lays claim to humans as their creator. Thus, whereas Locke promotes religion as alienable and convertible, this brisk trade is stabilized by the consensus that each human, as a creature of God, is the bearer of an inviolable and inalienable transcendence that cannot be subsumed, enslaved, or destroyed. In addition, this same God has yielded punishing power to humans and no longer threatens humans with the specter of eternal punishment. This God has no need to have his honor avenged; no purported heretics need be punished or killed to preempt their own and others' eternal punishment. Locke's political theology is a softer patriarchalism. Like his deity, Locke's human patriarch (political and familial) is also made beholden to the protection of human bodies or properties. The state is not exactly neutral, then, but receives its legitimacy precisely through its recognition of citizens as divinely endowed with inalienable rights.

Locke provides a thorough rethinking of God's power as complementary to his political philosophy of consent. Indeed, Locke's writings on religion, theology, political theory, and epistemology continually return to the issue of force or power. What I find most instructive about reading Locke without the encumbrances of the binaries of church and state, soul and body, and private and public, is discovering just how keen he is to the ambience and variation of force. Locke is adamant that the difference between church and state is a difference in power. But for Locke this is not a case of powerlessness and powerful; rather, it is about types of power. For Locke church, public, and state employ *persuasive* power; the state alone employs *punitive* power. Yet beyond these Locke also describes the absolutely compelling force of empirical knowledge and emotional trauma as well as the possessive force of childhood experiences and lessons. He summons the liberty, as well as the public censure and judgment, signified by "fashion." Moreover, he is sensitive to the subtleties of force in persuasive power that can feel like "rough usage"; he acknowledges that words can be weapons, and when challenged, insists, much like he does with regard to political power, on the necessity of consenting to such encounters.

Locke's God represents power (both the unmistakable force of sensible data, such as the fact that one cannot avoid seeing the sun, and the solicitous, reciprocating character of consensual power), and Locke is prepared to employ power to inculcate his political theology. But, again, the power or force in question is varied and subtle and, Locke implies, does not violate consent (which is not to say that Locke is beyond challenge on this or that there are not troubling tensions in his work). He recognizes the right of appeal to God to justify rebellion; he urges the social and economic shunning of atheists; he lists those who cannot be tolerated (albeit he does not mention punishment); he endorses, as state policy, religious education for various "outliers" (the able-bodied poor, Natives, and African slaves); and he develops a detailed pedagogy for instilling his political theology in children. I suggest that Locke's pedagogical writings are an early instantiation of what Foucault has argued with regard to the rise of a rule of "governmentality" in the eighteenth century: that the patriarchal family shifts from being a model of appropriate rule to being deployed as a tool for producing self-governing subjects. Indeed, Locke calls "religious" that power which insinuates itself early and deeply, before the onset of articulate speech. In other words, Locke wants it both ways: religion lifted up and away from the body and subject to reentering that body only by consent, and religion embedded deeply into the body before consent is even at issue.

My logic here is somewhat similar to that of Ethan Shagan, who argues that during the course of seventeenth-century England, "toleration" went from being widely regarded as extremist to "moderate"; moderation entailed not calm or temperance but the active constraint of excess. Shagan specifically mentions Locke's denunciations of licentiousness and debauchery in his arguments for toleration.[11] I envision Locke's and others' condemnations of promiscuity as evidence not simply of the restraint entailed in toleration but of a more encompassing anxiety triggered by social, religious, economic, and political dislocations. Locke offers, I suggest, strategies for cultural and subjective formation that will both capitalize on and offset these dislocations of the secular. In other words, I regard Locke as consistently seeking to mitigate the very risks he courts: a sacred patrimony to enable religious dissensus and ground rights; a political and theological justification of consent to manage circulating currents of force; and a softened familial and political patriarchalism to curb promiscuous publics. Thus, on the one hand, Locke beckons subjects to break free from the patriarchal reproduction of political, religious, and sexual orders and to seek forms of intimacy unbent to immediate political and familial agendas. On the other hand, his incipient encouragements to promiscuity alternate with restriction, protection, and confinement. Perhaps, then, it is best to speak in terms of a "dialectic of the secular" (to echo the title of the famous Horkheimer and Adorno book, *Dialectic of Enlightenment*). In this telling the secular is characterized not by towering walls or even sturdy boundaries but by countervailing pressures. It is characterized not by a feeling of freedom but by ambivalence.

What follows is, however, no origin story. I do not claim that Locke is responsible for the secular.[12] Rather, in loosening the grip of a dominant reading of Locke's relationship to contemporary conflicts as consisting in the struggle to privatize religion, I wish to highlight less noticed features of contemporary struggles over religion. Thus I draw suggestive parallels between Locke's political theology and contemporary conflicts. These parallels consist in ongoing struggles over religion's commodification, circulation, and depreciation as mere persuasion or fashion, the surreptitious reliance on familial inculcation of religion to cement societal and political bonds, debates about the force of religion, especially in relation to religious speech and proselytization, and the influence and institutionalization of universal human rights. I do not enter into exhaustive discussion of these correlations. I touch on a couple here and there and devote the final chapter to developing the issue of force and religious speech in the context of an apparent hegemony of human rights. My hope is to be suggestive of future projects that might experiment with configurations of secular conflicts that no longer bow to the public-private logic attributed to Locke.

I do not presume that my interpretation of Locke's oeuvre yields Locke's real intentions. Rather, I reconstruct what I take to be a coherent and plausible reading of Locke's published and unpublished writings. I acknowledge shifts in his thinking between earlier and later phases of his writings. I also point out tensions and contradictions where relevant. I have sought to provide historical contextualization for those aspects of his work on which my reinterpretation is most dependent, for example, his conversion of religion to opinion, argument, and fashion, his denunciations of promiscuous behavior, and his consequent return to the family in his pedagogy. Thus, on these points I trace related debates among Locke's interlocutors and highlight pertinent themes in contemporaneous literary sources.

My argument builds and expands on that body of work which highlights the centrality of theology in Locke's corpus.[13] What I add to these arguments is a detailed linkage between Locke's theology and his avowal of human rights, a careful delineation of Locke's understanding of the relationship between God, religion, and power, and a reassessment of contemporary liberalism in light of my reconstruction of Locke's political theology. I draw from unexpected sources (e.g., Locke's puzzling discussion of miracles and his widely influential pedagogy) and from expected ones (Locke's debates with Proast and his writings on the law of nature) to show that Locke sought to make congruent divine power and consensual political power. Although there are commonalities between my account and those who spy in Locke the makings of a civil religion, I argue that Locke's project is more accurately termed a political theology rather than a civil religion.[14]

To assert that Locke produces a political theology is to court the question of what is Christian about Locke's project and, more generally, about my reading of the secular. Sommerville describes secularization processes as reflecting a Protestant desire to "purify" religion from other cultural sectors. Talal Asad sees the secular as entailing the interiorization of religion as "faith" or "belief," which he attributes to the dominance of Protestant Christianity. Locke's project is rooted in monotheism, but he repudiates much of Christian theology (e.g., original sin, the centrality of the will, incarnation, atonement). He feels compelled to cite and interpret scripture in formulating his vision of God's power, but he is far from being a biblical literalist and explicitly condemns this in the education of children. I agree that there is an isomorphic relationship between types of Protestant Christianity and secular projects to convert religions into discursive, textual, and even spiritual formations and delineate a common denominator underlying particular "manifestations" of religion. This certainly puts certain strands of Christianity at an advantage and other strands and religions at a clear disadvantage. At the same time it is important to keep the following points in mind. First, Christianity is not a monolith reflecting an essentialized logic. Second, it is important to acknowledge just how broad the category "Protestant" is. Third, Christianities are also subject to the disciplinary mechanisms of market forces, multimedia, and the concomitant global flows of peoples. Fourth, analyses of the secular that amount to smoking out Christian loyalties or affinities underestimate the multidimensionality of the secular and mistakenly assume that this kind of critique amounts to an overcoming of or at least critical leverage over the secular. That Locke's worldly religion takes shape amid his immersion in Christian theological sources is undeniable. So too is the fact that much of the backlash directed against forced religion, which I discuss in Chapter 6, involves Christianity. My aim, however, is to convey the complexity and persistent tensions of the secular and not simply track the not so secret collusions between Christianity and secularization.

For John Dunn, what is living or relevant in Locke is certainly not his Christian theological baggage; in the end, Dunn decides that only Locke's contractarian approach to political authority is still firmly alive.[15] But this view reflects presuppositions about the secular that are not beyond challenge. Locke remains relevant not just because he is continually appropriated to authorize various readings of the secular but because he countenances the force of religion and because he knows that the political does not consist in overcoming or segregating religion but in staging their mutual authorization.

In Chapter 1 I reconstruct Locke's argument that true religion's primary medium is not bodies but rather persuasion and argumentation. Locke is seeking to make dissent nonthreatening and to have diverse bodies consent to productive interaction. In other words, Locke's true religion is of a piece of his promotion of the economic and political mixing of bodies in an enriched England and its enlarged colonies. Adherents of Locke's true religion no longer *identify* with their religion but rather have a measure of critical distance toward it as fashion or mere persuasion. Religious claims are to be placed in circulation, as other competing market goods and political claims are, and are to be submitted to the discipline of public opinion. I then draw on my reading of Locke's efforts to reconfigure religion to explain more recent patterns of conflict over religion that defy framing as skirmishes over the boundaries of public and private.

In Chapter 2 I discuss the debates surrounding the emergence of a discursive and textual culture, specifically, the issue of whether authority is passed through bodies or texts. In doing so, I establish that the conversion of religions into arguments, texts, and fashions was not peculiar or uncontroversial. The writers I assemble here are interlocutors, critics, and fans of Locke—for example, John Tillotson, John Sergeant, Isaac Watts, and Moses Mendelssohn. I examine and compare these writers' attempts at reconnecting religion and the body through ritual and inherited tradition to establish and augment societal and political obligation.

In Chapter 3 I attempt to explain why Locke insists that "the taking away of God, tho but even in thought, dissolves all." I argue that Locke sees human rights as grounded on the supposition that humans are the bearers of an inalienable transcendence qua property of God. I note affinities between Locke's political theology and that of covenant theologians and also delineate the ways in which Locke's political theology resists categorization. I show that Locke repudiated a punitive and juridical deity and sought instead to make God's power compatible with his understanding of legitimate political authority. I conclude by comparing Locke's political theology to that of Carl Schmitt, addressing Schmitt's objection to what he terms liberalism's neutralization of the political.

In Chapter 4 I take up Jonas Proast's challenge to Locke regarding the imperative of force for true religion. Although a number of commentators have found Locke's apparent rebuttal of Proast unsatisfactory, I draw out that Locke concedes Proast's point: the efficacy of force in religious matters. I connect this concession with the ubiquity and subtlety of force throughout his corpus: in his epistemology and in his discussion of rhetoric and religious speech. Nonetheless, Locke insists that such force be authorized through consent. At the same time, I discuss those instances in which Locke was willing to bypass consent in converting individuals to the gospel of "sacred property."

In Chapter 5 I first set the context for Locke's return to the family as a conduit for his political theology (after having argued that true religion was not passed down through families). I draw on seventeenth-century literary sources (especially English comedies) to illustrate the anxieties that attended the actual and imagined familial, sexual, economic, social, and political realignments brought on by colonialism, religious conversions, expanding markets, and emergent urban publics. A number of these explorations end with a rededication to patriarchal familial arrangements. Similarly, Locke challenges traditional familial arrangements by insisting that religion is not inherited, but he backs away from the repercussions of such liberty by calling on parents to pass on to their children a benevolent yet ever watchful deity and to liken his and their power so as to make submission to power feel natural, inevitable. I conclude by examining Locke's recommendations in light of both William James's and Stephen Macedo's understanding of the role of religion in the formation of modern citizens.

In the sixth and final chapter I move into the contemporary period to sketch recurrent conflicts over the force of religious speech—conflicts that have led a number of scholars to describe the contemporary context as riddled with holy wars. I suggest that such conflicts indicate the difficulty of distinguishing word and body, persuasion and force, and war and politics in the secular context. Moreover, these conflicts persist despite or perhaps in part because of the near universal consensus as to the preeminence of human rights. In conclusion, I analyze the affinities between John Rawls's overlapping consensus and my reconstruction of Locke's political theology. I do so to highlight the sources of sacrality that continue to animate liberal secularism and to evaluate whether they are sufficient for distinguishing holy wars from politics.

1

Fashionable Religion

Stanley Fish insists that the debates on the separation of church and state have "not advanced one millimeter beyond the terms established by John Locke."[1] Moreover, he argues that Locke's use of the Christian binary of body and soul entailed his reconstruction of religion as private belief. Fish blames this Lockean legacy for the fact that contemporary liberal theorists consistently seek to keep religious participants and their arguments out of the political process.[2] Paul Morris also blames Locke, among others, for his embrace of a metaphysical dualism of mind and body, in which religion is privatized and in which "politics is the management of bodies."[3] Morris's most poignant concern in this regard—and one not to be dismissed—is his claim that by confining religions to the margins of privacy, liberalism effectively marginalizes its ideological rivals. In addition, Fish and Morris insist that liberalism cannot claim the high ground of neutrality; liberalism is as much a disciplinary regime bent on inculcation as are the religious communities it aspires to rise above.

Locke is also faulted for liberalism's inability to contend with the rise of global militant religiosities. Mark Juergensmeyer, whose writings have examined the rise of religious nationalism and religious terror around the globe, has sought to mediate some of the differences between these movements and modern liberal democracies. He speaks to the fact that members of liberal democracies are flummoxed by contemporary combinations of religion and violence and surprised that political parties with explicitly religious agendas are winning adherents and even elections. To account for this failure of understanding on the part of citizens of liberal democracies, he observes that "the ideas of John Locke about the origins of civil community . . . had the effect of taking religion—at least Church religion—out of public life."[4] Juergensmeyer does not explain what he means by distinguishing "religion" from "Church religion." Nor does he elaborate on what he means by the "public life" from which religion has been evacuated. Perhaps for Juergensmeyer public life is not synonymous with civil society or politics but with "the state."

According to Clayton Crockett and Creston Davis, Locke does not simply privatize religion; he banishes it to the mind. They conclude that, post-Locke, religion is not even to be talked about.

Faith, on Locke's view, does not actually exist in any material or concrete way; for it only ever exists "in the mind." Faith is thus an idealized non-thing or even void. Thus, Locke moves faith away from a "way of life" that is public and inextricably political to an internal disposition that is literally nothing at all. Consequently, the communal aspect of religious faith is utterly abolished, and *religion is removed from a public discourse altogether.*[5]

For Crockett and Davis the public realm is aligned with space, efficacy, influence, and power. Locke's removal of religion from the public means that religion is not to be heard or seen; it is not supposed to take place or take up space. Religion is nowhere and therefore nothing.

I agree with these critics that Locke's influence is still very much with us. I am convinced, however, that Locke's strategies for securing religious toleration are more complicated than his critics describe. I am further convinced that unpacking this complexity offers resources for understanding and addressing the contemporary conflicts that beset secularization.

I argue that Locke embarked on a reconfiguration of religion. Such a reconfiguration goes way beyond either recommending tolerance as a virtue or advocating a policy of toleration predicated on a separation of church and state. Locke develops a political theology that transcendentalizes sacrality so as to enable religious dissent to circulate publicly. Locke's political theology is predicated on a consensus on the sacrality of humans qua property of God. It is this consensus that grounds human rights, more specifically, the liberty and equality of all human beings. Locke's political theology entails a repudiation of all political theologies in which the divine inheres in certain bodies or

16   *Fashionable Religion*

literally in scriptures, in which God is susceptible to injury and whose majesty requires avenging that injury.

This theological consensus on sacrality makes possible the translation of *religions* into opinions and fashions, subject to consensual trade and dispute, and posing no risk to bodies—individual or corporate. Locke does not entomb religion in the mind but places it into *circulation*. Locke does not privatize religion but converts it to *public speech*.[6] Thus, although Locke used the term *secular* perhaps once, I argue that his conversion of religion amounts to making religion secular, that is, making religion worldly.[7] Religion was to be subject to public censure and dispute.

The specific contours of Locke's political theology is a topic for a later chapter (Chapter 3). In this chapter I first discuss Locke's specific remarks on religion and privacy. Second, I set these remarks within the context of changing communicative practices that mark a transformation in the practice and understanding of publicness. Third, I discuss Locke's efforts to reconstruct religion so that it is coincident with (rather than in opposition to) the increasing circulation of ideas and people in early modern England and its colonies. Locke repudiates dominant portrayals of religion in which religion is aligned with the will or body. He insists instead that religion is speech and argument which makes appeal to the understanding and that religious differences and alterations are analogous to fashions. Religion as a species of signs is lifted up and away from bodies; it no longer links them across generations as families, "races," or churches of the elect; nor does it point toward them as weapons. Time and again Locke insists that religion neither forces nor injures[8]—not because it is to be privatized or turned into an inert faith, I submit, but because it will be constituted by circulating signs and styles. Nonetheless, as I elaborate in the concluding section of this chapter, Locke's reconstruction of religion as speech and fashion retains religion's proximity to the body and its ambience of power.

The idea that Locke's political platform was responsible, in part, for sweeping religion from the public sphere and into the private is absurd when one considers, for instance, that in the early modern Netherlands, Catholics and Jews could not have public houses of worship or hold public office.[9] Similarly, throughout Europe Socinian and Quaker meetings of any size were forbidden and their writings were prohibited from circulating. In his *Letter Concerning Toleration* Locke asks, "If we allow the *Jews* to have private Houses and Dwellings amongst us, Why should we not allow them to have Synagogues? Is their Doctrine more false, their Worship more abominable, or is the Civil Peace more endangered, by their meeting in *publick* than in their private Houses?" (54; second italics added). Despite this crystal clear repudiation of religion's privatization, numerous interpreters of Locke would have us believe that Locke insisted that the peace of civil society necessitated religion's retreat to private spaces. Indeed, toleration is superfluous if religions are privatized. What is left to tolerate if religion is hidden behind doors or sequestered in hearts and minds?

Locke nowhere provides a systematic definition of private and public. In certain instances he seems to regard private matters as those that have no bearing on others or in which there are no overlapping jurisdictions. The selection of a marriage partner for a family member qualifies as private, as do individuals and churches in relation to one other.[10] The key distinction between church and state is not that of private and public but in their respective use of force. Governmental or magisterial power is distinguished by "prescribing laws and compelling by punishment." Therefore the ultimate aim of religion (the care of souls) must not be corrupted by legislating or punishing certain religious convictions and practices. This does not mean that Locke thinks that care of souls, or religion, is wholly private or that the magistrate must be neutral and cannot care about religion. Indeed, Locke enjoins all people, including the magistrate, to attempt to persuade fellow citizens of their religious error. He writes, "Charitable care which consists in teaching, admonishing, and persuading, cannot be denied unto any man." The constant effort to persuade individuals as to the error of their ways is, according to Locke, "the greatest Duty of a Christian."[11] Religious power is persuasive power. Locke is not looking to sequester religion but to alter the force associated with it.

Indeed, Locke is not just permitting religion in public; he is insisting on it. Locke nowhere suggests that religion's mere publicity constitutes harm and its privacy, safety. Note that Locke insists that the "taking away of God, *tho but even in thought*, dissolves all."[12] Moreover, Locke spies danger in religions driven to privacy: "When, therefore, *men herd themselves into companies with distinctions from the public*, and a stricter confederacy with those of their own denomination and party than other [of] their fellow subjects, whether the distinction be religious or ridiculous matters not, otherwise than as the ties of religion are stronger, and the pretences fairer and apter to draw partisans, and therefore the more to be suspected and the more heedfully to be watched."[13] The particular danger of religious partisanship is avoided by publicizing religion. Locke believed that religions could be erroneous, ridiculous, and dangerous; the way to regulate them was to encourage their subjection to the judgmental and disciplinary pressure of the law of opinion.[14] Better to have a religious position aired and challenged than to have it fester, mislead, and mobilize resistance in private.

Locke no more relegates religion to privacy than he reduces knowledge to innate ideas. Locke repudiates the inwardness and presumptuousness of "innate ideas." For him all knowledge is produced by data from the world without. So, too, his ideal of reason is that it entails subjection to the scrutiny of public argumentation. Like his friend Robert Boyle (1627–1691), Locke envisions reason, and the scientific method specifically, as eminently public practices. Rationality for these writers was not a coincident characteristic of privilege but one of probative arguments. Thus, whether Locke is discussing the production of knowledge or upright Christian citizens, he favors the scrutiny and sharing entailed in public argumentation.

Moreover, Locke's insistence on the appropriately public character of religious speech was in keeping with contemporary trends in publishing. One must not lose sight of the sheer quantity of printed texts produced in seventeenth-century England. More texts were produced in the twenty-year period of 1640–1660 than in the prior history of printing in England from 1485 to 1640. In 1642 alone, 2,134 items were published, most of which were about religion.[15] In the midst of this near explosion of the publication of religious debate, does anyone really think that Locke was looking to put the genie back in the bottle and privatize religion? Locke's writings on religion must be read against the backdrop of seventeenth-century changes in communicative practices—changes that David Zaret convincingly argues mark the emergence of the modern public sphere. This emergence is marked by several developments: the shift from norms of secrecy and privilege to appeals to public opinion, the recognition of the right to petition the government, and printing's imposition of dialogical order on political (and religious) conflict.[16] This imposition of dialogical order offset sixteenth-century English Puritans' fear of the public as a "multitude," a many-headed monster beholden to Satan.[17] At the same time, members of the English monarchy worried that repeated exposure to publications showcasing religious argument instructed readers to fancy themselves as interpreters and nudged them to formulate their own opinions. In short, whether it was welcomed or vilified, the printing and circulation of religious dissent was recognized as tremendously powerful. As John Foxe was to remark in 1570: "The Lord began to Work for his Church, not with Sword and Target, to subdue his exalted Adversary, but with Printing, Writing, Reading." For Foxe the pope would have to abolish printing, for printing "doubtless will abolish him."[18]

The key point is not simply that religion was going public in early modern England but that the understanding and practice of publicness and religion was undergoing fundamental change. Just as the image of the public was transformed from a many-headed monster to that of circulating opinions (from which readers could take up a critical distance), the image of religious dissent was transformed from brandishing a sword to picking up a pen. Locke is a witness to religion's increased circulation in printed material and the concomitant rise of the modern public as well as a proponent of the transformation of religion's medium from bodies to speech and text. Religion, Locke argued, was the stuff of argumentation, and these arguments moreover could conveniently circulate at a remove from vulnerable human bodies.

Religious intolerance and conflict is frequently attributed to an epistemological absolutism, which gives rise to competing claims to incommensurable truths or unwarrantable references to transcendent grounds of argumentation.[19] The problem with this attribution is that it already presumes that religion is a species of argumentation. It fails to account for the processes by which religion is transformed into signs—a transformation that is witnessed and advocated by Locke, although it is certainly not complete and certainly not uncontested. (I will have more to say on this in Chapters 2 and 6.)

Religious differences and their attendant flashpoints of violence were not, and frequently are not, matters of truth but matters of identity and of bodily and communal boundaries. The risks posed by religious dissent are not simply philosophical disagreement or even political deadlock. Rather, dissenters, particularly those labeled heretics and schismatics, were seen as infecting, injuring, polluting, or severing the sacred social-political body. Many were accused of sexual perversion, promiscuity, and licentiousness.[20] Given a presumption that bodies are linked by biblical kinship or incorporation in the redemptive body of Jesus, dissent was regarded as contagious. Thus religious dissenters had to be kept apart (jailed), decontaminated, or destroyed. As Calvin remarked, "Shall the whole body of Christ be mangled that one putrid member remain intact?"[21] Heretics were subject to penalties on their persons and properties precisely because the danger posed by religious dissent was widely imagined to be bodily. Given this context, it would not be enough to simply advocate for the delegation of bodies to the state and minds to religion. Rather, religion's relationship to bodies and wills would have to be reconfigured.

Accordingly, Locke insists that religion ought to proceed through harmless circuits of argumentation. But this is a beguilingly simple declaration. To recast religion as opinion or persuasion, Locke must also loosen its mooring in the will and in persecuted, inherited, endowed, ritualized, and divinized bodies. To do so, he argues that "true" religion cannot be forced because religion makes appeal to the understanding, not the will. Religion is epitomized by opinion, which by virtue of being in the province of the understanding, is impervious to outward force: "True and saving Religion consists in the inward perswasion of the Mind. . . . And such is the nature of the Understanding, that it cannot be compell'd to the belief of anything by outward force. . . . It is only Light and Evidence that can work a change in Mens Opinions."[22] With this argument Locke makes a significant departure from traditional Christian teaching as to the centrality of the will in Christian conviction and practice. This is not to say that traditional Christian teaching directed that one could be converted *at will*, but rather that one must surrender one's will; in other words, human willfulness was the central obstacle to religious orthodoxy. Locke sidesteps the will and insists that the key locus for religion is the understanding.[23]

Locke also insists that religion is altogether unrelated to the encumbrances and inertia of familial ties: "No body is born a member of any

Church; otherwise the Religion of Parents would descend unto Children, by the same right of Inheritance as their Temporal Estates.... No Man is by nature bound unto any particular Church or Sect.... No Member of a Religious Society can be tied with any other Bonds but what proceed from the certain expectation of eternal Life."[24] For Locke religious selves are made, not born. Religion is not about blood, land, or money but about words, persuasion, and conviction. Religion is no longer an identity with which one is born and is no longer passed along familial lines of inheritance. True religion is not inherited; it is not habitual or second nature but rather the result of critical reflection on the appropriate evidence.

Many people in the seventeenth century may have agreed with Locke that religion was not subject to the will, that it was not simply the result of choice. Nonetheless, they would have insisted that religion was appropriately spoken of as a matter of inheritance. Roger Coke claimed that Charles II's subjects were "Born and Baptized in a Christian Church." Edward Stillingfleet could refer matter-of-factly to "the Church we live in."[25] For Henry Barrow all Christians, indeed all people, "are from ancient descent within the covenant."[26] The sign of this ancient covenant was, of course, circumcision. The sign of the new covenant was infant baptism. Both of these signs are performed on the body and before the age of consent. (Infant baptism became required Christian practice from the time of Augustine of Hippo [354–430]). Supporters of infant baptism argued that it was a sign of the community's enduring bonds and pertained to the rights of Christian parents and children, as, for instance, in Robert Cleaver's 1624 *Patrimony of Christian Children*.[27] For some the right to infant baptism was comparable to the right of inheritance: "Children of believing parents have a right to the sacrament.... As in the title of lands at this day, a man does purchase lands to himself and his heirs after him."[28] For others effective consent to church membership was located in the past ratification of the biblical covenant; this consent on the part of ancestors was binding on all subsequent generations, permitting even state enforcement of membership.[29]

Locke's fundamental point is that toleration requires regarding religion not as the stuff of familial inheritance or spiritual patrimony but as circulating, alterable speech acts. Locke writes in his *Letter Concerning Toleration* that those who do "not own and teach the Duty of tolerating

All men in matters of *meer Religion*" signify their willingness to "seize the government and estates of their fellow subjects" (50; italics added). Those who do not recognize religion as alienable speech but rather bind tightly together word and body imagine religions as inalienable identities, races, or nations. Consequently, they regard dissent as injurious to the social body, as tantamount to warfare, and regard each "religion" as potentially hostile to any other. In contrast, Locke insists that we could all get along if we all recognized that religion wields only the power of persuasion. Locke unzips words and bodies not only to free those words so that they may circulate freely without offense and injury to bodies but also to herald opportunities for redeploying, reconfiguring, and regrouping those bodies. Locke is implicitly undermining religion's role in consolidating the political and economic prerogatives of patriarchal families and racial cosmologies. In short, religion in Locke is undomesticated. As Locke writes: "As people of *different perswasions* enjoy Lybertie of Conscience, so let people of all Nations be naturalized, and enjoy equal privileges, with the other English inhabitants residing there."[30] If one concedes that religions are not inheritable and inalienable identities but rather convertible persuasions, then one can be granted the magical identity that is "English." Purging religious identities as so many speech acts frees up those same bodies to affiliate as the enhanced, enlarged English. Religion as "meer Religion," as "persuasion," or as speech act, is made publicly available as part of the proverbial marketplace of ideas. Consequently, religion becomes one among other tradable goods in the emerging colonialist economy.

Locke downplays, again, obstinate religious divisions by insisting that the problem is really one of different languages. In the *Essay Concerning Human Understanding*, he observes: "For though it is generally believed, that there is great diversity of *Opinions* in the Volumes and Variety of Controversies, the World is distracted with; yet the most I can find, that the contending learned Men of different parties do, in their Arguings one with another, is that they speak different Languages" (3.10.22 [504]; italics added). Here Locke echoes Montaigne: "Our controversies are verbal ones."[31] What are thought to be fundamental differences of outlook or conviction are, instead, tussles over meaning and interpretation. At other points, however, Locke does not downplay but rather raises considerably the stakes of linguistic dispute.

To break in upon the Sanctuary of Vanity and Ignorance, will be, I suppose, some Service to Humane Understanding: Though so few are apt to think they deceive, or are deceived in the Use of Words; or that the *Language of the Sect* they are of, has any Faults in it, which ought to be examined or corrected, that I hope I shall be pardon'd, if I have in the Third Book dwelt long on this Subject; and endeavoured to make it so plain, that neither the inveterateness of the Mischief, nor the prevalency of the Fashion, shall be any Excuse for those, who will not take Care about the meaning of their own Words, and will not suffer the Significancy of their Expressions to be enquired into. ("The Epistle to the Reader," in *Human Understanding*, 10; italics added)

On the one hand, religious differences are mere linguistic puzzles and disputes. On the other hand, people hold onto their verbal habits with a conviction that is nothing short of "religious" (note the reference to "sanctuary" and "sect"). Woe to the person who wishes to dispute linguistic custom! But Locke is up for the challenge. Note that he is not advocating that sects retreat into cliques where they may babble in private codes to their hearts' content. He seems intent instead on examining differences in meaning and opinion and, ultimately, on knitting a common language among speakers and writers from multiple languages and sects.[32]

Locke's reconstruction of religion as word, text, or persuasion is nonetheless filled with ambiguity about the relationship between religious speech and power. He frequently uses metaphors of force when discussing religious speech. In the *Letter Concerning Toleration* he speaks approvingly of "Christian Warfare" waged by Jesus and his "Soldiers" in their "subduing of Nations." Locke hurries to add that neither Jesus nor his followers were "armed with the Sword, or other Instruments of Force, but prepared with the Gospel of Peace, and with the Exemplary Holiness of their Conversation" (25). At the same time, he speaks approvingly of the "press of Arguments" (27) and the "Arms of Exhortations, Admonitions, and Advices" (30), and he acknowledges the "strength of Arguments that may confound errors" (30). Nonetheless, he worries about the "rough usage of Word" (30) and the "intemperate Zeal [that breathes] nothing but Fire and Sword" (35); he also suggests that pens may be as guilty as swords.[33] Locke warns that when one is seeking to restrain people from their error, "all Force and Compulsion is to be forborn" and "nothing is to be done imperiously" (47). All these examples blur what appears to be a fairly straightforward distinction between force and speech, body and word. Nonetheless, ambiguity regarding the power of persuasion is not peculiar to Locke. After all, what exactly is meant by Jürgen Habermas's famous phrase, "the unforced force of a better argument?"[34]

Locke's tacit recognition, then, of the force of persuasive speech combined with his insistence that all people—citizens and magistrates—have an obligation to attempt to persuade their fellow citizens to what they regard as essential to salvation reveals that it is a serious misunderstanding to see in Locke's work either the privatization of religion or the separation of religion and power. As William Walker observes, "Locke places no limits whatsoever on who can use the effective means of changing and controlling religious belief, nor on those against whom these means may be brought to bear. . . . *The form of Christian society envisaged by the letter is a free-for-all,* within which everyone, including the magistrate, has the duty to use the effective means of changing the religious beliefs (and the practices that are dictated by them) of everyone else."[35] Locke is deeply aggrieved by the physical violence of religious intolerance; nonetheless, he has the stomach for intellectual combat in religious matters.

Nonetheless, Locke continues to dial down the stakes of religious dissent by comparing religious differences to matters of fashion. (Note his reference to "the prevalency of the Fashion," quoted earlier from "The Epistle to the Reader" in his *Essay Concerning Human Understanding,* 10). Locke's choice is fascinating. "Persuasion" and "fashion" are poor cousins to "truth" and "law" and have the added handicap of a feminine gender. This wording suggests the variable, superficial, albeit public, character of religion.

Penal laws, made about matters of religion in a country where there is already a diversity of opinions, can hardly avoid that common injustice which is condemned in all laws whatsoever, viz. in retrospect. It would be thought a hard case, if by a law, now made, all would have to be fined that should wear French hats for the future, and those also who had worn them at any time in the year past. It is the same case to forbid a man to be a Quaker, Anabaptist, Presbyterian, for it is as easy for me not to have had on the hat yesterday, which I then wore, as it is in many cases not to have the same opinions, the same thought, in my head as I had yesterday.[36]

Note Locke's analogy between religion, opinion, and style of hat. His point is not that changing religions is necessarily as casual or easy as changing a hat. Rather, he wishes to colorfully illustrate his conviction that although such changes are not wholly subject to the will, religious convictions, like opinions and fashions, are alterable. For Locke differences in religion are not the stuff of contagious diseases or "soul death" but of style. As he says in the *Letter Concerning Toleration*: "But now, if I be marching on with my utmost vigour in that way which, according to the sacred geography, leads straight to Jerusalem, why am I beaten and ill-used by others because, perhaps, I wear not buskins [laced, open-toed boots]; because my hair is not of the right cut; because, perhaps, I have not been dipped in the right fashion?" (35). Locke observes that what is most important about religious worship is what passes, unseen, between God and person. This spiritual commerce in no way disturbs the community. But Locke well knows that this is not the whole of religion. He also remarks, "For kneeling or sitting in the sacrament can in itself tend no more to the disturbance of the government or injury of my neighbor than sitting or standing at my own table; wearing a cope or surplice in the church can no more in its own nature alarm or threaten the peace of the state than wearing a cloak or coat in the market."[37] Note that the first part of this quote would suggest that the absence of injury is due to privatization ("standing at my own table"), yet the second portion refers to a public setting ("wearing a cloak or coat in the market"). This indicates that the absence of injury is attributable not to context (private versus public religion) but rather to the character of religion as fashion.

Locke's referencing fashion reflects a contemporary preoccupation. A number of seventeenth-century English broadsheets were published to be sung to the tune of "A Man of Fashion." At the same time a number of these sources reflect recurring anxieties about the reign of fashion and its takeover of that seeming antithesis to fashion, religion. Fashion is dictated by preference, which is always changing. Religion would seem to be dictated by an eternal and constant source. An example of a contemporary denunciation of fashion's triviality and its taking over religion is supplied by the Quaker leader George Fox, who denounces the tremendous energies given over to keeping in fashion—even in the context of Christian worship. People go to services, he bemoans, just to see what everyone is wearing. He implores his readers whether powdered hair and skin, gold and silver jewelry, and ribbons and points on clothes are the "marks of a Christians life, a Christians behavior, a Christians nature or disposition?" For Fox fashions are superficial, worldly ornaments that "pass away"; they are the "pollutions of the world." A true Christian lives from the precious faith that radiates from within. Fox asks: "What good do these great broade Cuffs do you that you wear.... What is the pleasures of ... the world, which are but for a time: and do you not go out of one fashion into another, continually inventing fashions, and they last but a season."[38] Fashion is the seduction of the ephemeral, which distracts humans from the eternal. Fashion clings to surfaces, whereas true Christianity is an inner nature or disposition. Over and over again Fox links fashion with the world. Fashion is the quintessence of worldliness—and thereby, I suggest, of the secular.

Worldly religion suggests its commodification, that is, its suitability for accessorizing, altering, comparing, and exchanging. Accordingly, it suggests religion's triviality or superficiality. Nonetheless, other seventeenth-century sources explore the more complex ramifications of envisioning religion as analogous to fashion. In one anonymous dialogue (published in London) between a Protestant "Monmouth-shire" and a Catholic "York-shire," religion is described as a seasonable garment. Nonetheless, the Catholic offers that the best way to wear religion is as a cloak because it can hide one's nature, character, and actions. This remark suggests that religious signs, appearances, and performances can be deceiving and may not at all reflect who one truly is. At the same time, religion as fashion is a cover, buffer, and protective layer allowing bodies and selves to circulate in public as well as to be public. Publicness presumes not only coverings of bodies but also coverings that are *fashion*, that is, signs to be read, compared, assessed. Fashions are not merely useful—they do not merely cover, protect, and warm the body—they solicit readers, interpreters, imitators, critics.

The debate between the Protestant and the Catholic continues. When asked from which "piece of Religion" he should wish to construct his cloak, the Catholic reveals that the Roman-piece is his preference for it is the "Original, and is most in Fashion all o're the World." The Protestant states his preference to follow the fashion in his own country and to follow what his father wore, which, he adds, was most certainly Protestant. The Catholic challenges him as to whether he could discover what religious fashion his father wore, given the new-fangled character of Protestantism. He asks, coyly, "Well with what Antiquary will you consult for the Fashion?" He then suggests that the pattern of the Protestant fathers' pants was probably that of Oliver's Half-Crown—a playful reference to the coins issued during Puritan Oliver Cromwell's rule as Lord Protector of the English Commonwealth (1653–1658). Having suggested that religion as fashion entails both deception and innovation, the Protestant (Monmouth-shire) and the Catholic (York-shire) turn accusatory and defensive regarding the relationship between religion and fashion. Monmouth-shire avers that his Protestant religion determines his fashions or practices, whereas it is the reverse for Catholics: "Prithee, what doest talk of Fashion? This is all the difference 'twixt ours and yours: We cut our Cloth according to Religion, you your Religion according to your Cloth; we make interest according to Religion, you Religion according to Interest." The Protestant objects to religious differences being reduced to differences of fashion (and fleeting market values), insisting that Protestantism retains the appropriate hierarchy by which eternal (and perhaps inward) religion dictates fashion and market valuation rather than the reverse, as in Catholicism. In his rejoinder to this rather stunning rebuke, York-shire, the Catholic, dismisses the Protestant as merely echoing "the Rabble" and voicing their "wavering Fancy."[39] On the one hand, the interlocutors exploit fashion as an entirely productive idiom for understanding and describing the public and communicative character of religion. Imperial Catholic Christendom's fashion is claimed to link people across the globe, whereas Protestant fashion is said to reflect regional or national custom. On the other hand, both the Catholic and the Protestant are quick to insist on their own religion's enduring power over and against wavering fashion.

Locke's description of religion as fashion courts the judgment that he trivializes religion. Even now fashion is regarded as more subject to whim and time than is culture. Fashion would seem to be culture lite. (Perhaps no more telling indicator of this is the ready association of women with fashion and men with culture.) Indeed, centuries later, in 1909, the editors of *Cosmopolitan* magazine denounced what they saw as the deterioration of standards and more specifically the diminishment of a sense of sacrality, as evidenced by the fact that "the change in one's religion to another is like getting a new hat."[40] It is ironic that more than 200 years earlier Locke had recommended just this for the sake of religious toleration. It is also ironic that this same "family" magazine would eventually be transformed into a women's fashion magazine.[41]

Indeed, having equated religious differences to not being "dip't in the right Fashion," Locke goes on to suggest, "Certainly, if we consider right, we shall find that for the most part they are such frivolous things as these ... which breed implacable Enmities amongst Christian Brethren, who are all agreed in the Substantial and truly Fundamental part of Religion."[42] Here, Locke uses fashion to highlight the superficiality of religious differences, indicating that they are insignificant or indifferent matters (*adiaphora*). Thus Locke sounds like a Latitudinarian here. But Locke's ambitious reconfiguration of religion goes beyond specifically Christian enmity. His use of fashion does not just convey that *differences* are frivolous or superficial but that religion is a communicative, convertible item.

Moreover, in the same way that Locke's reconstruction of religion as persuasive speech retains traces of force, his likening of religion to fashion and opinion evidences recognition of their governing power. In referring to public opinion as law, Locke signals his awareness that opinion can easily become the rule by which individuals unthinkingly live. This is why it is so important that opinion be subject to public scrutiny and debate. Locke also states that the "great governors of this world" are "example and fashion."[43] What Locke draws attention to, then, is not simply the triviality of fashion but its communicative and disciplinary qualities. Thus religion as fashion is evocative of a prevailing decorum. Fashion may be changeable, but it is no less potent an indicator of status. One keeps watch on what is out this season and what is in. Indeed, one might be accused of being a "slave to fashion." And one is also subject to being cast out of a group based on a "fashion disaster." This sense of fashion as entailing spectatorship and judgment comes out in Locke's *Essay Concerning Human Understanding*: "No Man scapes the Punishment of their Censure and Dislike who offends against the Fashion and Opinion of the Company he keeps, and would recommend himself to" (2.28.12 [357]). Because he does not state specific state penalties for atheists, the intolerant, and those who follow religious leaders that resemble heads of state, no doubt he imagines that religious fashion and opinion will serve up the appropriate discipline for these heretics! (Indeed, he explicitly says so in the case of atheists.)

Locke's likening religion to fashion indicates that he does not require that religions qualify as rational before they are permitted to go public. But, more important, it suggests that Locke envisages reason as an aspirational or ongoing project. Indeed, I suggest that Locke imagines rationality as bound up with what is shared or shareable. Insofar as the reality of religious pluralism and conflict reveals that we can no longer presume a shared religion or revelation, Locke nonetheless encourages the construction and expansion of what is shareable through public venues of scrutiny, judgment, and argumentation. In one text he suggests that persistent religious error rarely finds company and therefore ought not to be a source of worry.[44] The pressures of publicness and the constraints of custom are sufficient to keep religious differences civil. Privatizing or punishing religion, Locke insists, will not achieve this end.

Locke's comments on the disciplinary aspects of fashion echo those of Bishop Joseph Hall in a sermon from the 1620s. Bishop Hall refers to the world as "nothing but a mint of fashions," and he urges his audience not to fashion themselves to the variable and "outward form of . . . fancies, mis-opinions, misjudgments, heresies, novelties of devices, superstition." At the same time, Hall recognizes the significance of fashion in performing gender and marking class distinctions. Furthermore, he claims that the "fashions of morality, in good and evil, however, are fixed and perpetual."[45] Even morality is a matter of fashion?! Hall's specific point appears to be that the dictates of fashion are inescapable—best to don the ones that (appear to) resist the vagaries of history.

Hall's remarks suggest the possibility that some fashions are more than skin-deep—indeed, they are deep enough to rival the supposed eternity of religion or nature. In other words, some fashions may yet become a kind of second nature or quasi-religion. Locke gets at something similar regarding custom in his *Essay Concerning Human Understanding*. Custom "settles habits of thinking in the understanding, as well as of determining in the will, and of motions in the body . . . which once set a going, continue on in the same steps . . . and the motion in it becomes easy, and as it were natural" (2.33.6 [396]). A similar idea is reflected in a

1665 broadsheet critiquing the worldly mélange of Dutch toleration. The writer rails against the "hodge-podge Religion" of Dutch toleration. At the same time, the writer dignifies the diversity of Dutch toleration by likening it to a "University of all sorts of Opinions." Indeed, the writer does not suppose that a brisk trade in religious trinkets or opinions necessarily suggests Dutch indifference or frivolity with regard to religion. He goes on to reason that a man would "sooner convert a Jew than persuade a Dutchmen contrary to his humor; For Custome is his Law."[46] On the one hand, then, toleration makes of religion a mere mishmash of ornaments and opinions; on the other hand, religion as a market of fashions or an academy of opinions sinks as deep as any unshakeable habit or disposition. Partakers of Dutch toleration are less easily converted than the Jew, whose religion is akin to an identity.

Locke's reconstruction of religion as opinion, argument, and fashion counters Talal Asad's assertion that post-Reformation religion is divorced from power and thus is reduced to either private belief or inconsequential public speech. Locke presents religion as neither wholly internal nor wholly external; as habitual but changeable; as a peculiar kind of power or force—not at all violent and more subtle than coercion. Thus Locke's portrayal of religion's relationship to force is a more nuanced view than is usually associated with religion in the modern West. Gauri Viswanathan recently observed that "religious choice is as much a part of the logic of modernity as an increasingly differentiated individual subjectivity."[47] Of course, to the extent that heresy (from the Greek *hairesis*, signifying "choice") is decriminalized, this observation is almost a truism.[48] It is misleading, however, to portray religion as a straightforward, unconstrained choice. Locke argues that true religion requires assent. But Locke does not think we come to have convictions "at will." (If our religious convictions could be changed "at will," then we could be forced to change our beliefs—a notion that Locke vehemently denies.) One might argue that the ambiguity here reflects the complexity of religious conviction—a complexity similar to falling in love. We find ourselves moved, possessed, overcome by a religious conviction. So, too, we *fall* in love, yet we are also said to choose our own partner. And in the same way that Locke rejects prearranged governments, he rejects prearranged marriages and prearranged religiosities. We are not forced to marry a given person; we are not forced to remain a Presbyterian. Still, in both instances these decisions are constrained. The fantasy of a modern self who stands before a range of religious (and nonreligious) choices and who resists external force in negotiating these choices is a bit misleading. Moreover, it is undeniable that the authenticity of one's religion dictates the relinquishment of that fantasy. We do not, as Steve Bruce has persuasively argued, choose a religion in the same way that we choose which car or which breakfast cereal to buy.[49]

Despite Locke's repudiation of religion as the result of choice, he is nonetheless cited as endorsing the idea that one chooses what to think or believe. Wendy Brown depicts this presumption of choice as the "conceit" of liberal tolerance.

> Across Lockean, Kantian, Millian, Rawlsian, and Habermasian perspectives, rationality transcends, or better, exceeds embodiment and cultural location to permit a separation between rational thought, on one side, and the constitutive embodiment of certain beliefs and practices, on the other. For deliberative rationality to be meaningful apart from "culture" or "subjectivity," the conceit must be in play that the individual *chooses* what he or she thinks. This same choosing articulates the possibility of an optional relationship with culture, religion, and even ethnic belonging; it sustains as well the conceit that the rationality of the subject is independent of these things, which are named as contextual rather than constitutive elements.[50]

For Brown the conceit or perhaps illusion of choice is cashed out as the superiority of Western liberals who believe that they may *have* religious beliefs but that others *are* their religion, that they are walking embodiments of it. In other words, outside the "tolerant liberal West," religion is "saturating or authoritative."[51] Brown's choice of words reminds me of a comment I have heard again and again from students of religion: "Over there, religion is, like, in the water they drink or the air they breathe!" The tendency for those toward the liberal end of the political spectrum to regard identity as exceeding embodiment is surprisingly prevalent. For instance, in New Zealand the ruling Labour Party regards the Maori as a "cultural group" and the conservative National Party regards them as a "racial group." (Maori, however, belong to both parties!)

Brown may be wrong that Locke argues that we choose our religion and culture, but her description of a separation between thought and the constitutive embodiment of certain beliefs and practices resembles the Lockean reconstruction of religion I have described in this chapter. I insist, however, that Locke's effort is not an intellectualist conceit. What Brown's analysis fails to account for are the stakes of the Lockean project and the evidence that such a project was not designed to demarcate the West from the rest.

It is true that Locke's casting religion as speech and style entails religion's subjection to the rationalizing discipline of publicity and its (potentially critical) distance from embodied selves. Nonetheless, Locke's aim is not unencumbered selves but rather the dissolution of political theologies that visit injury upon bodies and impede the circulation, affiliation, and economic productivity of those bodies. Consequently, he attempts to loosen religions' hold on bodies: their ability to dictate where bodies begin and end, what is "natural" to them, who counts as kin or neighbor, and which acts unleash divine fury and its corresponding state punishment and war making. Accordingly, he reconstructs religion as "meer persuasion" or changeable "fashion." In other words, Locke attempts to create some distance between *vulnerable* bodies and religious dissent (although fashion still evokes proximity to the body).

Moreover, Locke does not suggest that his reconstruction of religion would demarcate the Enlightened, European, or English over against "them." Locke imagines his reconstruction of religion as mere persuasion enabling "all Nations" to be naturalized in colonial America. In other words, Locke anticipates the export of his understanding of religion. Locke's "religion" suggests the commodification, conversion, and exportation of religions and cultures. In other words, it reflects and augments capitalist and colonialist logics. This reading of Locke helps us to detect overlooked and ongoing conflicts surrounding religion, to delineate patterns between these conflicts, and to begin to understand the ways in which the secular does not solve religious conflict but instigates it.

For instance, Mohandas Gandhi (1869–1948), leader of the nonviolent Indian independence movement against the British, flatly declared: "Religion is not like a house or a cloak, which can be changed at will. It is more an integral part of one's self than one's own body."[52] Locke and Gandhi agree that religion is not the sort of thing that one changes "at will." Nonetheless, for Gandhi religion is constitutive of identity, whereas

Locke's reconstruction of religion as "fashion" may be read as an attempt to defuse the volatility of religious differences construed as being analogous to "identity politics." The immediate context for Gandhi's comment was Bhimrao Ramji Ambedkar's conversion to Buddhism. Weeks before he was to die in 1956, Ambedkar, leader of Dalit efforts for a separate electorate movement in post-independence India, led one of the largest mass conversions (of mostly Hindu Dalits to Buddhism) in modern history. He had declared that whereas he had no choice in being born a Hindu, he was resolved not to die as one. Ambedkar's primary objection to Hinduism was its providing sacral authorization of caste. For Gandhi, however, one cannot simply alienate that which has been thoroughly internalized. One cannot cast off that which has constituted him or her. One becomes oneself through immersion in a familial-cultural-religious milieu; hence one cannot emerge from this and simply peel off layers of oneself like articles of clothing. Religion, for Gandhi, is *who* you are; it is your identity. Religion, for Locke, is "meer opinion" or fashion.[53]

Locke's styling of religion as fashion and Gandhi's repudiation of the same may be merely coincidental. Yet it is difficult to resist the supposition that the logic I detect in Locke—whereby religions and identities are continuously disembedded from bodies in order to circulate as texts or "free speech" in an increasingly global marketplace of ideas—suggests affinities with capitalist and colonialist logics. If the goal is to extend the reach of commerce and colonial rule, then it would not do to allow what various communities regard as sacred, perhaps as something to die for, to burrow more deeply into the bodies and psyches of their populations. Rather, the goal would be to convince these populations to alienate their traditions as speech and text, subject to circulation, critical scrutiny, and conversion, all the while convincing them that nothing sacred or essential has been lost in the process and praising their Enlightened efforts at conceptual clarification and critical distance. At the same time, bodies unmoored from long-standing religious disciplines or rituals would get freed up for all sorts of gainful employment.

These kinds of conversion efforts occur in several domains, including education. During the period of colonial rule (1824–1948), the British attempted to convert Burmese Buddhist monastery education to a British model of schooling. The colonial officials assumed that this task would be rather easy in light of the long-established textual basis of Burmese Buddhist tradition and the high literacy rate. The British expected that the Burmese would share their assumption that the chief significance of religion consisted in preserving textual content and expanding literacy. As Alicia Turner points out, however, the Burmese resisted these efforts, which included free textbooks on traditional British subjects, the circulation of certified teachers, and grants and in-kind gifts based on student performance on achievement tests. To the dismay of the British, the monks were not interested in simply preserving teachings in texts but in maintaining the merit-making value of the rituals (including memorization for the sake of interiorization), which were also designed to foster detachment from the world. Colonial officials were seeking to train the Burmese population in capitalist values; they had not anticipated that their efforts would be subsumed into a monastery education that steadfastly inculcated a discipline antithetical to capitalism.[54]

As the case of Burma indicates (and Gandhi's denunciation may reflect), British colonialist policy regarding education sought to preserve traditional texts, to produce scholarly commentary on them, and to introduce them to populations formerly restricted from accessing them. These efforts do not reflect attempts at privatizing something regarded as analogous to religion. Rather, they are concerted efforts to train the Burmese to regard their traditions as largely textual, symbolic, or ornamental; to see themselves in a critical, distanced relation to these circulating objects; and to become accustomed to the circulation and competition of their cultures with other items called "religion." In other words, institutions, practices, and rituals that suggest archaism, inefficiency, or nationalism can be dismantled or depreciated even as "religions" are meticulously recorded and preserved as circulating media.

In reconstructing religion as mere persuasion and changeable fashion, Locke is, of course, not responsible for subsequent British colonial policies. Nonetheless, my reconstruction of overlooked arguments and themes in his work provides theoretical tools for examining the complexity of the secular that go beyond its purported opposition to the religious. Much attention has been devoted to examining Christian conversion efforts in colonial contexts, and some of these accounts have examined the influence of the Protestant emphasis on word and text as the authoritative basis of religion. My project has an affinity with these latter efforts; nonetheless, I seek to set this emphasis within a broader context. This context includes consideration of the political and economic interests driving the conversion of religion and culture to signs and texts, the reservations attending such a conversion, and forms of resistance to ongoing attempts to convert and package indigenous cultural practices as market-friendly religions.

In the next chapter I discuss the critical reception of Locke's and others' attempts to reconstruct religion as speech and text. I note that Locke voiced concerns about the efficacy and authority of words and texts to create enduring bonds between citizens. As I will show, no early modern thinkers, not even those associated with the Enlightenment, believed that religious and political obligation could be reproduced without deploying the body. Thus they set for themselves a particularly difficult challenge: delineating a variant of power that penetrated bodies without violating those bodies. In the final chapter I revisit the affinities and differences between the ways that Locke imagined religious and political conflict and its remedy, and the ways various constituencies currently imagine and attempt to fix them. Far from being accomplished facts or political and philosophical solutions, logics of toleration and secularization continue to spark and exacerbate conflict.

2

Wordish Ways and Ritual Bodies

Stephen Carter has claimed, rightly in my view, that "speaking—which always implies the possibility of convincing others—is at the heart of liberal politics."[1] Liberal political theorists consistently invoke a cozy scene of conversation partners gathered around a table. Everyone is supposed to play nice, exerting themselves only in the interests of pious political persuasion. This unwavering confidence in the power of speech strikes some critics as naive. Paul Kahn, for instance, criticizes the liberal presumption that the bonds of political society are spun from a verbal or textual contract.[2] But if contemporary liberals betray a peculiar trust in the power of words to fashion and sustain societies, this was not the case for one of liberalism's purported architects.

In the previous chapter I argued that rather than privatizing religion, Locke sought to publicize it. He encouraged public discussion aimed at persuasion—both between citizens and on the part of state representatives. I also argued that Locke insisted on depicting religions as speech, more specifically as circulating signs and fashions (one might even say commodities), so as to uncouple the association between bodily harm and religious dissent. I posed this as Locke's attempt to secularize religion. Religion circulating as argument, sign, and fashion achieves just enough distance from vulnerable bodies to allow those bodies a wider range of social, economic, and political intercourse. At the same time I noted the various ways in which Locke's apparent switch to the sign, and to the understanding as against the will, retained vestiges of force, that is, words as weapons, sectarian language as guarded sanctuaries, fashion and public opinion as law.

In this chapter I elaborate on Locke's ambivalence regarding the efficacy of signs to penetrate, discipline, and affiliate disparate bodies. I also introduce and compare a number of Locke's contemporary and later interlocutors, whose writings and debates evidence similar concerns about language, body, force, and authority. The purpose of this extension is not simply to cast light on writers who have been overshadowed by the prodigious scholarship on and reputation of Locke. Rather, it is to supply evidence of a sustained debate regarding a perceived disjunction between word and body in religion—a disjunction that Locke simultaneously denounces and augments. To put it another way, in the previous chapter I read Locke as attempting to disembed religion from the body and to portray religion as circulating signs (if only, as I substantiate in later chapters, to reconnect them in more subtle and far-reaching ways). In this chapter I assemble witnesses to and ushers and denouncers of this very process.

Locke, as well his critics and admirers, noted again and again the failure of mere language to conduct clear and stable meanings on a given occasion, let alone over long periods of time or expanses of territory. In addition, they continued to fret over and debate the relative power of the word to secure lasting political and societal bonds. For these Enlightenment thinkers the vaunted "republic of letters" is not an unqualified celebration of the emergence of a textual culture. What we see instead are sustained examinations of the relative force of speech and text to establish and maintain communal ties. I discuss these doubts and the ways in which they continued to imagine the body—human or divine, literally or metaphorically—as a source, site, or conduit of authority that had to be enlisted to offset the liabilities of mere speech. Moreover, I show that this debate with Locke continued into the eighteenth century with Moses Mendelssohn's (among others) recommendation of ritual to supplement the fragility of a textual culture.[3] I conclude by comparing Locke's project to these efforts to construct a civil religion in order to respond to the repeated contention that Locke's project is a civil religion and to lay the groundwork for my claim that his is instead a political theology.

Although it has been claimed that liberalism's inauguration of political contract "ushered in an age dominated by the power of discourse rather than force,"[4] abundant evidence shows that the valorization of the word as bond of society predates liberalism.[5] The idea that one's word affords obligatory power is prevalent from the Middle Ages to the Restoration. Indeed, Cicero had already conceived of language as a source of obligation and the means to subdue irrational conflict; Hugo Grotius qualified this point by noting that the consistency of meanings is itself the result of a verbal contract.[6]

Nonetheless, advocacy of verbal contract was not without attendant concerns about the risks of doing so. Doubts about the reliability of oaths appear to increase at the beginning of the seventeenth century. As early as 1605 James I insisted on an oath that nonetheless conveyed the disjunction of word and meaning in equivocation: "And all these things I doe plainely and sincerely acknowledge and sweare, according to these express words by me spoken, and according to the plaine and common sense and understanding of these same words, without any Equivocation, or mentall reservation whatsoever."[7] Why insist on a speech that declares the fragility of that same speech?

The poem "Hounslow-Heath 1686" also indicates the error of imagining early modern England as a straightforward installment of the authority of the word over that of the body or persuasion over force. The poem offers pointed commentary on the recent addition of Catholic officers to the standing army of James II. The poem challenges the purported shift from physical force to word.

> Not rais'd (as ill men say) to hurt ye,
> But to defend, or to convert ye,
> For that's the method now in use,
> The faith Tridentine to diffuse,
> Time was, the Word was powerful;
> But now 'tis thought remiss and dull,
> Has not that energy and force,
> Which is in well-arm'd foot and horse.[8]

The poem evidences a sophisticated suspicion of those who would claim to seek merely conversion through speech, suggesting that although there had once been a common faith in the power of words, that faith has been broken by a militant Catholicism.

Of course, recourse to the body was not an English Catholic innovation. A number of Puritans in the sixteenth century advocated not just the scriptural word but the embodied word. They recommended preaching, not just to instill biblical faith but as an able instrument of social control that ought to be of interest to the secular authorities. Puritan reformers declared that consistent preaching in a plain style directed toward edification was the only means by which to keep the public peace. Indeed, such preaching supplied what was lacking in the external coercion available to the state; it prompted "inner loyalty," the inward conformity of the heart to mobilize the outward conformity of the body.[9] In other words, authoritative deployment of religious speech would effect *consensual* submission to authority: "The preacher enters into the very soul and mind of man . . . and frames it unto inward obedience unto God, out of which springs and issues the true outward obedience unto his civil magistrate."[10] In some instances the language is bolder. In one example from 1549, the writer recounts that the old religion (i.e., Catholicism) is now forbidden and that the new reformed religion is not yet printed where it needs to be printed: "in the stomachs of eleven of twelve parts of the realm."[11] Another cleric remarked that the 1569 revolt would never have happened had preachers been able to "*beat into their* [parishioners'] *heads* what obedience faithful subjects owe, first to God, and next to their prince."[12]

Nonetheless, Locke has his doubts about the efficacy of preaching and its purported special power to penetrate through bodily boundaries. He questions the expectation that true Christians might be formed by their passive listening to a weekly sermon.[13] Locke's doubts about the ability of words to connect people and to be the instruments of a promiscuous public result from his misgivings about the clarity and consistency of language. For Locke language is artificial and the connection between signs and things or ideas is arbitrary. He is convinced that words are external signs for internal thoughts, that words are vessels carrying meanings across the divide of bodies (Locke refers to language as that "great Conduit" in his *Essay Concerning Human Understanding* [3.11.1, 5 (509–10)]).[14] According to Locke, intelligible words are those that "excite ideas" in the hearer; the words that are most suited to this effect are those of "long and familiar use" rather than the esoteric or disinterested language of the learned. As Locke writes in his *Essay Concerning Human Understanding*: "There comes by constant use, to be such a Connexion between Sounds, and the Ideas they stand for, that the Names heard, almost as readily excite certain Ideas, as if the Objects themselves, which are apt to produce them, *did actually affect the Senses*" (3.2.6 [407]; final italics added; see also 3.11.11 [514]). Only common, clear language, directed toward practical ends, approaches the force that objects have in intuitive, certain knowledge. In these instances language more easily gains entry into the mind of another; its power to penetrate, excite, and generate ideas is potent but barely noticeable. In this case language functions as it is intended: as pipes conducting water to the public (3.11.5 [510]), as knots keeping parts from scattering (3.5.10 [434]).

Despite his commendation of familiar words in civic or practical contexts, in the *Essay Concerning Human Understanding* Locke consistently draws attention to language's obscurity and plurality of meaning: "Revealed Truths, which are conveyed to us by Books and Languages, are liable to the common and natural obscurities and difficulties incident to Words" (3.9.23 [490]). Locke goes on at length about how even a simple substance such as gold is associated with numerous qualities and nuances, making vain the assumption of an unequivocal meaning.[15] As Richard Vernon emphasizes, Locke takes the plurality of ideas (with which even the same words are associated) to be an undeniable reality of human life (3.9.8 [479]).[16] For Locke the inexpugnable gap between different people, even the dearest of friends, necessarily entails their connecting different ideas with the same words. Locke is aware that despite even love's lubricant, speech faces a formidable challenge in its circuit between people.[17]

Locke also voices serious misgivings about rhetoric. Following the long philosophic tradition of seeing rhetoric as striking or seductive speech, Locke warns that rhetoric "strikes" a person's fancy with beauty and wit. Rhetoric is a kind of enchantment—suspending reason's labor to detect the truth of a given discourse (*Human Understanding*, Epistle, 8; 2.11.2 [156]; 4.17.4 [675–76]). Locke suggests, however, that rhetoric's spell is only superficially powerful. It fails to penetrate to reason and to prompt the generation of ideas. Rhetoric may be a lovely woman, but she is only a woman, or to keep company with the metaphor, she is barren.

Having already noted the particular challenge of consistency of meaning with regard to philosophical or speculative ideas—which certainly does not bode well for productive religious argumentation—Locke also critiques the religious enthusiasts' inability to produce genuine knowledge from mere metaphors. The enthusiasts claim to be infused with the clear light of revelation. They claim to be the embodiment of the force of prophecy. For Locke, however, the gushing enthusiast is like the beguiling enchantress of rhetoric. In both cases the gossamer web of words lacks the force of objects on impressionable bodies, or the fecundity to produce fertile ideas that, by being shared over and over again, will reproduce themselves and give birth to new ones.

Locke was not alone in his doubts about language's powers of persuasion and penetration or in his refusal to take refuge in the apparent clarity and universality of innate ideas. One of his critics (whom Locke mentions) was an English Roman Catholic priest, theologian, and controversialist named John Sergeant (1623–1703 or 1710). Sergeant wrote a repetitive critical analysis of Locke's *Essay Concerning Human Understanding*, but he had high praise for Locke's intellect. Sergeant also rejects innate ideas, but his main objection is that Locke fails to account for how it is that the mind can process sense data. He offers his own quite fabulous theory: The mind has a "feminine seat" that is just sticky enough (but not too sticky or else the distinctness of the object would be lost) to receive the effluvia or particles sent out from the object. Thus, although both Locke and Sergeant see sense data as a result of the force of objects making impressions on the mind, Sergeant provides the juicy details of this productive collision. Locke, however, never responded to Sergeant in print. But Sergeant's other writings warranted critical responses from several noteworthy people, including Archbishop John Tillotson. These exchanges reflect broader concerns about religious authority amid the increasing circulation and exchange of speech and text. These concerns are articulated through repeated, albeit varied, recourse to the binary of word and body. The interlocutors in these debates are agreed as to the goal of a truly authentic and spiritual faith, yet even as the word is touted as the appropriate vehicle of such a faith, the efficacy of that faith is conveyed by its subtle conspiracy with bodily force.

Tillotson and Sergeant clashed over what was the appropriate rule of faith for Christians.[18] For Tillotson it was the Bible; for Sergeant it was "tradition." According to Sergeant, for something to serve as a rule of faith, the following conditions must be met: Its existence must be evident; its ruling virtue must be self-evident; it must have power to falsify doubters; and it must *not* be subject to endless interpretation. Sergeant's argument is that scripture fails all the tests for being a rule. The reasons for this failure are the following: The biblical canon was (and is) contested; the text may be corrupted; most people do not know the original languages; it contains anthropomorphic imagery; and it has garnered an endless stream of interpretations and commentaries (which themselves call explicitly or implicitly for a rule). Tillotson counters that all these same things can be said about tradition. Moreover, Tillotson, sounding like Locke (at least in Locke's explicit statements), insists that faith is not an inheritance but a persuasion or assent of mind "wrought in us by argument."[19]

Sergeant, however, raises a number of weighty objections. He asks about the rule of faith for the illiterate and for those who became part of the Jesus movement before the establishment of the scriptural canon (which was not until the fourth century). Moreover, he asserts that children learn not by texts but by example. In his *Sure-Footing in Christianity* he mocks Biblicists and their "Letter-Rule" and "wordish way of Grammar and Criticism" (147) and their reliance on "shreds and fragments of words" (105). He argues that a rule can only be had by the "immediate delivery of Tradition" (48), which consists in daily practice passed "hand to hand" (103) in sense impressions that entail no mediation (53–55), in the "spectable Majesty of outward Ceremonies" (63)—all of which are discoverable by "the noon-day Sun of *self evidence*" (56; italics in original). The "inerratability of Tradition" that is "riveted into [a man's] Soul by so-oft repeated sensations" is a "force of Nature" (54). Through tradition Christians are "suck't in Christianity" (83). Sergeant uses the example of someone trying to read and understand Aristotle's texts. Failing to understand Aristotle, the student is not impressed by this ancient Greek's authority. If a learned teacher of Aristotle should, however, "by word of mouth" explain Aristotle's philosophy to the student, that student has "as it were new Eyes" to understand Aristotle and to feel the full force of his authority. For Sergeant textual exegesis of the Bible does not conjure the force of authority; what is gained is "dim, dry and uncertain" (148). Sergeant argues that what is needed is the authority that is of "force to cause Faith and Assurance" (136). Sergeant jams his text with bodily imagery. Authoritative tradition is eyes, mouth, breast, hand, ritual. As Sergeant writes, "It is not possible that men should be *ignorant* of that to which they were *educated* of that which they dayly *saw* and *heard* and *did*."[20] For Sergeant the biblical text, qua text, cannot summon this kind of authority. As he points out, all Christian sects agree in the outward letters of scripture but differ profoundly in their beliefs and acts and are prepared to die for these differences. Hence he concludes that the bare letter cannot possibly be the rule of faith.

Sergeant often portrays the Protestant reliance on scripture as "mere words" and "wordishness" that is evanescent and without authority (read: embodiment). He argues that Protestants try to offset this airiness by suggesting volume or mass. They supply, for instance, a great number of citations or proofs so that they may "bubble up their books to a voluminous bigness," yet they have no force or weight. They also "talk gaily" of "sacred or grave authority." But for Sergeant this is all affectation, for they really adhere to "dead unsenc't words."[21] Moreover, Sergeant cleverly reverses the binary whereby Catholics are associated with materiality and Protestants with spirituality. For Sergeant it is because Catholics rely on the embodied conveyance of tradition that they are able to have a truly spiritual faith.

> Hence, we carry, for the main of our Doctrin, and as far as 'tis antecedent to written Authority, our Library in our *Heads*; and can as well study in a Garden, as sitting in a Library stufft with books; whereas your way of Learning ties you to turn over leaves of Authours, as children do their Dictionaries, for every step of your discourse. . . . If your Notes, you have with much pains collected, hap to miscarry, you are utterly at a loss; so that little of your Learning is *Spiritual* and plac't in your Soul, as true Learning should be, but in *material* and perishable paper and characters.[22]

For Sergeant a truly spiritual religion is one that is fully internalized, an internalization that can only be had through the force of authority daily insinuating itself through the body's senses and intimate relationships.

Critics of Sergeant conceded that Puritan reliance on preaching was ill-fated. Méric Casaubon (1599–1671), who held a seat of honor at

Canterbury Cathedral and was known for his editions of classical works, acknowledged that instruction in childhood is far more powerful than preaching to adults. Casaubon writes of Puritans that their "endeavor hath always been in all places to set up their *lectures* and *Pulpit-Preaching*, instead of Catechising; whereas three moneths [*sic*] right Catechising will make more Christians, I am confident, then Forty years Pulpit-preaching."[23] Nonetheless, Casaubon misunderstood Sergeant to be insisting on merely the *oral* conveyance of tradition. Thus he denounced Sergeant's "monstrous" opinion, which would reduce the "oral tradition" of Christianity to that with which "mothers flatter their children." Sergeant made a case not only for the early oral conveyance of tradition but also for its emotive, visual, and tactile conveyance.

George Hughes (1603–1667), a Presbyterian clergyman, writer, and chaplain to a baron and an earl and another critic of Sergeant, quite nicely phrased Sergeant's objection to scripture as "letter unsenc't." Nonetheless, he misunderstood Sergeant (as did Casaubon) to be endorsing the spoken word over the written word. Hughes writes, "Whereas they [Papists] mean by tradition . . . Oral speech or words without sense or matter. It is left to your judgment to discern, what a new, nothing this invention is. . . . Words are but wind."[24] Hughes believed the scriptures are endowed with the force of sense through God and not through other people, such as parents: "the scriptures being spirited by God as so truly senced."[25] He also argues that the Papist insistence on lending sense to tradition "seems to make Christian Religion too much like a *Mechanical Trade* to be hammered out by sensation."[26] For Hughes this insistence on the body to supply the force of tradition is primitive and corrupts the spiritual with the sensible.

We deny expressly that natures stroaks upon senses can make direct impressions of knowledge unto faith in any man: How many eies and ears do receive sensible impressions by Scriptural and oral revelation, and yet never come to the true apprehension of the doctrine of Christ? *This impression must be made by an Almighty arm*, to make man beleeve. Yet we deny not, but that mans sense is helpful to his understanding in its measure; therefore sights and sounds may be a good means to bring things heard and seen to the understanding; *but matters of faith are proper objects of intellectual faculties*, if we speak as men. We judge it a brutish assertion, that the sound of the Oral Tradition of Christ's Doctrine to eies or ears, should make such impressions of knowledge naturally and necessarily, as the affecting of senses, to feel heat, cold, pain, pleasure, or any other material quality: For these are proper to sense; but the matters of faith far above. Sense takes the sound not the Faith.[27]

Note that Hughes wants to insist on the spiritual character of faith over and above the sensible world. Yet he nonetheless makes recourse (which he does repeatedly in this text) to the image of the arm of God as the only truly effective power. This "Almighty arm" is to be applied to human intellectual faculties to keep them to the way of truth. Hughes (and Locke) agree that the force of conversion and of faith is ultimately the prerogative of God, but Hughes's God is a victorious pugilist.

Sergeant's most sophisticated and astute critic, however, was William Falkner (d. 1682; rector, stalwart defender of the Church of England, and critic of toleration).[28] Falkner reproduces faithfully Sergeant's concern to produce a tradition that is demonstrable as to its ruling power and that conveys the faith from generation to generation. Nonetheless, he sarcastically quips that Sergeant is convinced that "the Causes to preserve Faith intire, are as efficacious as those laid for the propagation of mankind."[29] (This critique resonates with Locke's insistence that one does not inherit religion from one's parents.) Whereas the reproduction of religious convictions may not be equivalent to sexual reproduction, Sergeant is certain that the former relies on the familial bonds begat by the latter. For Sergeant any religion that wishes to survive must be modeled on patrimony. Indeed, Sergeant finds bewildering Protestant idealizations of their tradition as composed of rational and reflective adherents who are successfully indifferent to prejudice.

And when they come to Maturity, pray tell us truly, how many of your *Sober Enquirers* have you met with in your life, who endeavor to abstract from all the prejudices they have imbib'd in their Minority, and reducing their inclin'd thoughts to an equal balance of Indifferency.... I doubt, if you would please to answer sincerely, you would seriously confess you scarce met with such a one in your life; that is, never met with any one who *rely'd* upon Scripture's Letter *practically* for his Rule of Faith.... Or can any be so blind, as not to see, that 'tis the following the natural way of Tradition, or *Childrens believing Fathers* (that is, indeed, of Education) that such multitudes in several places, continue still of the same perswasion; and that you consequently owe to this way, which you decry in Catholics, that any considerable number of you do voluntarily hang together at all?[30]

For Sergeant the familial inheritance of religion is the surest conveyance of tradition. Persuasion relies not simply on argument but on daily practice imbibed since childhood. Nonetheless, critics suggested that reliance on inheritance, familial or apostolic, signified a less authentic faith; Daniel Whitby charged that Catholics regard faith not as a result of convincing argumentation, as do Protestants, but as a "Patrimony handed down from Apostles to Fathers."[31]

Falkner acknowledges Sergeant's claim that books may be burned, torn, blotted, or worn out. Nonetheless, he points out that memories fail and understandings falter, that a copy of scripture is more durable than the life of a man, and that, besides, there are so many copies of scripture in circulation. Falkner wonders where Sergeant got the idea that an imperishable tradition was the key to human salvation and asks him why humans should bother keeping any written records if they are so vulnerable. He also casts doubt on the supposition that any human speech or practice can actually secure the sure conveyance of doctrine, for any tradition in this human world is, he reminds Sergeant, subject to error. If Sergeant had responded to precisely these points, I suspect he would have cited that place in his text where he asserts that skepticism is the "acutest way of Wordishness" and necessarily follows for those who salute authority but are hard pressed to establish it.[32]

Worries about wordishness and religious authority persisted into the eighteenth century. Writing almost a hundred years later, Moses Mendelssohn (1729–1786) concluded that Locke attempted to settle violent religious conflicts by portraying them as conceptual disputes.[33] Mendelssohn gently mocks John Locke for what he takes to be Locke's naïveté regarding language: "Very well! If the dispute allowed itself to be settled by a verbal definition, I would know of none that is more convenient; and if by this means one could have talked the agitated minds of his time out their intolerance, it would not have been necessary for the good Locke himself to go into exile."[34] Like Locke, Mendelssohn is at pains to separate religion from coercive, punitive power—which is, he agrees, the prerogative only of the state and to be used only for the promotion of the public good. Indeed, for Mendelssohn the antithesis of coercion and religion (*Jerusalem*, 72) is best exemplified not by Christianity but by Judaism, which nowhere in its scriptures commands that one believe anything but only that one perform certain actions (and thus is a revealed legislation not a revealed religion) (90, 100). On this point Locke and Mendelssohn agree.[35] And again, like Locke, Mendelssohn's rhetoric reveals that he recognizes the power of persuasion, its "irresistible force" (75), in matters of religion: "[Religion] does not prod men with an iron rod; it guides them with bands of love. It draws no avenging sword, dispenses no temporal goods, assumes no right to any earthly possessions, and claims no external power over the mind. Its *weapons* are reason and persuasion" (73; italics added). Yet again, like Locke, Mendelssohn suggests that words are weapons even as he denounces the use of the latter. Nonetheless, Mendelssohn's concerns go beyond facing the formidable challenges of religious violence; he is deeply troubled by what he perceives to be an increasing reliance on the power of speech to knit together societies.

Mendelssohn also believes that language is artificial and that the connection between signs and things or ideas is arbitrary. He, too, imagines words as external signs for internal thoughts that must be conveyed across individuals (*Jerusalem*, 66–67). Yet Mendelssohn supplies a revealing theory of the evolution of language—one that conveys his ambivalence about the relationship between bodies and signs, whereby the body blocks but also delivers and retains meanings "from mouth to heart" (119). In the first phase things themselves are signs, as, for instance, doctors carrying snakes to show that they can render the harmful harmless; in the second phase images of things come to stand for the things; in the third stage outlines are used as representations of things; in the fourth phase hieroglyphics stand for composites; and in the fifth phase an alphabetical script is developed (107–117).[36] According to Mendelssohn, in the first four stages there is a liability to idolatry given the embodiment of the sign. There is always the tendency for the thing or image to draw attention simply to itself rather than pointing away from itself as a sign. With alphabetical script the chance of idolatry is nonexistent given the disembodied and abstract character of letters. Letters humbly, steadfastly deflect our gaze elsewhere. Nonetheless, with the advent of text cultures there is for Mendelssohn a profound danger of social fragmentation as relationships are reduced to the fragile chains of words, letters, and texts (119).

The preacher does not converse with his congregation; he reads or declaims to it a written treatise. The professor reads his written lectures from the chair.

Everything is dead letter; the spirit of living conversation has vanished. We express our love and anger in letters, quarrel and become reconciled in letters; all our personal relations are by correspondence; and when we get together, we know of no other entertainment than playing or *reading aloud*. (103; italics in original)

Here is a surprising critique of that darling of the Enlightenment: the reading public.[37] If the word is to usher in a new polite decorum in societal bonds, Mendelssohn has his doubts about the staying power of such a new world order. (How his critique resonates with contemporary anxieties regarding texting!) Mendelssohn warns his readers that no society can afford to leave the body behind in fashioning collective ties and obligatory bonds. Mendelssohn wishes to avoid the polar dangers of idolatry and alienation. He is seeking an alternative mode of cultural transmission that avoids the inertia of images and the weightlessness of words.

Although Mendelssohn worries about fashioning a common good, he is emphatic that we ought to resist the efforts to construct a universal faith, a single religion of humanity or state. Why? Recall the worry that is opposite to his worry of alienation: idolatry. Micah Gottlieb argues that by insisting on a plurality of meaning-making communities, Mendelssohn preempts the liability to idolatry—that this one set of signs is indeed an adequate representation of God.[38] But Mendelssohn's arguments against a universal faith reveal, again, his unexpected ambivalence about the power of speech. Mendelssohn argues that religious universalism would actually compound the fragility of language. It would only further unravel already tenuous bonds.

The unifiers of faiths want to join forces; they wish to squeeze, here and there, the meshes of words, to render them so uncertain and broad that the concepts, regardless of their inner difference, may be forced into them just barely. In reality everyone would then attach to the same words a different meaning of his own. . . . None of us thinks and feels exactly like his fellow man; why then do we wish to deceive each other with delusive words? We already do this, unfortunately, in our daily intercourse. (*Jerusalem*, 137–38)

Mendelssohn's comments here cast some doubt on Gottlieb's thesis. Mendelssohn appears to reject the possibility of a presumed univocality of speech that would be universally understood to adequately represent God. Rather, Mendelssohn suggests that such efforts are an attempt to mask the diversity that God has stamped on the world's faces and tongues. Any attempt to establish universal meanings and communities, albeit seductive, is bound to strain the already tenuous ties of speaking and reading publics.

Mendelssohn, I suggest, makes explicit what is only implicit in Locke: that to truly persuade someone, appeal must be made to affection as well as to reason, to the body as well as to the mind. In *Jerusalem* Mendelssohn declares, "In fact the most essential purpose of religious society is *mutual edification*. By the *magic power* of sympathy one wishes to transfer truth from the mind to the heart; to vivify, by participation with others, the concepts of reason, which at times are quite lifeless, into *soaring sensations*" (74; second and third sets of italics added). Scholars of religion will no doubt be reminded of sociologist Émile Durkheim's notion of collective effervescence, in which collective religious ritual generates a contagious enthusiasm and sense of power to each member, revivifying their loyalty to the group. Like Durkheim, Mendelssohn argues that only religion can provide this kind of visceral and persuasive power; hence it supplies the defect of the state, which, in relying on the idiom of law, does not produce conviction. Mendelssohn writes, "And it is here that religion should come to the aid of the state, and the church should become a pillar of civil felicity" (43).

Mendelssohn identifies at least two ways in which the religious body shores up the fragility of speech. First, Mendelssohn speaks of eternal truths that appeal to reason and are proclaimed directly by creation (read: the obvious testimony of the senses). In this instance God simply sidesteps language in communicating eternal truths. God instructs us "not by sounds or written characters, which are comprehensible here and there, to this or that individual, but through creation itself" (*Jerusalem*, 93); one simply beholds the sight of the heavens "declaring the majesty of God" (126). Perhaps to shore up their power, Mendelssohn adds that God "inscribed [these eternal truths] in the soul with a script that is legible and comprehensible at all times and in all places" (126).

Second, Mendelssohn looks to religious ritual or the ceremonial law to stabilize meaning and promote the sociability and connection of persons. (In this case he echoes Sergeant.) Ritual performance by a community of bodies brings to life the laws and rites revealed in scripture:

"Men's actions are transitory; there is nothing lasting, nothing enduring about them that, like hieroglyphic script, could lead to idolatry through abuse or misunderstanding. But they also have the advantage over alphabetical signs of not isolating man, of not making him to be a solitary creature, poring over writings and books. They impel him rather to social intercourse, to imitation, to oral, living instruction" (*Jerusalem*, 119). The beauty of ritual is that it allows for the continuous socialization of a people without danger of taking on a life of its own, without becoming an end in itself. Mendelssohn's recourse to the body to supply authorizing power to speech and to establish social ties within and across time reflects his perception of participating in a text-based culture and, moreover, the fragility of that culture.

Mendelssohn was not the only thinker to recommend the civic purposes of ritual. Locke's trusted peer Archbishop John Tillotson remarked, "For is there any *Civil Society* or *Corporation* into which persons are admitted without some kind of *Solemnity*?"[39] Whereas Tillotson insisted the Bible was the "rule of faith," he also advocated what he referred to as the "Religion of an Oath," and specifically corporeal oaths in which the "sign or ceremony of it is performed by some part of the body."[40] Similarly John Wilkins (1614–1672), Bishop of Chester, founder and secretary of the Royal Society, and head of colleges at Oxford and Cambridge, reasoned, "It is natural for men who are joined together in Civil Societies to join likewise in Religious worship. And in order to do this, 'tis necessary that there should be publick Places and solemn Times set apart for such Assemblies."[41]

Tillotson's recommendation of a "Religion of an Oath" was further developed by the famous English Nonconformist hymnist, poet, theologian, and logician Isaac Watts (1674–1748). Watts composed songs for children that were inspired by Locke's pedagogy. He was full of praise for Locke, citing expressly his "Letters of Toleration."[42] He agrees with Locke that theism is necessary to civil welfare and that all people, even governors, have a duty to attempt to persuade others as to what they understand to be religious truth, without, however, "compulsion or force or terror."[43] Nonetheless, like Tillotson, Watts was convinced that government requires oaths, for the "bond" of an oath is the "ultimate Resort of Men," which is an appeal to a "superior and invisible power" (*New Essay on Civil*

Power, 14). To be effective, oaths must be administered by the magistrate "with the utmost solemnity" (15). For those who doubt the efficacy of oaths, Watts counters that oaths have generally had so little force because they commonly mention only God's potential blessing rather than God's wrath. If persons utter only "So help me God," Watts reasons that the "Curse is conceal'd and only imply'd at a distance; so that very few who take an Oath have such an awful Sense of their Transactions with an Almighty and avenging Power" (15–16). (He acknowledges, however, that people may not be willing to pronounce a curse upon themselves.)[44] He also admits that "the scrupulous" (he refers to the "Quakers") will be uncomfortable with "ceremonies invented by Men" (17). Nonetheless, as another installment of this "Religion of an Oath," Watts recommends that upon reaching the age of 21, children born of parents who are members of the nation visit the magistrate to declare, first, their veneration of God and, second, their obedience to moral and civil laws. This ritual will constitute their complete membership in the nation. Moreover, knowing that this event lies ahead for their children, parents will be constrained to provide religious education for their children and to attend required public lectures given by preachers of natural religion (which are to be funded by taxes).[45]

For his part, Locke does not recommend a "religion of the oath." (Mendelssohn, too, had nothing good to say about oaths; see his *Jerusalem*, 64–65.) Locke agrees with Sergeant that when God clothes his will in *words*, there is doubt and uncertainty—as testified by the volumes of biblical interpretation and commentary (*Human Understanding*, 3.9.23 [489–90]). This is, after all, the liability of this kind of "Conveyance" (3.9.23 [490]). Nonetheless, Locke notes that God clothes his will in other media. Whereas Locke forgoes the reassurance of innate knowledge, he suggests that evidence of God's existence and our comportment toward it is as obvious as the fact that the sun shines.[46] In creating the world, "God hath spread such legible Characters of his Works and Providence" (3.9.23 [490]) that God's existence cannot possibly be doubted. According to Locke, the "script" that is God's creation appears to be less liable to diverse interpretation and uncertainty. Locke goes further, however, and argues that God not only clothes his will in words (as scripture) and in sensible signs (in creation) but also in flesh (as Jesus). He adds that the last instantiation is a more efficient conduit of meaning than mere words or even nature's signs. (Locke elaborates on this point in his discussion of the miracles of Jesus; I discuss his argument in Chapter 3.)

Locke, however, does *not* advocate ritual as an instrument of religious authority or civil solidarity. Locke agrees with the many Christian writers of the Reformation and Enlightenment who insist on the distinction in the Hebrew Bible between the "parochial," "trifling" (Hegel), and dispensable Mosaic or ceremonial law and the universally binding moral law.[47] Locke is consistently critical of religious ritual in his *Reasonableness of Christianity*. In this text he is utterly dismissive of mostly pagan ritual. Priests press on the people their "invented Rites" (144) in order to secure their own "Empire" (143). The priests did not teach that the gods were pleased by virtue; instead they insisted that the gods cared only if "they were diligent in their Observations and Ceremonies; Punctual in their Feasts and Solemnities, and the tricks of Religion" (147). Rather than enjoining a good life, people were told to offer an "expiatory Sacrifice, that attoned for the want of it" (147).[48] For Locke such tricks of religion sap resources and soak up labor. He bemoans "Stately Buildings, costly Ornaments" and "pompous, phantastical, cumbersome Ceremonies" (159). To Locke such materializations are a colossal waste. Locke argues that God, who is spirit, wants none of this but our spirit only (160).[49] Locke goes so far as to claim that Christianity largely dispensed with ritual! In a late (1698) unpublished piece titled "Sacerdos," he writes:

Jesus Christ, bringing by revelation from heaven the true religion to mankind, reunited these two again, religion and morality, as the inseparable parts of the worship of God, which ought never to have been separated, wherein for the obtaining the favour and forgiveness of the deity, the chief part of what man could do consisted in a holy life, and *little or nothing at all was left to outward ceremony*, which was therefore *almost wholly cashiered out of this true religion . . . all pompous rites being wholly abolished.*[50]

Locke is seeking to spare bodies from the ritual labor entailed in the sacralization of political entities so that those bodies might be more "gainfully" employed.

Nonetheless, Locke's repudiation of ritual seems incongruous, given his acknowledgment that recourse to the body supplements the liability of words in forging intersubjective ties. I suggest that Locke's reasons for disavowing the ritual body are both political and theological. Locke's disdain of ritual is congruent with his apparent predilection for tacit consent as opposed to explicit political consent. I suspect that Locke fears that ritualistic displays of consent to membership in the polity are in danger of highlighting the contrived character of political obligation. Locke wants political obligation to *feel* natural even as he insists it is not natural. Locke makes a distinction between tacit and express consent as applying to the difference between, on the one hand, visiting a country, owning property in that jurisdiction (and hence having an extension of one's body within the boundaries of that government), and traveling through it, and, on the other hand, being a full member of that country (see *Two Treatises*, II: 119–22 [392–94]). Yet Locke never gets around to describing particular acts of express consent in this text; this lacuna in Locke's text has prompted a significant amount of scholarship.[51]

Locke does, however, supply additional instances of tacit consent. Locke claims that the formation of language, specifically the common association of certain words with certain meanings, entails tacit consent.[52] He asserts that the introduction and use of money reflects tacit consent. He also attributes the widespread practice of children inheriting their parents' property (instead of returning it to a common pool of potential property) to tacit consent. Locke also describes the history of political societies as entailing tacit consent to the rule of the father. Such consent to the father's authority and government would be "almost natural" and "scarce avoidable" given the "tenderness" of the father (*Two Treatises*, II: 75 [360]).[53] In this discussion Locke's analysis echoes the fact that the word *consent* is derived from *consentir*, which means "to feel with or across." In relationships in which the other is seen as an extension of oneself (or at least as not hostile or antagonistic) or in which the power of that other is seen as reciprocally enabling to one, there is a sense of "feeling with" and thus a trust that the other acts to secure one's interests. In such cases consent would not need to be expressed, for it would be performed by the relationship itself. It would be confirmed in the daily habits of mutual care. Indeed, when Locke speaks of members of a new generation giving their tacit consent "separately in their turns" (he is referring to inheritance), he adds that "people take no notice of it, and thinking it not done at all, or not necessary, conclude *they are naturally Subjects* as they are Men" (II: 117 [391]; italics added).

Elaine Scarry suggests that the prominence of tacit consent in Locke reflects his commitment to the body serving as the locus, or perhaps, lever, of consent.[54] Govert Den Hartogh likens consent in Locke to a "convergence of expectations" to "common practices" and "convention" and relates it to "reciprocity."[55] Peter Josephson insists that for Locke tacit consent is expressed in everyday customs and common practices that generate a "sentiment of obligation" or "sentiment of attachment."[56] Consent emanates from and in turn augments myriad instances of good faith and mutual solicitude; it is the "feeling with," the trust, that prompts cooperation and mutual assistance. Such a tight weave of felt obligation is wholly incongruous with the supposition of a singular occasion of a spoken formula on the threshold of political membership or even of a common transfer of a population from the "state of nature" to political society. This is why Locke's history of the nearly imperceptible steps of tacit and "scarce avoidable" consent that "before remembrance" led from parental authority to political authority is far more relevant to his theoretical account of the legitimacy of political power than is usually supposed. Because for Locke obligatory ties are fashioned by repeated actions and by daily transactions with others, economic and affectionate, it is a mistake to attribute to Locke the idea of consent as a matter of "attitude" or as a single action accomplished by an "isolated agent acting upon the world from a position of unfettered autonomy."[57]

On at least one occasion Locke insisted on the necessity of a performance of explicit consent. Writing in the 1690 post–Glorious Revolution context of internal turmoil and threats from foreign powers (chiefly France), Locke recommends the following to be expressly consented to by all: (1) a general act of oblivion for all guilt of association with previous administrations; (2) the repudiation of the doctrine of divine right of kings; (3) a public condemnation of the miscarriage of former reigns; (4) an acknowledgment of William's having with armed force recovered "our liberties, laws and Religion"; and (5) the declaration that William is king by right and not only by fact. Locke emphasizes that the time is one of disunity—a disunity so great as to threaten the nation.

Complaints are everywhere soe loud and the apprehensions that people droope under are soe visible. . . . They are our divisions, which throw a dred amongst us, and everyone sees and says unless we are better united we cannot stand. . . . I appeal now to every true Englishman whether the preservation of our peace, the safety of the King's person, and the security of the Kingdom doe not all center in the points I have here mentioned. Those who refuse to unite in these, do they not declare they are separate from the government and will be noe friends to its continuance? . . . The presse openly scatters doubts and every one finds a great many questioning without knowing any that are *in heart and persuasion* for the government.[58]

Palpable alienation and the threat of war necessitate the stronger medicine of explicit consent. Locke adds to this argument for express consent the suggestion that the consequence of his fellow Englishmen's unwillingness to offer such consent to William will be a personal and traumatic experience of the epitome of nonconsensual power: "Will he be satisfied with what he has don when he sees his children stript and his wife ravished?"[59] Locke's comments on this occasion suggest that express consent is necessary to overcome endemic estrangement and hostility, whereas tacit consent reflects the preferred context of familiarity and fondness.[60]

For Locke, then, express consent is the exception and tacit consent is the rule. Whereas acts of express consent draw attention to the boundaries between bodies (even as it performs their overcoming), Locke idealizes the power that passes imperceptibly across bodily boundaries. Locke is looking to articulate the bases of both power's legitimacy and its efficacy. On the one hand, he insists that power must be legitimate and thus distinguished from the body and held up for inspection and deliberation. Legitimate power is neither passed through bloodlines nor aimed at those bodies like a sword. On the other hand, Locke recognizes that power's efficacy resides in its imbrications in bodies—to the extent that it appears inextricable or inalienable from those bodies. Locke sees the body as the repository of obliging power—not the body in contrived or foregrounded rituals but more specifically the body employed in quotidian activities of reproducing a commonwealth. It is in these contexts that power is made real, one might say natural or effortless. Bruce Lincoln's theory of authority illumines the implicit logic of Locke's understanding of legitimate and effective power. Lincoln argues that authority consists of both persuasive power (i.e., consent) and coercive power (i.e., arms) *in latency*. In other words, someone's authority is being contested precisely when that someone must either work at persuading others to consent to his or her authority or must call in the troops to regain order.[61] Authority is operative precisely when it need not call attention to itself, when compliance to it is automatic, like taking one's seat and remaining quiet when a prime minister rises from her chair to speak.

What is new in Locke, then, is the imperative of consent combined with a repudiation of religious or political ritual as a mechanism for performing this consent. Given this repudiation of ritual, I disagree with Michael Zuckert and Mark Goldie that Locke proffers a civil religion.[62] The phrase *civil religion* first appears in Jean-Jacques Rousseau. For Rousseau civil religion is eminently simple: existence of God, a future life, the reward of virtue and the punishment of vice, and probation of religious intolerance. So far Rousseau sounds like Locke, but he goes beyond Locke in recommending civic ceremonies directed to the rapid transmission of feelings to the masses by appealing specifically to the eye.

More recent scholarly discussions of civil religion have added the centrality of sacrifice, both as shared memory and as ritual. In the late 1960s Robert Bellah appropriated Rousseau's phrase and argued that American civil religion is constituted by both creed and deed: a collective faith in a transcendent deity who calls America to account and the cyclical celebration of national holidays. These holidays, Bellah insists, consistently evoke the memory of shared sacrifice and trial as so memorably articulated by Abraham Lincoln. Paul Kahn argues that the only truly effective political bonds are those that flow to and from the will and beget feelings of love—a love strong enough to endure sacrifice.[63] Thus for Kahn enduring political societies are not composed of discursive agreements but of profound *personal* relationships that prompt members to risk death to preserve them. Indeed, for Kahn sacrifice is the definitive mark of the political. Similarly, Carolyn Marvin and David W. Ingle insist on the visceral character of the bonds between fellow citizens. They argue that producing this "felt nation" requires the periodic performance of sacrifice in war or, with less risk, in the bloodless contrived crises of presidential elections. According to Marvin and Ingle, the necessity of sacrifice to the reproduction of the nation goes unacknowledged for several reasons, including the assumption that modern societies are built on texts as opposed to primitive societies, which are built from the body. For Marvin and Ingle this is a modern conceit; in their view all groups are built on the body and require the willingness of their members to perform (enabled by the memory of having done so) the blood sacrifice of some members if they wish to endure as a group.[64]

In contrast to these contemporary political theorists' insistence on the necessity and centrality of sacrifice to the maintenance of modern nation-states, early modern Protestant divines were adamant that sacrifice would play no role in their civil religion. For instance, John Wilkins references the claim that the near universal practice of sacrifice suggests the "light of Nature," but he disputes this, declaring that sacrifice is suitable for ruder peoples immersed in sensible things and that the true God is best served by "virtuous minds."[65] For Archbishop Tillotson, Jesus's sacrifice puts an end to the bloody sacrifice that is the epitome and shortcoming of Judaism. He insists that God made recourse to the gruesome sacrifice of Jesus (body) rather than a gentle general pardon (speech) for three reasons: to vindicate the honor of God's laws; to create in us a horror of sin and knowledge of God's infinite mercy; and to condescend to the primitive and ubiquitous religious ritual for expiating sin, that is, bloody sacrifice. Nonetheless, Jesus's sacrifice was the sacrifice to end all sacrifice: "to put an end to that barbarous and inhuman way of serving God." Tillotson goes on to claim, erroneously, that in all the parts of the world in which Christianity was to prevail, sacrifice was to be terminated.[66] (He conveniently forgets the Catholic sacrificial understanding of the Eucharist.) Thus, for those Protestant divines who seek to offset the transience and indeterminacy of words by returning to the body by means of civic ritual, this recourse to the body emphatically excludes the affirmation, let alone practice, of sacrifice.

Locke, as I have already argued, rejects civic ritual (apart from provisions for explicit consent in rare and specific circumstances). In doing so, he departs from his contemporaneous Protestant divines and some of his subsequent Enlightenment readers. He also differs from them (or at least the Christians among them) in that he does not depict Jesus's death as a sacrifice, let alone a redemptive one. Nor is there anything in Locke's writings to suggest his agreement with the notion that Jesus's sacrifice was "the sacrifice to end all sacrifice." In fact, it is fair to say that Locke goes out of his way to suggest that

Jesus's death was no sacrifice and to avoid mention of Abraham's near sacrifice of Isaac.[67] Locke appears convinced of the relationship between the performance of sacrifice and absolute patriarchal-political power. Thus he seems intent to exonerate Judaism and Christianity of this vision of divine and human power and to suggest that absolute patriarchal-political power is a phenomenon of non-Western political theology.

In the next chapter I elaborate on Locke's political theology and make clear the reasons that it is not reconcilable with sacrifice. Whereas Locke may have harbored a distaste for sacrifice, given its proximity to religious persecution and violence, he puts forth a vision of God and God's power that is clearly inimical to the power or glorification of sacrifice. In terms of the human-divine relationship, Locke emphatically rejects notions of guilt, debt, and juridical punishment. But, more important and expressly, Locke seeks to avoid the sacralization of a polity, which follows inevitably from the insistence on the necessity and centrality of political sacrifice.

I began this project by portraying Locke as a pivotal figure in the modern attempt to construct a secular public composed of signs—the spirit-filled "republic of letters"—so as to significantly reduce both the perception and the occasion of injury, profanation, and pollution. In this chapter I have begun to uncover the doubts and anxieties that attend such an undertaking—doubts that surface in Locke, in debates among his interlocutors, and in eighteenth-century responses to his work. These doubts pertain to the efficacy of words alone to establish lasting religious and political bonds. Although Locke rejects civic ritual, I argue in subsequent chapters that Locke articulates a political theology that will undergird the circulation of religions as so many diverse fashions. Moreover, he recommends several opportunities for the diffusion and internalization of this political theology through the venues of state and family: the state's ongoing imperative to persuade the populace as to the "true religion," the state's implementation of religious instruction especially to the poor and the colonized, and parents' theological education of children from "their very cradles."

3

Liberal Political Theology

Locke nowhere else conveys the same measure of clarity and urgency as in his startling assertion, "The taking away of God, tho *but even in thought*, dissolves all."¹ If toleration was to work, Locke was adamant that atheists could not be tolerated. Some commentators regard Locke's theism as a bit of outdated nonsense evidencing Locke's irrelevance to contemporary efforts to manage a peaceable religious pluralism. But Locke's intolerance for atheists is not dramatic, at least for those who reside in England.² No punishments or penalties, no overt coercion (how impolite!). Just the subtle coercion of a tacit understanding that proclaimers of atheism will be excluded from polite society: their word simply not believed, their name wholly without credit. If such people cannot be trusted, then no one will do business with them (or vote them into office!).³ Locke's policy on atheists is reminiscent of former president Bill Clinton's policy (now repealed) regarding gays and lesbians in the military: "Don't ask, don't tell!"

Locke's theism finds him plenty of company in the contemporary period. Pace Mark Lilla, I do not think that most Americans, for instance, when confronted by references to "our shared God"—the God who purportedly grounds liberty and equality and calls humanity to righteousness—"fall mute, like explorers coming upon an ancient inscription written in hieroglyphics."⁴ Lilla seems unaware that even today a large percentage of Americans are theists and that most of them will not vote an atheist into the presidency. Lilla claims, erroneously, that Locke was one of the architects of liberalism's "great separation" between traditional political theology and political philosophy. Lilla is not the only political theorist to presume that Locke abandons political theology. Calling for a comparative exercise in political theory that engages Islamic sources, Roxanne Euben explains the thought of Sayyid Qut'b (1906–1966), the executed member of the Egyptian Muslim Brotherhood and admired ideologue of contemporary militant Sunni Islam: "Equality is only possible under a divine sovereign, where each member is equal by virtue of their common submission to God. This is not the Lockean idea of equality whereby all persons are free and equal in that each has a natural right to life, liberty, and property. Rather, it is the case that since all are equally subject to God's call, they are therefore equal."[5] Euben is mistaken; her description of this Islamic political theology is entirely accurate when applied to Locke's political theology. Locke refers to humans as submitting to God as God's servants beholden to God's law. Hence, to reconstruct Locke's political theology is to open up new avenues of cross-cultural and cross-religious exploration and debate.[6]

Of course, I am not the first to notice that God is central to Locke's project.[7] His theology has been variously characterized as Calvinist, Latitudinarian, Socinian, Arminian, Manichean, and independent. His God has been called both a tyrant and a liberal.[8] According to a number of Locke scholars, Locke looks to God to establish the priority of human rights. Jeremy Waldron concludes that Locke's God provides "some sort of leverage" for arguments endorsing human equality.[9] According to John Perry, "Locke forbids atheism not for theological reasons but because it, in some ultimate and indirect sense, threatens rights."[10] Why so indefinite? Why the qualifiers? For Kirstie McClure, Locke presumes consensus on a hierarchical and "morally-marked world of God's design," which makes manageable the adjudication of individual rights.[11] Yet McClure insists elsewhere that Locke is convinced that the truth of religious claims cannot be empirically demonstrated, and thus the *consequence* (but not the premise) of Locke's approach is the relegation of religion (including, therefore, the conviction of God's existence) to the status of subjective conviction.[12] For John Dunn, Locke's God is the necessary frame for the intelligibility of human rights.[13] How does Locke's God frame rights? What precisely is the connection between Locke's God and Locke's rights?

Liberal Political Theology 61

In what follows I provide a reconstruction of Locke's political theology to establish the centrality of theism to Locke's *liberal* political theory. Theism for Locke grounds rights and, moreover, establishes the legitimacy of the state. Therefore it is misleading to see Lockean liberalism as predicated on separating religion and politics or as establishing government "neutrality."[14] I first address Locke's proofs for God's existence and his position on natural law. Next, I elaborate on the centrality of Locke's God to his political philosophy of consent by explicating Locke's understanding of God's power. Finally, I delineate the features of Locke's liberal political theology as a rejoinder to Carl Schmitt's critique of liberalism. In making my case, I cite writings that span Locke's career, some of which he chose not to publish. Clearly, then, these writings reflect varying investments on Locke's part. While mindful of this fact, I seek to reconstruct a plausible picture of Locke's God—plausible in the coherence it draws from his writings rather than in an assumption as to what his "real" intentions were.

For Locke human rights are part and parcel of natural law.[15] Because Locke rejects a teleological account of nature, he must rely on something outside nature—that is, a transcendent God—as the basis of natural law.[16] Locke insists that the idea of God, like all other ideas, is *not* innate. He acknowledges that the idea of God requires care and attention. He reasons that humans arrive at a proper *idea* of God by enlarging the properties of existence, power, and wisdom by using the idea of infinity.[17] Locke also argues that the existence of God is the reasonable conclusion to the question as to the cause of human existence—the existence of which is beyond challenge.[18] In addition, he claims that God's existence is indicated by nature's design. Locke's arguments are not beyond challenge and not without inconsistencies—nature evidences intelligent design *and* decay and death—yet rather than anticipating a Humean theodicy that would call the supposition of intelligent design into question, Locke cites the fact of human mortality as yet more evidence that we did not make ourselves (because we would have certainly endowed ourselves with immortality).[19] Locke does not seem to be wholly satisfied with his arguments for God's existence; he chastises readers who expect him to hit upon one conclusive argument, suggesting that such an important topic was deserving of several points of approach.

Michael Zuckert argues that Locke knows his proofs for God's existence are unsuccessful and, moreover, that he does not actually need God or natural law. According to Zuckert, Locke innovates by claiming that humans are rights bearers because they are self-owners.[20] Pace Zuckert, I dispute that Locke makes humans self-owners. Moreover, I strongly disagree with another of Zuckert's contentions: that reason for Locke is merely calculative.[21]

Locke's workmanship argument is emphatic that each human is the property of God.

> The State of Nature has a Law of Nature to govern it, which obliges every one: And Reason, which is that Law, teaches all Mankind, who will but consult it, that being all equal and independent, no one ought to harm another in his Life, Health, Liberty, or Possessions. For Men being all the Workmanship of one Omnipotent, and infinitely wise Maker; All the Servants of one Sovereign Master, sent into the world by his order and about his business, they are his Property, whose Workmanship they are, made to last during his, not one anothers Pleasure. And being furnished with like Faculties, sharing all in one Community of Nature, there cannot be supposed any such Subordination among us, that may Authorize us to destroy one another, as if we were made for one anothers uses, as the inferior ranks of Creatures are for ours.[22]

It is difficult to put aside Locke's contention that God has an ownership in humans. Humans are distinguished from the rest of God's creatures in their recognition of God's existence and their concomitant reliance on God. Thus, although this fact elevates humanity, it also indicates their dependency on God. For Locke humans are not wholly at their own disposal. If this were the case, they might very well trade in their rights; they might sell themselves, sell or consume their children, and transfer to the state the authority to dictate "true religion." I suggest that Locke sees humans and God as sharing jurisdiction over humans. Locke declares that humans have property vis-à-vis God—that is, their persons—even as God has a property in them (*Two Treatises*, II: 27 [328–29]).[23] Locke consistently balances powers rather than absolutizing them, and the same goes for human and divine power. Locke inaugurates individuals who are equally distant as discrete individuals and equally proximate as the property of God or as the "Community of Nature." In other words, Locke distributes sacrality, as a portion of divine property, to each person qua a creature of

God. Locke also balances this individuality by linking humans as God's common property, as God's body, so to speak. This sacrality, however, is to remain transcendent; that is, it cannot be embodied in any person, group, or political regime.

Although Locke entertains the idea that nontheistic nations may enjoy stability, I suggest that a theistic conviction is for Locke a, if not the, chief criterion of one's humanity and rationality.[24] Whereas Locke argues that religion is not the result of or amenable to force (at least when arguing against persecution), recognition of God's existence appears to indicate one's susceptibility to force or to the pressure of impressions from without. Locke points to the "visible marks of extraordinary Wisdom and Power [that] appear so plainly in all the Works of the Creation" and claims that he cannot help but wonder how a mind could fail to discover a deity.[25] Moreover, to have an idea of such a deity is to "certainly know that Man is to honour, fear, and obey GOD, as that the Sun shines when he sees it. . . . Nor can he be surer in a clear Morning that the Sun is risen, if he will but open his Eyes, and turn them that way."[26]

As I describe in more detail in Chapter 4, Locke's epistemology poses the mind as an entity susceptible to force. Moreover, Locke correlates certainty with the amount of external force relative to the exertion of the mind. That which is certain is irresistible in its power to compel knowledge. Indeed, as Locke writes in the *Essay Concerning Human Understanding*, certain knowledge, had by intuition, does not admit of doubt (4.2.5 [533]). Certainty of God is like the sun's rays pressing on our eyes. It is distinguished from faith or opinion in which the mind is active and can regulate its assent. Locke's arguments suggest that he would have his doubts about the humanity of someone who is so *insensible* as to miss seeing evidence of God. I suggest that for Locke a rational person is one who is amenable to the unforced force of sunshine, evidence of God and natural law, and keen argumentation. Indeed, Locke remarks, "It seems stranger to me that a whole nation of men should be anywhere found so brutish, as to want the notion of a god; than that they should be without any notion of numbers, or fire" (1.4.9 [89]; italics added; see also 1.4.15 [93]). This comment indicates that Locke regards knowledge of God's existence as akin to knowledge of numbers and fire. The absence of the knowledge of God's existence makes Locke skeptical about such a person's or people's ability to feel the *force* of other evidence and thus begin to build a common fund of knowledge, a shareable reason. Reason is not merely calculative in Locke. To be reasonable for Locke is to inhabit a particular disposition toward the world. To be reasonable is to be capable of receiving impressions, of acknowledging the claims of others, of feeling beholden. If people wish to have knowledge, relationships, and political stability, then they must be responsive to the impressions of objects and people without. (As I elaborate in Chapter 5, Locke's pedagogy is directed precisely at the formation of such subjects.)

In his *Letter Concerning Toleration* Locke insists that "Promises, Covenants, and Oaths, which are the bonds of humane society, can have no hold upon an Atheist."[27] But why does Locke believe atheists cannot be trusted to keep their promises? Locke avers, "Ultimately all obligation leads back to God."[28] For Locke there is no obligation without law. For law to be effective or for obligation to take hold, it must be based ultimately on something unmade or transcendent. Standards of action are effective insofar as they are (or appear to be?) "not . . . ideas of our own making, to which we give names, but depend upon something without us, and so not made by us."[29] Thus all law is ultimately derived from natural law. Moreover, Locke insists that there is no law without a lawmaker and his enforcement of that law. God is the maker and enforcer of the law of nature of which promise keeping is a part. Locke writes, "The original and foundation of all Law is dependency. A dependent intelligent being is under the power and direction and dominion of him on whom he depends and must be for the ends appointed him by that superior being."[30] If one does not see, feel, and respond to the evidence of a wise and good deity, then one may well imagine oneself a god beholden to no one—a notion that makes that person no better than a beast. A person impervious to the imprints of nature's God suggests his or her status as an outlier to the human community. Locke worries about the fictional status of civic obligation that his theory of consent epitomizes; he supplements it with the obligation generated by the certainty of our gratuitous making by the unmade Maker.

Locke's God is not merely a placeholder for sacrality. What God represents to Locke is *power*. To use language supplied by Jeremy Waldron, the token of one's relationship to God is not the capacity for abstraction but a *feeling* of being dependent and obliged, a feeling or recognition of creatureliness. I think David Gauthier is closer to the work God does in Locke when he writes: "Why ought one obey God? We are unwilling to be his creatures; indeed, we are unable to be his creatures because we have forgotten the meaning of the status of creaturehood. Locke's theocentrism is an answer we no longer understand, but insofar as it is an answer to the question of the foundations of morality, our failure to understand does not remove the problem."[31] Although Gauthier may have overlooked the fact that the world is filled with plenty of theists who have not forgotten creaturehood, his point is certainly applicable to liberal theorists who assume that liberalism's integrity rests in part on its atheism. For Locke one must not only *believe* God exists but also *recognize* his or her dependence on a power to which he or she is obliged: "He that believeth one eternal, invisible God, *his Lord and King*, ceases thereby to be an atheist."[32]

But what kind of power does Locke's God exemplify? Some critics are deeply troubled by Locke's God and see it as inimical to his political philosophy. J. B. Schneewind, for instance, claims that Locke "could admit no difference between God's rule and that of a benevolent despot."[33] Schneewind's concerns seem justified when reading Locke's earlier texts: "God has created us out of nothing and, if he pleases, will reduce us again to nothing."[34] Schneewind's concerns are more difficult to reconcile, however, with the picture of God that emerges in Locke's later writings; as I have already noted, Locke insists that humans have a property in themselves—a point that contradicts the notion of despotic power as a rule over those without property. Vivienne Brown lodges a similar complaint, but sees it as a problem specific to the later *Two Treatises*. She argues that, whereas in the *Essay Concerning Human Understanding* Locke stresses unknowability as the index of God's infinitude, in the *Two Treatises* the figure of God becomes politicized; God in the *Two Treatises* takes on all the power relationships of elite individuals: father, judge, king, master. Brown is particularly troubled by the analogy between divine and princely power, insofar as Locke accommodates the prince's "prerogative" (i.e., power that is above the law).[35] Locke's endorsement of princely prerogative evokes Carl Schmitt's rendering of secularized political theology whereby sovereignty is equated with the imperative of deciding on the exception, on that which is outside the law, a power that Schmitt likens to the power formerly associated with the divine and with a situation analogous to the miraculous. But Brown does not take into account Locke's insistence that the prince's prerogative must be for the public good, and she does not cite passages in the *Two Treatises* that declare that God too is tied by contract.[36]

Whereas Schneewind and Brown claim that Locke's God is antithetical to Locke's political philosophy, Greg Forster claims that Locke's God is foundational to his political philosophy. Forster argues that Locke worked to establish a position of moral consensus as the pivot point of a robust pluralism. For Forster Locke's God is at the center of this moral consensus.

> Locke's God is ultimately bound by no law but his own and accountable to no one but himself. God is the ultimate arbitrary ruler—to take the most extreme example, it would arguably be consistent with Locke's proofs if God were a sadistic tyrant who created us so that he could torture us for his own amusement. Of course, Locke does not actually believe God is indifferent or hostile to humanity.... [Nonetheless] voluntarism is a necessary consequence of Locke's epistemology of moral consensus, and in turn it helps support the moral and political aspects of moral consensus.[37]

Forster insists that Locke is a voluntarist (i.e., one who understands morality as a reflection of God's will) as opposed to an intellectualist (i.e., one who understands morality as a reflection of reason and thus a standard to which the divine, too, is "subject").[38] For Forster voluntarism generates consensus because it "takes off the table all questions of justifying God's pronouncements. If we all agree that God commands a certain thing—for example, that we are not to murder one another—we need not argue over God's reasons for doing so."[39]

There are several problems with Forster's analysis. First, Forster seems to think that argumentation comes about only when people seek the *reasons* for God's pronouncements. But surely there is disagreement over what constitute God's pronouncements and whether divine authorization is warranted at all. Furthermore, if a conception of God cannot rule out that this God created us merely for his sadistic voyeuristic pleasure, this conception cannot ground agreement that God commands us not to murder each other. (Indeed, it seems such a God would hope that we would not heed such a command.) Second, Forster is incorrect that "voluntarism is the only sound approach to explaining God's authority." Voluntarism does not *explain* God's authority; it simply asserts it. Third, Locke does not just believe that God is not hostile to humanity; he insists on this point. Locke is explicit that God's authority consists in his creating and preserving humanity. Locke asserts—albeit in a paradoxical formulation—that "unlimited power cannot be an excellency without it be[ing] regulated by wisdom and goodnesse."[40] Although I agree with Forster that Locke believes pluralism pivots from theological consensus, I insist that Locke emphatically rejects the depiction of God that Forster presents.[41]

Here, we would do well to recall what it is that Locke objects to in Sir Robert Filmer's *Patriarcha*. What Locke objects to in Filmer is, first, his insistence that the Bible contains God's explicit transfer of God's power to Adam and his heirs and, second, his depiction of that power as absolute, unbent to any law, and thus producing the natural subjection of humanity. As is well-known, Locke rebuts Sir Robert's argument that political power is an extension of the paternal power passed on by God the Father through *his seed* Adam and on down the line through successive father-kings. According to Locke, such a vision of political-religious power amounts to nothing less than the visible installation of God's body on earth.[42] Locke remaps the political-religious body. He starts not with the sacred body of Christ or its representation in the sovereign body of the king but with the many bodies of sovereign individuals—endowed with punishing power—who will supposedly consent to unite into a common political body. Phrased differently, our sovereignty is a fragment of the transcendent God. Locke makes us, politically speaking, bastards; at the same time, he insists that we are religious kin, submitting to God our Father, our Maker and Master. Although Locke's God is distant, we are allowed to console ourselves with the thought of being all God's children. The price of Locke's political theology is that one can no longer claim intimacy with the divine—whether political (there can be no visible installation of God's body on earth) or personal (Locke will not countenance "the god within" of so-called enthusiasts).[43] Locke resembles an exorcist; convinced that divine imposters pose a threat to the bodies of others, he casts out the spirits of the possessed bodies of kings and enthusiasts. Thus, whereas Augustine insisted on the universal inheritance of a corrupt will, he nonetheless argued that we could enjoy the infinite object of our infinite desire, that is, God. Locke repudiates original sin but declares that the object of desire is foreclosed. Condemned to exist in a state of perpetual uneasiness for the absent good/God, Locke urges us to exploit this unease so as to be more productive. We may not come close to God, but we can, indeed we must, imitate his prodigious creativity.

Locke also objects to Filmer's portrayal of sovereign power. Locke writes, "His [Filmer's] absolute Monarchy . . . erects it self to an height, that its Power is above every Power . . . so high above all Earthly and Human Things, that Thought can scarce reach it; *that Promises and Oaths, which tye the infinite Deity,* cannot confine it."[44] Locke overlooks the fact that Filmer states that the ruler is bound by the law of nature to preserve those whom he rules.[45] This proviso, however, is boxed in by many statements that mitigate its notice, let alone force. According to Locke, Filmer's depiction of absolute patriarchal power is zero-sum; it is antagonistic to those over whom it rules. Such power is not accountable to the preservation of bodily boundaries but rather enjoys invasive prerogatives vis-à-vis vulnerable bodies. Thus, if he so wishes, the absolute ruler may castrate or sell any of his subjects. Locke also notes that Filmer focuses more on the generation of monarchs than of the people, suggesting that providing for the monarchs may be at the expense of the people.[46] Indeed, to bring home the point, Locke instantiates this arbitrary absolute power by reference to reports of Peruvian parents eating their children and to biblical passages in which parents sacrificed their children.[47] Locke goes on to note that God does not endorse Filmer's notion of "Absolute Fatherly Power."

Locke contrasts Filmer's conception of absolute power with his (Locke's) theology whereby God is "tyed" by promises and oaths. The idea of a God being bound seems unthinkable from a voluntarist viewpoint; certainly Locke's invocation of a tied (up? down?) "Omnipotency" or a God who swears by God sounds more than a trifle dissonant. Nevertheless, Locke's insistence on God's being bound to humans does not contradict the interpretation of Locke as a theological voluntarist. In a painstaking analysis Francis Oakley suggests that we read the voluntarist and intellectualist echoes in Locke as reflecting his acquaintance with the distinction between God's absolute power and God's ordained power—a distinction made by late medieval voluntarists such as William Ockham (c. 1287–1347) and Pierre d'Ailly (1351–1420). Accordingly, the binding power of the natural law—a power binding God and humans—does not suggest that the law is supreme even to God but rather that, in creating the order that God has created, God has chosen to be bound to the necessities of that order.[48] This seems to be what Locke is getting at in the following passage: "The bonds of this law are perpetual and coeval with the human race, beginning with it and perishing with it at the same time."[49] Moreover, Locke writes in the *Essay on Toleration* that God cares so much for the preservation of government that he "does sometimes . . . make his law in some degrees submit and comply with man's."[50] God can do anything God wants; nonetheless, God chose to make this world and is thus bound to honor its conditions. Oakley reasons that Locke is more indebted to late medieval thought than his interpreters usually suppose, noting in addition that he shares with the voluntarists an emphasis on the ineffability of God.[51]

Oakley is correct that Locke insists on divine ineffability; nonetheless, I suggest that Locke's political theology bears a greater resemblance to early- and mid-seventeenth-century covenantal theology than to late medieval theological thought.[52] Clearly, covenantal theology echoes Oakley's descriptions of the late medieval distinction between God's absolute and ordained power. Yet covenantal theology goes a step further by foregrounding God's acknowledgment of his accountability to law in establishing a covenant with humans. Perry Miller writes of the covenantal theologians' God:

He has placed himself under a yoke. In His nature he remains above all law, outside all morality, beyond all reason, but in Covenant he is ruled by a law, constrained to be moral, committed to sweet reasonableness. . . . Having created the universe, the creator takes His place within it upon the same level with His creatures, becoming morally responsible and liable, should he ever take unfair advantage of His might, to be arrested, prosecuted, and fined.[53]

The affinity between covenantal theology and Locke's political theology consists in a vision of God as decidedly noncapricious and as accountable to reason and human embodiment.

A divinity whose sovereignty consists in his being outside the law is one who is liable to instantiate that power by hurting human bodies. A divinity committed to being answerable to human reason and embodiment forsakes a show of power through scenes of hurt bodies. As Perry Miller quotes: "He [God] conducts the affairs in a manner 'answerable to the nature of man, not with blowes, but with reasonings and disputes.'"[54]

Note that divine sovereignty is depicted as either injuring or saluting the body and that it is the injurious display of power that is rejected. Here it is helpful to summon the analysis of Elaine Scarry in her book *The Body in Pain*. Scarry sees biblical texts as struggling to maintain the people's faith in an unseen, transcendent deity. Scarry draws attention to two biblical models for depicting the reality of that power. In the first model transcendent divine power is portrayed as antagonistic to corporeality. To make real and thus sustain belief in the almighty albeit unseen divinity, the divinity's commanding voice is paired with (indeed is said to cause) the wounded or destroyed bodies of faithless and idolatrous people. This first version of power bears some resemblance to aspects of what Foucault refers to as sovereign power. Sovereign power is on display; it is theatrical and sometimes makes itself visible on the bodies of its (injured, tortured, or executed) subjects.

In Scarry's second model divine power is portrayed as compatible with creation and especially human embodiment. Hence in this model divine power is not antagonistic to creation but is reciprocating toward it. God's power is made real through its embodiment, whether in "Passover artifacts" that prompt God's killing power to "pass over" the people (although it should be pointed out that in these cases this same killing power destroys Egyptian bodies even as it spares Hebrew bodies) or in Jesus, who is purportedly God's embodiment and who feels empathy with suffering human bodies and heals those bodies. Already in the Old Testament, God initiates the authorization of his power by offering the covenant to the Hebrew peoples. He makes his case by appealing to his astonishing rescue operation: "I am Yahweh your God who brought you out of the land of Egypt out of the land of slavery" (Exodus 20:1 [*Jerusalem Bible*]). In the Christian scriptures divine power is authorized or made real by the many healed bodies of Jesus's ministry and by the proclamation of resurrected bodies. Scarry sees the shift from the first model of divine power (antagonistic to human bodies) to the second model (reciprocating to human bodies) accomplished in the pages of the Bible. Yet it is obvious that the two versions of divine power continue to circulate in the histories of Judaism and Christianity and Islam; indeed it is these two models of divine power that are cited in the covenant theology of the seventeenth century.[55] Again, Miller: "Therefore union with god promised to be no more a torturing uncertainty, not a ravishing of the surprised soul by a terrifying power, but a definite legal status, based on *quid pro quo*."⁵⁶ Like the covenant theologians, Locke expressly rejects the first model of power for both divinity and magistrate. This first model of power is the absolute, antagonistic power that worries Locke in his treatment of Filmer's "Absolute Fatherly Power."

Nonetheless, Locke's God is significantly different from that of covenantal theology. Locke nowhere endorses a judicial providentialism whereby a wrathful God punishes the sins of individuals or nations.⁵⁷ Locke rejects a model of God's power as what Foucault refers to as "juridical." Juridical power entails the drawing up of a schedule of crimes and their respective punishments. Locke objects solemnly to the idea of God counting up our sins: "I cannot conceive it to be the design of God nor to consist with either his goodnesse or our business in this world to log the actions of our lives even the minutest of them."⁵⁸ And he cannot countenance that God would punish those who have not received the purportedly salvific message of Christianity. Thus Locke goes beyond covenantal theology's tenet that God submits his will to the law; he argues that God refrains from punitive action that might flow justifiably from the law.

Some portions of Locke's works would have us believe that God's obligating power consists truly in the threat of divine punishment or incentive of divine reward (as reported in scripture). Locke writes that the ground of morality is the "Will and Law of a God, who sees Men in the dark, has in his Hand Rewards and Punishments, and Power enough to call to account the Proudest Offender" (*Human Understanding*, 1.3.6 [69]). Locke refers to the motivating power of divine rewards and punishments throughout his writings.⁵⁹ These references are, however, difficult to reconcile with the following facts. First, Locke is explicit that the threat of punishment does not produce obligation.⁶⁰ Already in his early *Essays on the Law of Nature*, Locke insists that obligation does not consist in punitive power but rather in authoritative power. And in God's case his authority arises from his capacity as creator and preserver.⁶¹ We are obliged to God not simply because our future well-being depends on God (revelation) but because God created the world (evidence of senses). Second, Locke takes pains to critique much of Christian theology that portrays God as a punitive God. Locke speaks of God offering "rivers of pleasure," not blasts of fire. He repudiates the idea of eternal torment, asserting that God punishes "only for the good of the creature, [he] cannot remain forever in torment but shall suffer greater and longer proportionable to his sins and shall come out as soon as [he] has paid the utmost farthing."[62] Third, Locke himself appears to dismiss almost entirely the efficacy of such future consequences. He observes that hardly anyone gives a thought to future divine sanctions; rather, everyone cares much more about the immediate regard of his or her peers![63]

Locke's political theology is, I submit, strikingly original. For Locke a subject is free or is an agent insofar as that subject has a conscience, which consists in an inescapable sense of accountability to a higher power. Other thinkers have noted this dialectical relationship between subjectivity and subjection to divinity. Louis Althusser, for instance, insists that the discursive formation of subjects (what he terms interpellation) necessitates the "Unique and central Other Subject" (God). According to Althusser, each subject is *a subject through the Subject and subjected to the Subject.*[64] Nonetheless, this sense of accountability is not, for Locke, equivalent to original sin. John Dunn writes, "The human mind was to be made free in order that men might grasp the more clearly their ineluctable confinement in the harness in which, ever since the delinquencies of their first ancestor, God had set human beings in the world."[65] Dunn burdens his insight into the dialectic of freedom and subjection in Locke by tying it to original sin. Locke quits original sin. That dependency begets freedom is for Locke the result of humanity's insight into its creatureliness, not its precocious delinquencies. For Locke there is no hereditary blame; that would be unjust and would eviscerate human agency. As Timothy Stanton convincingly argues, Locke's repudiation of original sin and his assertion of humanity's natural adequacy to the discovery of God's law enables Locke to break the conspiracy of church and state—a conspiracy required if fundamentally corrupted humans were to live upright lives.[66] Thus with the dismissal of the doctrine of original sin goes the rationale (hapless concupiscence) for absolute rulers.

Locke also departs from the predominant (Catholic and Protestant) Augustinian conception of the human will. According to this conception, conversion from sin consists in accepting that God is the only true power, indeed the only actual being, and thus, in recognizing that freedom and peace of mind, consists in submitting to that power, to do God's will and forsake one's own flawed, even impotent, will.[67] Locke, however, rehabilitates the human will, arguing that God concedes the boundary of the human will and, moreover, endorses the possibility of an antagonism of human and divine wills.[68] Indeed, Locke boldly proclaims, "God himself will not save men against their wills."[69] This position is strikingly different from that of Calvin, who writes: "When he wills to save, the free will of no man can resist Him. . . . Again, when He wishes to bring men, does He bind them with physical chains? He works inwardly . . . draws them by the wills *which He has wrought in them*."[70] Although Locke asserts that humans are God's property, he also insists that each person has a property in his or her own person. God must honor the integrity of the person and weigh his or her actions accordingly. Otherwise, for Locke, morality is rendered meaningless. Locke wishes to account for the production of human agents in a theocentric universe: "The infinite and eternal God is certainly the cause of all things, the fountain of all Being & power. But because all was from him can there be nothing but God himself? Or because all power was originally in him can he communicate nothing of it to his creatures? This is to set very narrow bounds to the power of the Almighty; & by pretending to extend it, takes it away."[71] Locke's point is strikingly similar to one Hegel will make many years later. Locke's point is that conceptions of infinite power, whereby it simply proceeds in every direction without distinction or determination, actually limit that purported infinitude. If God is truly powerful, then God can afford to bestow some of that power on humans without feeling threatened. Indeed, Locke is sarcastic in his portrayal of the view he opposes.

And so whatever a man thinkes, God produces the thought, let it be infidelity, murmuring or Blasphemy, the man does nothing, his minde is only the mirror, that receives the Ideas that God exhibits to it, & just as God exhibits them, the man is altogether passive in the whole businesse of thinking. A man cannot move his Arme or Tongue, he has no power, only upon occasion the man willing it, God moves it. When man wills, he does something, or else God upon the occasion of something which he himself did before, produced this will & this action in him. This is the hypothesis that clears doubts & brings us at last to the Religion of Hobbs & Spinoza by resolveing all even the thoughts & will of men into an irresistible, fatal, necessity. For whether the original of it be from the continual motion of the Eternal [all-doing] matter or from an immaterial being which having began matter & motion continues it by the direction of occasions, which he himself has also made, as to Religion & Morality, it is just the same thing.[72]

Putting aside his particular take on Hobbes's and Spinoza's repudiation of the notion of "freedom of the will," this passage illuminates clearly that Locke insists on human agency and appears to understand it in the sense of a space of initiation or of a sphere of power that is distinguishable from God.[73]

Locke rejects a sovereign God, understood as unbound to law, and a juridical God, preoccupied with reckoning sins and meting out punishments. He also rejects the doctrine of original sin and its concomitant corruption of the will. Thus it should come as no surprise that Locke rejects atonement theology—that is, that God accepts the sacrifice of his son Jesus in exchange for the forgiveness of humanity's sins. (This fact distinguishes his position from that of Arminianism.)[74] Locke opts not for the scapegoat Jesus but for the prophylactic Jesus. For Locke the new covenant signifies the revelation that belief in Jesus serves as "cover" for humanity's inevitable failures to uphold the law.[75] Moreover, for Locke Jesus delivers not from sin but from parochial and divisive political and theological jurisdictions. Where Paul's letter to the Ephesians (2:16) reads: "And that he might reconcile both unto God, in one body, by the cross, having slain the enmity thereby,"[76] Locke comments:

So he [Jesus] might make or frame the two, viz. Jews and Gentiles, into one new society, or body of God's people, in a new constitution, under himself, so making peace between them; And might reconcile them both to God, being thus united into one body, in him, by the cross, whereby he destroyed that enmity, or incompatibility, that was between them, *by nailing to his cross the law of ordinances*, that kept them at a distance.[77]

Locke is unwilling to serve up an image of Jesus's passive body nailed to the cross. Instead, it is Jesus who nails the ritual laws to his cross. From this act a new constitution, an incorporation of two formerly hostile bodies or peoples, was to issue forth. Locke sees redemption as consisting not in Jesus's sacrificial death but in the destruction of alienating theocratic distinctions and incorporation in universal natural law.

Locke argues that before Jesus's coming, all that was needed for morality was a source of obligatory power. Pagan philosophers had no authority to back up their talk of virtue; the priests cultivated relations with divinities—albeit by means of wasteful ceremonies—but did not speak of virtue. Only Judaism combined divine authority and morality. Yet, apparently, Judaism's vision of an obliging and all-powerful God was blocked from view. Locke argues that the Jews' experience of a rescuing God as the basis of moral obligation could not be widely publicized, for a "Wall of Partition" had been built around the Jews. Locke is frustratingly evasive as to the foundation of this wall. On the one hand, he implicitly indicates barriers of geography and trade by noting that the Jews were relatively unknown. On the other hand, he asserts that Jews were condemned and thought vile by other peoples (and thus lacked the power to convey their message). Finally, he preempts both these suggestions by stating that the very law that was concomitant with their revelation of the one true God "excluded them from Commerce and Communication with the rest of Mankind."[78] In other words, Jews' adherence to the law establishes impenetrable boundaries around them as a religious and political body and preempts their indiscriminate mixing with other populations. Locke insists, however, that this wall is destroyed by Jesus, who took his message and miracles to the Gentiles. In Jesus the word delivered to the children of Israel becomes the "WORD published throughout" the area.[79] Before Jesus the word of God delivered to the Jews remains blocked by political division. Jesus heralds the broad circulation of that word. Note that what was parochial is now public, esotericism is supplanted by publication, and taboo commerce and communication between different bodies gives way to promiscuous mixing.[80]

For Locke, then, the power of Jesus consists not in his redemptive death but in both the reach and solicitousness evidenced by his ministry. More specifically, for Locke divine authority is exemplified in Jesus's performance of miracles. At first sight it looks as though Locke's recommendation of miracles comes down to the need to impress the illiterate masses. But he goes on to claim that "as it [the performance of miracles] suits the lowest Capacities of Reasonable Creatures, so it reaches and satisfies, Nay, enlightens the highest. The most elevated Understandings cannot but submit to [this] Authority . . . as Divine."[81] Patrick Riley argues that, according to Locke, divine law is known by the few through reason and by the many through revelation and miracles. He also suggests that divine law (natural law) is preponderant in Locke's early works and that consent and contract are prevalent in his later works, yet they ought to be seen as working in equilibrium or as an ensemble. I suggest that Locke's exposition on miracles explicitly aligns divine law with consent, rights, and contract.[82]

Miracles exemplify for Locke not the exceptional character of divine power (à la Carl Schmitt) but rather divine accountability to vulnerable bodies and to the imperative of consent. Locke speaks of God's miracles as analogous to "credentials" to an "embassy."[83] (Recall God's offering his credentials to the Hebrew people, "I am Yahweh your God who brought you out of slavery.") On the one hand, this seems a merely logical point. Power is abstract; it is made tangible and real through its signs. On the other hand, Locke's point is political. Credentials are solicited by individuals with the authority to ask for them, in other words, in a context whereby consent is the measure of political legitimacy. For Locke it makes sense to speak of miracles as credentials only when they are sent by "one only true God," and thus only Moses and Jesus performed genuine miracles (to cover his monotheistic bases, Locke states that there are no reports of "Mahomet" having performed them for the "vouching of his mission"). Apparently all other religions have produced only "wild stories," "so obscure, or so manifestly fabulous, that no account can be made of it."[84] Although it may be supposed that this indicates the circularity of his argument as to authoritative power and miracles, I think rather that Locke is implying that miracles cannot serve as credentials in the case of multiple gods, which suggest confused and overlapping jurisdictions. (Perhaps Locke has in mind something like Hume's later argument that the different religions' testimonies of miracles tend to cancel each other out.) Nonetheless, this tedious portion of Locke's argument should not cloud a fundamental point he makes with regard to the kind of divine power evidenced by miracles.

Although a number of commentators have read Locke as saying that miracles simply point to God's supreme power, they have overlooked the fact that Locke is careful to note the character of that power.[85] To convince his audience of God's overwhelming power, the Gospels could have portrayed Jesus as destroying cities or conjuring blazing fires. To convey the exceptional character of God's power, the point of Jesus's ministry of miracles might have been to showcase his prerogative to interrupt the laws of nature. Instead, as Locke remarks, Jesus accomplished the following: "The healing of the Sick, the restoring sight to the Blind by a word, the raising, and being raised from the Dead."[86] In short, it all comes down to the transformation from the former to the latter: "sick and well, Lame and sound, dead and alive." Bodies are cared for, healed, protected, fed, restored. This is for Locke the mark of authoritative as opposed to absolute or arbitrary power. There are no spectacular routings of enemies and no retreating of raging waters. No erecting boundaries around a "pure" people and no interrupting the laws of nature.

That Locke feels strongly about the authority of miracles consisting in their demonstration of God's accountability to human vulnerability is evident in his anonymous (on his part) debates with Jonas Proast. Jonas Proast, the Anglican clergyman and one-time chaplain of All Soul's College, Oxford, argued that "true religion" did not stand to gain through a policy of toleration. Rather, true religion required a measure of force if it was to gain a hearing. He adds that in the early years of Christianity, this force was largely supplied by miracles, and when they ended, the civil power of Christian empire supplied an analogous force. Locke's criticisms of Proast are manifold (I treat them at length in Chapter 4), but I wish to draw attention here to just one. Whereas Proast does not differentiate the force of miracles from the coercive power of empire, for Locke the power of miracles is wholly different from empire building. In response to Proast's conflation of the power of miracles with the power of state, Locke sarcastically remarks: "But men were not always *beat upon* with miracles." And in reply to Proast's contention that kings and queens are nursing fathers and mothers to the true church, Locke disagrees, adding (again sarcastically), "unless you can find a country where the cudgel and the scourge are more the badges and instruments of a good nurse than the breast and the bib."[87] The power to which miracles testify is responsive to vulnerable bodies; indeed, such power seeks to alleviate this vulnerability. In contrast, the power of the state, particularly the one cloaked in "divine right," has been, according to Locke, inimical to vulnerable bodies.

Like the voluntarists generally and the covenant theologians specifically, Locke insists on God's transcendence; he is adamant that God does not inaugurate a political regime in his name. No ruler and no enthusiast may claim to be an embodiment of the divine. Indeed, he insists that this is one of Jesus's most important teachings: that God abjures coercive power and has not built a kingdom of this world.[88] At the same time, Locke recognizes that for consent to function, power must have a sign. (A wholly hidden God is of no relevance to a consensual polity.) He argues that the sign of legitimate power is that it be accountable to properties and bodies. Ian Harris argues that authority in Locke derives chiefly from intellect and that "Locke did not subject the authority of God to revision."[89] I disagree. Locke's earlier works point to God's punitive power and prerogative for destruction. (Yet, already in the *Essays on the Law of Nature* he distinguishes authority from the power of punishment.) In his later writings Locke produces a surprisingly sophisticated rendering of God's authority—and one that grounds, elaborates on, and enriches his liberal political philosophy.[90] God has authority because God creates humans and makes promises to them, because God feels compelled to serve his credentials to them, and because his power is testified to not by the specter of their hurt bodies (or of royal bodies or ecstatic bodies) but by their healed bodies. Through Jesus God feels beholden to surrender his appropriate documentation to the very people who are illegal, who will inevitably fail to carry out the law. Nonetheless, their belief in these signs will, in turn, supply *their* credentials.

Contra those who insist that liberalism represents the official end of political theology, Locke makes his theological claims do political work. First, Locke and writers almost too numerous to mention claim that God is utterly transcendent, and moreover, they exploit this claim as a way to curb human pretensions to divine illumination and thus the potentially intolerant and coercive measures such a conviction might engender.[91] Locke's insistence that the deity does not inhere in kings or scriptures or consecrated hosts voids attempts to wrap state power in a sacred cloak of "divine right." Whereas James I claimed that "kings are called Gods . . . because they sit God upon his Throne in the earth," Locke is adamant that God has no body on earth.[92] God's transcendence means that God is not susceptible to offense or injury, nor is his word univocal.

God does not avenge challenges to God's magnificent power; indeed God bestows his punishing power on each individual, who, in turn, consents to hand this over to the state.

Second, Locke's God funds the distinction, equality, and sacrality of all individuals. Accordingly, *all* individuals are equally creatures (and not gods) and *all* are simultaneously God's property as well as their own—a status that renders illegitimate any attempt to incorporate another person as a slave or to cross his or her boundaries without permission or consent. Locke's political theology is a repudiation of political theologies in which only certain bodies are sacred (say, the king, the priests, the elect, or, to move way beyond Locke, the English, whites, the *Umma*, the born-again, heterosexuals, etc.) and other bodies polluting. Locke's political theology is also a repudiation of political theologies in which all bodies must be incorporated into the sacred body of Christ. No longer connected by the inheritance of original sin or the corresponding atonement attained through Jesus's sacrificial death on behalf of all humankind, Locke offers to individuals the possibility of being "adopted" by God in light of our actions and belief in Jesus.[93] According to Locke, God does not mandate universal salvation but offers salvation as an opportunity addressed to the individual.

Locke's political theology is significantly different from that of Carl Schmitt. For Schmitt the political question is the decision between who is a friend and who is an enemy. Schmitt acknowledges that the political reflects a negative anthropology of humans as given to hostility and conflict. Schmitt also notes that Christian theology's doctrine of original sin evidences a similarly negative anthropology that necessitates Jesus's redemptive sacrifice. The consequence of this purported foundation in anthropology is that the political is prior to any law and thus will necessitate law's suspension. Although Schmitt suggests the possibility that this will not necessarily always be the case, he also insists that the "seriousness" or stakes of having to sacrifice and kill to protect a particular way of life is what makes of life a meaningful and human life.[94]

Locke rejects a negative anthropology and its Christian correlate of original sin. He also insists that each individual is sacred qua property of God and thus is a bearer of inalienable rights. Moreover, Locke is clearly insistent on the priority of law. Thus, although he speaks of law's efficacy as owing to humanity's sense of dependence on an all-powerful God, Locke insists that divine omnipotence is nonetheless regulated by wisdom and goodness; in other words, God is also answerable to the law. For Locke this political theology serves as the consensus enabling the circulation of religious differences as persuasion, argument, or fashion and the circulation of peoples and goods in capitalist colonial development. With this political theology in place, religious difference need not entail violence or sacrifice.

It is these very features that prompt Schmitt, although not discussing Locke's work specifically, to declare that liberalism neutralizes the political. This is so because liberalism invests in individualism and translates the political concept of battle to economic competition and intellectual discussion.[95] My question is whether it is possible to see in Locke not the neutralization of the political but the secularization or worlding of the political. The significant difference between Schmitt and Locke for my purposes here is their respective takes on the relationship of the political to sacrality and to sharing. For Schmitt the political task reflects a fundamental negative anthropology whereby sharing is difficult, perhaps impossible, and actually undesirable. He sees our humanity as consisting in our struggles to protect precious ways of life and to avoid their dilution (through indiscriminate sharing). Thus for Schmitt the identity of a people is sacred; what this means for Schmidt is that protecting this identity necessitates violence, for it cannot be readily shared or accessed without destruction. Moreover, for Schmitt the sacred becomes present or immanent in sovereign will or power. Political theologies that depend on immanent sacrality—whether that of an executive or "the people"—tend to set up hierarchical and competitive structures of differential access to this sacred. For Schmitt managing this access would simply be part of the political process. For Locke it would be difficult to imagine how such an arrangement would not deteriorate into war.

In contrast, Locke attempts to dematerialize and democratize the sacred and sovereign. Locke's political theology insists on the *shared* conviction or consensus that individuals are the sacred property of a transcendent and benevolent Creator God. If everyone has a piece of sacrality, then there is no longer a basis for the distinction between pure bodies and polluting bodies. If there could be consensus about this—if this could become a shared theological conviction—then *salvation* would become private, religions could become shareable (read: public), and religious dissent would be *merely* political as opposed to criminal or bellicose. Locke's political theory, as is the case with the Enlightenment's valorization of reason, is predicated on the virtue of amplifying the shareable. Locke sees our humanity as consisting not in our willingness to kill and sacrifice to protect a sacred way of life but in increasing comfort with indiscriminate mixing among diverse individuals (who are nonetheless all creatures of the divine). For Locke, then, the political is no longer an end in itself, no longer a staging ground of the heroic and sacrificial acts of the sacred.

Similar to Schmitt's critique of liberalism, Thomas Pangle criticizes Locke's political philosophy as marking the end of Republican virtue and the rise of the "prosaic society." What Pangle means by this is that the political becomes merely an instrument to protect preexistent and individual rights, liberties, and preferences.[96] I suggest that what is described as the neutralizing or deflating of the political is best understood as a secularization of politics that makes possible the rule of law. The rule of law applies to all; it is common and unexceptional. It lacks the intensity, drama, and capriciousness of Schmittian sovereignty; it lacks the masculinism implied in Republican virtue. Nonetheless, Locke's political theology prompts us to reconsider the insistence that the stature of the political or of the theological consists in sacrifice, in that which exceeds law, rather than the protection of vulnerable bodies. Moreover, as I show in Chapter 5, Locke's pedagogy is directed to developing the attitudes and habits of civic-mindedness, not individual preferences.

In this chapter I have argued that Locke's God not only grounds and sacralizes human rights but also models consensual power. In other words, not only does God supplement the artifice of polities fashioned by consent, but also God's power is authorized by consent and specifically by a solicitous regard for vulnerable human bodies. This model is most vividly supported by Locke's reading of Christianity and of Jesus's ministry in particular. Although this suggests that Locke's political theology evidences both universal accessibility and application (natural law) and a particularistic supplement (Christian revelation), Locke insists on their congruence. Locke, of course, does not presume consensus on his political theology. He supplies criteria for distinguishing the tolerable from the intolerable. But rather than recommending punishment, he recommends several strategies for converting enemies to friends. These strategies evidence various modalities of force. Thus, although Locke may have transcendentalized, distributed, and sequestered the sacred, force continues to circulate throughout his corpus. In the next chapter I draw attention to the role of force in his epistemology, his recognition of its efficacy in religion, and his willingness to use it for converting the poor, migrant, Native, and African.

4

Force at a Distance

In the previous chapters I discussed the basic contours of Locke's secularization of religion. Locke insists that religion's circuit is not bodies, whether through injury or familial inheritance or original sin or incorporation in the body of Christ. Rather, religion's circuit is the sign, that is, speech, persuasion, or fashion. Locke's secularization of religion makes way for his own political theology, which entails a sacralization of individuals qua property of God—a God who is both transcendent and benevolent. Thus, whereas the first move reflects Locke's efforts to construe religion as the sort of thing to which one does, indeed must, consent, the second reflects Locke's conviction that his particular political theology is what grounds and enables consent in the first place.

My analysis in this chapter confirms and extends my longer running argument that the conventional view of Lockean toleration is insupportable. This conventional view has Locke making absolute distinctions between private and public, church and state, soul and body, and relegating religion to the first of these binaries. In this chapter I add to these binaries those of persuasion and force, consent and coercion, and politics and war. For these pairings I argue that Locke advocates for religion's affiliation with the first of these oppositions. Nonetheless, there are signs, again, that it would be mistaken to portray Locke as an absolutist on these matters. Although it is widely assumed that Locke sought to separate religion from power, he is consistently bringing them together. Like a number of his peers, Locke is looking to get beyond religious violence while preserving the power of religion to instill discipline and to tie individuals together. In other words, Locke is tuning into force's frequencies in order to graph and exploit its various sallies, secretions, and subtleties. As I delineate, Locke (and his interlocutors) catalog graphic horrors of force at close range and struggle to imagine force's efficacy at a distance. They denounce force that strikes and injures bodies and cheer on force that stealthily slips across those same bodily boundaries. To recognize Locke's (and his contemporaries') sophistication regarding the circuits of force is to realize that they are not naive enough to assume or to wish that force could be contained within imagined or institutionalized walls. Locke recognizes that force is inseparable from what counts, epistemologically, religiously, and politically. He is also convinced that force inevitably solicits the body. The imperative, then, is to recalibrate force in order to lend weight to a new political theology, with its attendant attachments and aspirations as well as its social, economic, and political practices.

Many credit Locke with laying the foundation for what has come to be referred to as the wall of separation between church and state: "Because the Church it self is a thing absolutely separate and distinct from the Commonwealth. The Boundaries on both sides are fixed and immovable. He jumbles Heaven and Earth together, the things most remote and opposite, who mixes these two Societies; which are in their Original, End, Business, and in every thing, perfectly distinct, and infinitely different from each other."[1] Locke's spatial metaphors in the 1689 *Letter Concerning Toleration* reproduce the literal spatial presentation contained in a 1674 journal entry on the "definitions of the nature and extent of civil and ecclesiastical power" in which "Civill Society" constitutes the left-hand column and "Church" constitutes the right-hand column. The two columns, separated by a consistent gap of white space, are additionally described as "The Paralel" [sic].[2] But whether bounded by printed columns or spatial metaphors, Locke bores several holes in the reportedly insuperable boundary between state and church and, by extension, between body and speech and force and religion.

For instance, Locke identifies three sorts of opinions or positions that cannot be tolerated in the name of toleration (the concluding section of his *Letter Concerning Toleration*). First, Locke insists that those opinions that are intolerant or seditious are not to be tolerated: "No opinions contrary to human Society . . . are to be tolerated" (49). Second, those who do "not own and teach the Duty of tolerating All men in matters of *meer* Religion" signify their willingness to seize the government and estates of their fellow subjects. Third, Locke insists that atheists are not to be tolerated. The implication of Locke's list of intolerables is that it is going to take some force to keep force out of religion!

Locke's anxiety about these intolerable opinions is rather astonishing. Does not Locke insist that religion is mere opinion? And yet here mere opinion is dangerous, including apparently the opinion that would abjure the phrase "meer Religion." Notice also that despite the lack of evidence of worldly injury, Locke is convinced of the alacrity with which opinion materializes as coercive power over others.[3] Let us say that I am of the opinion that I ought not to have to tolerate all people's religions. Is this, as Locke suggests, evidence of my willingness to seize the government and estates of my fellow citizens? Or perhaps I am convinced that my ideology ought to be the ruling ideology. Does my possession of this conviction make me dangerous—or is it merely my belief?[4]

One cannot help but notice that Locke's insistence on these "particulars," that is, the groups that cannot be tolerated, contradicts his argument that religious beliefs or opinions are not subject to the will and thus cannot be subject to regulation or punishment.[5] A person holding any of these three positions might be convinced that she cannot take any other position. And she might make appeal to Locke to argue that just as she cannot be made to fall in love, she cannot be made to renounce these beliefs. The sting of this criticism of Locke's inconsistency is neutralized by the fact that Locke nowhere specifies state punishment for these particular groups of people. He simply says that they are not to be tolerated. (Although in the case of atheists he elsewhere comments that they should be shut out of society on account of this "crime.") Perhaps Locke would defend his position by arguing that he is not seeking to change these people's position but simply seeking to curtail the circulation of their particular ideas.

The fact that the boundaries between state and church (and thus of body and soul, force and speech) appear unstable in Locke's *Letter Concerning Toleration* is not at all surprising or unusual in light of his corpus. Locke's various texts relentlessly complicate the relationship between religion and force. Despite the fact that Locke separates religion and power in the *Letter Concerning Toleration*, he insists in the earlier *Essays on the Law of Nature* that morality needs a generous helping of theistic power to produce moral obligation, or, to shift to his metaphor in the later *Reasonableness*, beautiful virtue needs a dowry if she is to be "wed" or, in a less than felicitous restatement, "bought."[6] This raises a key question: What varieties of force is Locke willing to permit, or even insist on, for the sake of true and tolerant religion?

Jonas Proast prodded Locke on just this issue, although Proast was unaware of Locke's authorship of the *Letter Concerning Toleration*. Proast states that like the author of the *Letter*, he abhors recourse to physical injury as a means to produce religious conversion. Yet he wonders whether some milder forms of force, what he calls "force indirectly and at a distance," might not prove efficacious, *if not to produce belief*, at least to prompt persons to seriously consider the true religion.[7] Proast is hitting Locke at a vulnerable spot. Although in his *Letter Concerning Toleration* Locke asserts that belief is not subject to the will and therefore is not amenable to force, in his *Essay Concerning Human Understanding* Locke accepts that although we cannot believe at will, we can will that to which we turn our attention. It is within one's power to direct one's attention to certain items and to attend to them more closely rather than distantly.[8] Thus the will has a role to play in the acquisition of knowledge and belief. And this is precisely what Proast is getting at.

In his subsequent anonymous replies to Proast, Locke again and again asks Proast for some specifics as to this "force at a distance," a phrase that Locke repeatedly quotes with a sarcastic tone (*Third Letter*, 6: 214, 379–80). He also refers mockingly to "your beloved force" (*Second Letter*, 6: 132). Proast never supplies specific examples, and he admits that such a delineation of degrees of force would be controversial.[9] Locke offers numerous critiques of Proast's position. He insists that it is impossible to detect religious error because none of us is privy to a person's mind or God's judgment. Moreover, he points out that there is no way to ascertain whether someone has sincerely and seriously considered the evidence, as Proast insists is the goal of his force at a distance. Thus Locke concludes that conformity, not impartial reflection, is the real goal of Proast's arguments: "For, pray tell me, when any dissenter conforms, and enters into the church-communion, is he ever examined to see whether he does it upon reason, and conviction, and such grounds as would become a Christian concerned for religion and not simply in order to keep his house or obtain a license to sell ale?" (Locke, *Second Letter*, 6: 73).

Although Proast acknowledges the subjective element of religious conviction, he continues to insist on the objective evidence of true religion. Tantalizingly, he critiques Locke's epistemology (again, unaware that Locke is his interlocutor in these debates) in order to challenge a hard and fast difference between belief and knowledge. Proast states that, according to Locke, knowledge is the effect of strict demonstration and is to be distinguished from belief or opinion as a sort of assent or persuasion. Proast objects to this binary opposition and asserts:

There is a third sort or degree of Perswasion, which though not grounded upon strict Demonstration, yet, in Firmness and Stability, does far exceed that which is built upon slight appearances of Probability; being grounded upon such clear and solid Proof, as leaves no reasonable Doubt in an attentive and unbyass'd mind: So that approaches very near to that which is produced by Demonstration, and is therefore, as it respects Religion, very frequently and familiarly call'd in Scripture, not Faith, or Belief onely, but Knowledge, and in divers places, Full Assurance.[10]

Although it is difficult to suppress the thought that Proast's description of "full assurance" applies to Locke's wavering arguments for God's existence, Proast never supplies any specifics as to this "clear and solid Proof" that constitutes full assurance. A similar claim to a kind of certainty that is not grounded on intuition or demonstration is graphically articulated by George Hickes, Dean of Worcester (1642–1715). Hickes sees two kinds or degrees of certainty. (He is apparently not particular about the distinction between quality and quantity.) To the first he assigns both ostensive certainty and demonstration, which leave no room for objection. The second he says results from "*violent* presumption." This is the case "where the objections on one hand are insufficient to move, or at least to turn the Balance, if put in the scale against the other, which is weighed down with the Authority of the Universal Church."[11] Proast would no doubt agree with this way of putting the point, as he is insistent that when he refers to true religion, he has in mind the Anglican Church. Such an established tradition is difficult to budge; so many people just cannot be wrong, no matter, apparently, how strong the objections.

Locke is outraged by Proast's sloppy epistemology. He insists that his own category of persuasion includes Proast's degrees of persuasion, although he adds that if degrees of firmness of persuasion constitute kinds of persuasion, then there are at least 300 sorts of persuasion (Locke, *Fourth Letter*, 6: 559)! He adds that no matter how firm one's belief, no matter how widely shared one's belief is, belief does not mutate into knowledge. Locke argues of knowledge and belief that "their boundaries must be kept, and their names not confounded." Yet, here again, a consideration of Locke's epistemology reveals fairly muddy waters. The lack of clarity is attributable, in part, to the centrality of force in Locke's epistemology.

Locke consistently describes the mind as an agent that "registers force."[12] This is especially the case when he wishes to convey the passivity of the mind in relation to the certain knowledge of intuition. In the *Essay Concerning Human Understanding* Locke describes the mind as "wax" receiving "impressions" from a "seal" that ought to have "sufficient force" (2.29.3 [363–64]). When it comes to simple ideas, the mind is "wholly confined to the Operation of things upon it," so that, for instance, "there is a *power* in Sugar to produce those ideas [of whiteness and sweetness] in our Minds" (2.30.2 [373], 2.31.2 [375]; italics added; see also 2.31.2 [376]). Locke speaks of this part of knowledge as "irresistible, and like the bright Sun-shine, forces it self immediately to be perceived . . . the Mind is presently filled with the clear Light of it" (4.2.1 [531]; see also 4.11.5 [632], 4.13.1–2 [650–51], 4.20.16 [717]). Locke correlates certainty, then, with the amount of external force relative to the exertion of the mind. That which is certain is irresistible in its power to compel knowledge. Indeed, certain knowledge, had by intuition, does not admit of doubt (4.2.4–5 [533]).

There is, however, another variety of certain knowledge in addition to intuition. It is that knowledge which is afforded by demonstration. In this case, though, doubt is possible and "pains and attention" must be applied to secure intervening proofs for the agreement or disagreement of any ideas (*Human Understanding*, 4.2.4 [532]). Locke writes of mathematicians that they are able to "force their way and make truth prevail by irresistible demonstration."[13] Thus in the case of demonstration the mind is active rather than passive. Still in both instances it is the relative force of the object, impression, or demonstration that is the index of knowledge.

Whatever comes short of these two forms of knowledge, and most things do, is faith or opinion. Faith or opinion pertains to that which is probable rather than certain. In his introduction to the *Essay Concerning Human Understanding*, Locke states that his aim is to search out "the *Bounds* between Opinion and Knowledge" and to ascertain, where we do not have certain knowledge, how we "ought to regulate our Assent, and moderate our Perswasions" (1.1.3 [44]). Unlike the irresistible force of certain knowledge (delivered by intuition or demonstration), faith or opinion or assent is subject to regulation. Whereas we are passive recipients of the force of intuitive knowledge (like the sun on our upturned faces) and sometimes skeptical or inattentive observers finally routed by demonstration, we are, or at least ought to be, resistant to the pressure of opinion.

A similar distinction, albeit helpfully elaborated, is expressed by Daniel Whitby (1638–1726), an Arminian minister in the Church of England and late correspondent with Locke. Whitby argues that whereas science compels assent, faith does not.[14] For Whitby this lack of decisive force is what makes faith a virtue. He writes, "Yea this it is which rendreth Faith *rewardable* that 'tis an act of the believers choise (and not irrefragably induced) however it be abundantly confirmed with arguments *extreamly probable*, and such as render it *perverseness* and *obstinacy* to resist."[15] Nonetheless, Whitby hints at the pressures exerted by public opinion in the "free" formation of faith.

Locke appears to realize that relying on relative external force as the criterion by which to distinguish knowledge from faith is insufficient. So he adds another: We are made *to know* by the things themselves; we are made *to believe* by people. He writes in the *Essay Concerning Human Understanding*, "That which *makes me* believe, is something extraneous to the thing I believe; something not evidently joined on both sides to, and so not manifestly shewing the Agreement or Disagreement of those Ideas that are under consideration" (4.15.3 [655]; italics added). The extraneous force of opinion or belief arises from the authority of the source from which the testimony is received (4.15.1 [654]). Despite its emanating from an extraneous force, the force of personal authority is a mighty one. Indeed, Locke argues that the authority of a "Man of credit" is so powerful that simply "hearing" his testimony, one assents to it. Furthermore, Locke admits that such authority, rightly or wrongly, is the foundation of religion: "And if the Opinions and Perswasions of others, whom we know and think well of, be a ground of Assent, Men *have Reason* to be Heathens in *Japan*, Mahumetans in *Turkey*, Papists in *Spain*, Protestants in *England*, and Lutherans in *Sueden*" (4.15.6 [657]; first italics added). Locke's comment signals his awareness that continuous exposure to or immersion in the religious opinion or persuasion of family and society is almost impossible to resist. This awareness suggests, in turn, his tacit recognition that the force of belief or opinion is as coercive as is that of knowledge. Moreover, how many individuals will differentiate the two by tracing the first to the authority of people and the second to the effect of objects?

Indeed, individuals are liable to mistake both the source and the degree of force of the impressions they claim to receive. Nonetheless, they assert their possession of certain knowledge. This is why Locke is so incensed by enthusiasm. Locke's comparisons are revealing. Like the mind of the certain knower, the mind of the enthusiast cannot admit of doubt: "They see the Light infused into their Understandings, and cannot be mistaken; 'tis clear and visible there; like the light of the bright Sunshine, shews itself. . . . [They] see it as we do that of the Sun at Noon" (*Human Understanding*, 4.19.8 [700]). Note that these are the same metaphors Locke uses to describe certain knowledge and to indicate the certainty of God's existence! Here, he scoffs at the metaphors: "When what they say is strip'd of the Metaphor of seeing and feeling, this is all it amounts to: and yet these Similes so impose on them, that they serve for certainty in themselves, and demonstration to others" (4.19.9 [700]). Because the force of certain knowledge and enthusiastic belief mirror each other (just as Satan can "transform himself into an Angel of Light," 4.19.13 [704]), Locke reminds his readers of his method for distinguishing the force of knowledge and that of opinion or belief: "For there are two ways, whereby Truth comes into the Mind, wholly distinct, so that one is not the other. What I see I know to be so by the *Evidence of the thing* it self: what I believe I take to be so upon the *Testimony of another*" (4.19.10 [701]; italics added). But of course the religious enthusiast will *not* attribute their powerful impressions or visions—which they perceive as having the force of bright sunshine at noontime—to the influence of other people. To the enthusiasts their conviction feels just the same, just as genuine, just as bluntly objective, as the force Locke identifies as constituting knowledge. But for Locke this is all just a play of metaphors lacking objective referents.

Insofar as Locke has granted that force effects knowledge and belief, he must answer to Proast's insistence that force "at a distance" might be effective in inculcating true religion. Locke offers two qualifications. First, he clarifies that the force that objects and individuals of authority exert on our senses and our minds is not that of corporal punishment or loss of property. Second, he reminds Proast that his so-called force at a distance is also available to God. Indeed, it is the preeminent prerogative of the divine. Locke writes, "But if God . . . would have men forced to heaven, it must not be by the outward violence of the magistrate on men's bodies, but the inward constraints of his own spirit on their minds."[16] Locke also points out that even in the case of God performing miracles to vouch for his authority, God's point is to make people *know of* the truths of religion, not to make them *believe* them. He argues that such is also the point of the authority of the professor of mathematics teaching Euclid's propositions. His aim is to make students aware of these propositions, not to induce their belief in them (*Third Letter*, 176; see also 439). It is as though the authority of God and that of the professor consist precisely in their not making it about them but about the content of their teaching. They are not looking to make a personal impression on their audience but rather an impression supplied only by the weight of propositions and demonstrations.

But Locke moves too fast here. Certainly the professor aims to have students able to use and apply these propositions. And to do so, the professor is expected to use various disciplinary mechanisms. For instance, if students do not complete their homework or fail their tests, they get reprimands, extra assignments, or low grades. Might Proast have something similar in mind? Indeed, in Proast's *Third Letter Concerning Toleration* he remarks "that force does some service toward the making of Scholars and Artists, I suppose you will easily grant" (17). As Proast clarifies, these disciplinary measures do not directly inculcate learning. Rather they prevail upon students to "receive Instruction and apply themselves" (17). The instructor can pressure a student to read a book or attend a lecture. Might the magistrate do the same? Jeremy Waldron notes that this is one of Proast's most serious challenges to Locke. Unfortunately, Locke did not respond directly to this analogy. Perhaps he would have, had Proast suggested explicitly that the penalties he had in mind for use by the magistrate were analogous to those at the disposal of the professor: required classes, tests, and grades! But perhaps Locke would still object. In *Some Thoughts Concerning Education* Locke counsels again and again on the need to make learning pleasant and not coercive.

Interestingly, both Proast and Locke scorn people who are impervious to the force of impressions as delivered by things and persons. Such persons are "stiff in their Prejudices" (Proast, *Argument of the Letter*, 10), and it is "onely their own Hardness and Insensibility, contracted by the custom of sinning, which render'd them incapable of any impressions from the greatest Evidence that could be given" (Proast, *Third Letter*, 32). Proast offers that the only means left (apart from God's grace) by which to make an impression on such people is to "lay Thorns and Briars" in their way. Such people are, he claims, "deaf to all Persuasions," and thus an application of force may at least induce an "uneasiness" in them that prompts them, finally, to lend an ear to the representatives of true religion (*Argument of the Letter*, 10–11). Proast wants to soften recalcitrant dissenters. He wants to get their attention, to make them amenable to direction. He reasons that the way to do this is to make them uneasy, to trouble them, to wound them so as to open them up a bit. A few thorns or briars will simply serve to make them a little vulnerable and thus a bit more receptive.

Locke, however, emphasizes God's prerogative in these matters. He insists that we leave our neighbors' stiff necks and hard hearts to God, arguing that it is ultimately God's power that effects a conversion. Moreover, he insists that there is no scriptural support for insisting that Christians are responsible for their neighbors' salvation. Finally, Locke is adamant that one cannot hand over the care of one's soul to another. For his part, Proast acknowledges the primacy of grace but offers that God is open to assistance. Proast agrees that we are not to divest ourselves of care of our own souls, but he is convinced that God has charged us with the responsibility to care for each other's souls (Locke, *Third Letter*, 6: 76–77). Locke acknowledges in the *Letter Concerning Toleration* that it is Christian duty to attempt to persuade others to the religious truth as one sees it. Again, however, persuasive words, not fines or sticks, not thorns or briars, are the only suitable instruments for making an impression on one's neighbor. Locke disagrees with Proast's approach to cracking the case of the religious hard nut.

Although in his writings on toleration Locke denies force's efficacy in generating religiosity, elsewhere he makes several comments in which religiosity is posed as the result of or as amenable to force. In the *Essay Concerning Human Understanding* Locke describes the errors, especially in religious matters, to which people of all stations in life are given.

And, however they may seem high and great, are confined to narrowness of Thought, and enslaved in that which should be the freest part of Man, their Understandings. This is generally the Case of all those, who live in Places where Care is taken to propagate Truth, without Knowledge; where *Men are forced, at a venture, to be the Religion of the Country*; and must therefore swallow down Opinions, as silly People do Empiricks Pills, without Knowing what they are made of, or how they will work . . . they are *not at liberty to refuse swallowing . . . or to chuse the Physician*, to whose conduct they would trust themselves. (4.20.4 [708–709]; italics added)

Whereas in the *Letter Concerning Toleration* the nature of the understanding is such that it cannot be compelled, in the earlier *Essay Concerning Human Understanding* this freest part of man is enslaved! Moreover, it is surprising that Locke here likens the affirmation of opinions, which, he insists elsewhere, is a wholly mental enterprise, to the physical ingestion of a remedy. The bodily metaphors only compound the explicit references to force. Hence, although Locke conveys the injustice of the situation by referring to the corruption of the sacred relationship of doctor and patient (which he strenuously insists elsewhere must be consensual), he certainly finds force to be wholly, albeit dreadfully, efficacious in inculcating religious conviction.

Locke's acknowledgement of the efficacy of force in religion appears even in his later works. Following the Glorious Revolution and his writing of the (first) *Letter Concerning Toleration*, Locke worried that if Englishmen did not unite and renounce the divine right of kings and publicly support William's right to rule, then such enemies "to our religion and nation" would open the door to French and Irish popery and arbitrary rule. Locke asked, "Will a French or an Irish master that turns him out of all and *forces even his conscience to a compliance* be mor [sic] tolerable than an English neighbor that would live quietly by him, though with some little difference in opinion?"[17] Again, Locke compounds the measure of force that is applied to the religious conscience by painting a terrifying scene of physical force: "Will he be satisfied with what he has don [sic] when he sees his children stript and his wife ravished?"[18] Forced religious convictions are like force-fed mouths, compliant consciences, and stripped and raped bodies. Locke—the person for whom religion can neither hurt nor result from hurt—vividly depicts victims of religious force. Either Locke is of two minds about the relationship between religion and force, or he regards French and Irish popery as undeniably more compelling than English reticence and courtesy. Indeed, as late as his *Second Letter for Toleration*, Locke admitted that plenty of people would "venture nothing in this world" for their eternal happiness; of them, he remarks, "These, the moderatest punishments you can imagine will make change their religion."[19]

Locke finally acknowledges that he cannot rule out that people's lives have been changed for the better by an inflicted violence, shock, or deprivation. He reasons that suffering, brought on by war, plague, persecution, or famine, might yield a spiritual transformation for the better. Moreover, he does not doubt that God has made use of these means as an occasion of good to many persons (Locke, *Second Letter*, 6: 69). (By that he means that the suffering or shock may prompt a change in one's habits or disposition; he does not argue that it will inculcate specific beliefs.) Locke also notes that apparently miracles were once useful to God in promoting the true religion, but apparently no longer are. Hence Locke reasons that demanding that God perform miracles again is at least as reasonable a proposal as Proast's. Locke continues to press the point, arguing that if usefulness constitutes lawfulness, then laypeople should be able to preach in churches and anyone, not just the magistrate, would be able to force another in matters of religion (6: 80). Usefulness is a relative term. Locke goes so far as to suggest that if castration is an aid to chastity and thus to the salvation of souls, then surely the king ought to make his subjects eunuchs for the kingdom of heaven (*Second Letter*, 6: 81; *Third Letter*, 6: 487)! Moreover, all kings, not just Anglican ones, ought to be able to make use of such measures—seeing how useful they are (*Second Letter*, 6: 69; *Third Letter*, 6: 151).[20]

Locke asserts that nowhere in his first letter on toleration did he (referring to himself in the third person as "the author") "say that it is impossible that force should any way, at any time, upon any person, by any accident, be useful towards the promoting of true religion, and the salvation of souls.... But that which he denies, and you grant, is that force has any proper efficacy to enlighten the understanding" (*Second Letter*, 6: 68). Because Locke acknowledges that force may indeed change lives for the better and may promote true religion, the emphasis surely lies with "proper" (and not "efficacy") in his denial "that force has any proper efficacy to enlighten the understanding."

Locke argues that the usefulness of force, which is certainly debatable and indeterminable (the dissenting citizen conforms to the national church but continues in debauchery), does not thereby establish its lawfulness (*Second Letter*, 6: 80; *Third Letter*, 6: 162–66). Indeed, he observes that Jesus did not authorize force and adds that Saint Augustine's advocacy of force was merely his opinion (*Third Letter*, 6: 434, 485, 529).[21] Locke offers a particularly compelling analogy to demonstrate that usefulness does not constitute lawfulness. He argues that although a patient is in need of surgery and although a skilled surgeon is available, this need and this skill would not constitute a special commission. Locke insists that only the patient's consent constitutes such a commission.[22] Proast insists that should a magistrate order skilled surgeons to operate on all those afflicted with a stone and determined to be in mortal danger, with or without their consent, "I am apt to think you would find it hard to prove, that in so doing he exceeded the bounds of his Power" (Proast, *Third Letter*, 54). For Locke such a magistrate would be exceeding the bounds of his power; no one ought to be forced to be saved, medically or religiously—at least not in this text.[23]

Proast and Locke cover a lot of ground in this debate. Locke concedes much. He acknowledges that there is force in knowledge and religion; indeed force (albeit of a particular kind) is necessary in the first case and possibly efficacious and even useful in the second. Nonetheless, he insists that force at a distance is the prerogative of God alone and that any human attempt to save another human must be by consent. Proast repeats that God did not rule out the cooperation of human power and that recourse to the power of the civil magistrate is not out of line because "all coactive power resolves at last into the sword" (*Argument of the Letter*, 23). Whereas Locke is suggesting a nuanced spectrum of force and the necessity of its authorization, Proast appears to be willing to collapse all force into that of the weapon. Proast may have been interested in force at a distance, but he seems unable to imagine force that is of a different quality or species than coercive injury and punishment. Locke agrees that all authoritative power derives ultimately from God, but as I elaborated in Chapter 3, he is at pains to insist that God's power is not signified by the weapon.

Locke's anonymous exchange with Proast is not the only instance in which Locke entertains an analogy between religion and medical therapy—an analogy that betrays the impossibility of separating religion from the body.[24] Of course, likening a dissenting religious conviction or practice to contagion or disease was fairly common in Locke's day. Nonetheless, Locke's comparisons shed light on the complex interplay of consent and coercion in his understanding of religion. Here he is responding to a potential persecutor:

If they are perfect innocents, only a little crazed, why cannot they be let alone, since, though perhaps their brains are a little out of order, their hands work well enough? "But they will infect others." If those others are infected but by their own consent, and that to cure another disease that they think they have, why should they be hindered any more than a man is that might make an issue to cure palsy, or might willingly have haemorrhoids to prevent an apoplexy?[25]

Locke evidences a sense of humor in this passage. He playfully calls into question the assumption that consent can only be offered by the fully rational agent who appears to transcend his or her circumstances or bodiliness. Far from being the act of a sovereign being in control of one's faculties, the consenting agent is already diseased and yet welcomes an additional infection. To be infected suggests passivity (invisible germs lurch and leap across bodily boundaries without first seeking our explicit consent), whereas consent suggests agency. Locke is obviously playing around with the sense of control frequently implied by consent. Locke also provides a bit of sting for those who would denounce religions they do not like as akin to an infection; this is their way, of course, of portraying the insidious force of (false) religion. Note also that Locke portrays religion as both illness and remedy to illness or as the toleration of one injury to offset another. The passage reinforces religion's ties to the body and to force. And once again Locke's prophylactic is consent.

Does Locke's recourse to consent introduce, however, an element of the will into that which he elsewhere denies has to do with the will? Surely, I would have to consent to the Jehovah's Witnesses' knock at my door, but is my subsequent becoming a Witness accurately termed an act of consent or an act of will? Recall that Locke insists that I cannot believe "at will." So, is the event of religious conversion closer to some kind of infection, or perhaps seduction? Or might it be, instead, God's invisible spirit, prompting me to see the light? Locke does not at all clarify these matters by stating in the quoted passage that individuals may be "infected but by their own consent."

William James also struggles to capture the nuances of coercion and consent in religious conversion and conviction. Nonetheless, more explicitly than does Locke, James preserves an element of agency amid the force that is religious conversion. In "The Will to Believe" James defends the "right to adopt a believing attitude in religious matters, in spite of the fact that our merely logical intellect may not have been coerced."[26] (Thus, like Locke, James sees the acquisition of knowledge and belief as a matter of force.) Yet in other writings James moves away from portraying religion as voluntaristic. In these other passages belief is the sense of reality; this sense is bodily, or more specifically, emotional: "If belief consists in an emotional reaction of the entire man on an object, how can we believe at will? We cannot control our emotions."[27] Thus belief appears to be a passive affair; James refers to beliefs as the result of an idea "stinging us," as "coerciveness over attention, or the mere power to possess consciousness." Indeed, how is it that individuals could authentically "consent" to that which they regard as "first in way of being and power," as that which "overarches and envelops," and from which "there is no escape."[28] In his well-known work *The Varieties of Religious Experience*, James insists on the primacy of surrender in religious conversion and on the "invasiveness" and "overpowering" of the religious emotion.[29] Nonetheless, James also sometimes insists on a measure of agency in belief by speaking of belief as synonymous with consent or acquiescence.[30] James remarks of religious conversion as a case of "throw[ing] ourselves upon it [the higher power] and consent[ing] to use it."[31]

James nicely captures the oscillation of body and mind and consent and coercion in religiosity. Perhaps this felicity of expression is attributable in part to his taking for granted what Locke cannot: that no one ought to be forced by another person or government in matters of religion. Nonetheless, Locke's insistence in his *Letter Concerning Toleration* that true religion is an act of the understanding responding only to the "Light" of evidence certainly takes a beating compared to his numerous acknowledgments of the efficacy (if not the lawfulness) of force in religion. Locke recognizes that many people come by their religion through steeping in a particular religious culture, through a traumatic shock, an invading army, and even, contagion.

Having delineated Locke's recognition of the inescapability of force in matters of religion, and his insistence on consent as the authorization of this force, I wish to return to the topic of Locke's intolerables. Locke declares that three groups of people are not to be tolerated. The first group consists of the intolerant, for whom there is one nation and one religion, under God. Convinced that political dominion is inseparable from religious faith and practice and thus that political membership is isomorphic with religious membership, they feel justified in exiling, punishing, or destroying those who differ from them in religious affiliation. The second group is composed of those who have de facto consented to the sovereignty of a foreign prince and thus are not members of the nation in which they reside. Such a description may apply to the Catholic hierarchy, who obviously answer to the pope, or to Muslims, who swear obedience to a foreign mullah. Given this loyalty to a foreign leader, they may be regarded as resident aliens. The third group is composed of those people who do not believe in God. As I explained in Chapter 3, Locke regards atheists as incapable of making promises or of being obligated to fellow humans and their sacred rights. Those who do not believe in God imagine themselves to be gods, wholly without accountability to anyone. Consent is meaningless to such a person. What links these intolerables is the absence of consent to a political power that will be entrusted with the protection of *all* individual bodies or properties. These intolerables cannot be tolerated because in the absence of this consent (which signifies their shared sense of sacrality), they are a threat to the bodily well-being of their neighbors. Locke's toleration is a regime in which force is authorized to protect property in the name of a property-holding God.

Locke is not, however, always consistent in his insistence on the centrality and necessity of consent. In addition to atheists, the intolerant, and members of international religious associations headed by a single leader, Locke's dissentient outsiders—one might even say heretics—include the poor, African slaves, and American natives. Whereas Locke insists that the first three groups are not to be tolerated, and atheists specifically ought to be shunned by polite society, he recommends that the second three groups be subject to religious instruction, without any apparent insistence on obtaining their consent.

In his "Essay on the Poor Law" Locke insists on the public's responsibility to provide basic necessities for the poor. He declares, "That, if any person die for want of due relief in any parish in which he ought to be relieved, the said parish be fined according to the circumstances of the fact and the heinousness of the *crime*" (*Political Essays*, 198; italics added). Locke has empathy for the poor, whom he considers unable to work. But for those poor whom he regards as able to work but who do not do so, he has none. Locke does not discuss contributing factors to poverty in his time; the population doubled between 1580 and 1680 amid periodic inflation and unemployment, and many people suffered from chronic ill health and from the London plague of 1665.[32] In fact, Locke asserts that God had blessed the times with plenty. Thus, rather than attributing poverty to demographic, economic, or epidemiological pressures or to a possibly indifferent deity, Locke attributes poverty to a character defect of the poor; the able-bodied poor are "drones" who attempt to live off others' labor (184, 189). For Locke poverty results from the sin of laziness. Moreover, as Locke asserts, "Sloth is infectious."[33] Recall that numerous justifications for intolerance in early modern England were predicated on stopping heretics or dissenters from spreading an infectious disease or engaging in licentious behavior. Locke portrays the begging poor who, he specifies, are able but unwilling to work as attacking the bodies of their fellow citizens; he laments the "pravity of Mankind," which is the desire to prey on another's property rather than suffer the pain of providing for oneself. For Locke, of course, this is tantamount to seizing and injuring the body of another. Such individuals have broken the social compact. Accordingly, Locke recommends that poor children be taken from their parents and placed in working schools or "houses of correction."[34] At these institutions children were to be subjected to long hours of labor, occasional punishment ("soundly whipped" if *above 3 and under 14* and caught begging outside their parish; 187) and religious instruction.[35] Locke writes: "Another advantage also of bringing poor children thus to a working school is that by this means *they may be obliged to come constantly to church every Sunday*, along with their schoolmasters or dames, whereby they may be brought up into some sense of religion; whereas ordinarily now, in their idle and loose way of breeding up, they are as utter strangers both to religion and morality as they are to industry."[36] Locke does not spell out the religious curriculum for these children and their adult caregivers. Nonetheless, he is confident that some sense of religion supplies the drive and discipline to labor. For Locke "idle and loose" individuals cannot be acquainted with religion; such people reveal for Locke their ignorance of their duty to be productive and thus answerable for themselves before God.

Locke insists on the priority of God's commandment in Genesis: that God gave the world in common to humanity for their preservation. But, to sustain humanity, the earth must be cultivated. Hence the world is specifically given to the "Industrious and Rational." And because the commandment extends to subduing the earth, those who labor on the earth thereby appropriate it.[37] Laboring bodies accomplish nothing less than the divine work of preserving and indeed augmenting and enlarging God's creation. James Tully urges us to consider that Locke sees labor as a moral activity. Insofar as humanity is created in the image of the making, working God, so is labor the duty of humanity, for it is the form of activity characteristic of humanity.[38] Similarly, according to John Dunn, the sweat of labor is a "sacrament" for Locke, constituting the very activity of salvation.[39] Workhouses and religious instruction, then, are inseparable remedies for the heresy or contagion of sloth.

Locke also recommends that the multitudes of English, Irish, and French Protestant poor be sent to work on colonial plantations. He urges that delinquents be sent there as well.[40] Perhaps Locke imagines that the drudgery of forced labor would be offset by the promise of English citizenship or kinship—an affiliation made possible by a shared political theology centered around the sacrality of property and the rites of labor. Recall Locke's comment: "As people of *different perswasions* enjoy Lybertie of Conscience, so let people of all Nations be naturalized, and enjoy equal privileges, with the other English inhabitants residing there."[41] This comment is contained in the 1697 document "Some of the Chief Grievances of the Present Constitution of Virginia, with an Essay Towards the Remedies Thereof." It includes the lament that "little care is taken to instruct the Indians and Negroes in the Christian faith." The proposed remedy reads:

> The Conversion and Instruction of Negroes and Indians is a work of such importance and difficulty that it would require a Treatise of its self. At present, I should advise, 1. That all Negroes be brought to Church on Sundays—2. That a Law be made, that all Negroes Children be baptized—catechized, and bred Christians—3. That as many Indian children be educated at the Colledge as may be; and these well instructed in the Christian Faith, (but with all keeping their own language) and made fit to Evangelize others of their nation and language.[42]

Will the conversion, instruction, and churching of Negroes and Indians be consensual? The document makes no clear provision for this. In his earlier *Letter Concerning Toleration* of 1689, Locke asserts that no native Americans are to be punished in "Body or Goods" for "not imbracing our Faith and Worship" (43). He goes on to write: "If they are persuaded that they please God in observing the Rites of their own Country . . . they are to be left unto God and themselves" (43).[43] One might reconcile these two documents by arguing that Locke requires education in theism but is flexible as to the particulars of theistic worship. Or, one might note that these comments reflect the fact that Locke entertains different notions of force: people can be encouraged, cajoled, pressured to attend services, but they cannot be harmed for not doing so.

Reading Locke's recommendations for the conversion and colonization of English, Irish, and French poor together with these instructions for converting Natives and Africans in the colonial context suggests the possibility that Locke endorsed several rules contained in the earlier Fundamental Constitutions of Carolina, particularly those pertaining to theism. Article 95 of this document reads: "No man shall be permitted to be a freeman of Carolina, or to have any estate or habitation within it, that does not acknowledge a God, and that God is publicly and solemnly to be worshipped." And Article 101 reads: "No person above seventeen years of age shall have any benefit or protection of the law, or be capable of any place of profit or honour, who is not a member of some church or profession, having his name recorded in some one, and but one religion record at once." Here we see the consequences of being a suspected atheist. Such a person would not qualify as a consenting citizen whose body was worthy of protection. Such a person is no body at all. In this case membership in the English nation is isomorphic with membership in a religious body. One cannot consent to one without the other. How might these poor and criminal populations—heretics all—be brought to the light of true religion? Article 97 of the constitution reads: "That heathens, Jews, and other dissenters from the purity of Christian religion may not be scared and kept at a distance from it, but, by having an opportunity of acquainting themselves with the truth and reasonableness of its doctrines, and the peaceableness and inoffensiveness of its professors, may, by good usage and persuasion, and all those convincing methods of gentleness and meekness suitable to the rules and design of the Gospel, be won over to embrace and unfeignedly receive the truth." What exactly is meant by this opportunity, and how is it to be secured? Just how different is this from Proast, who is looking to apply force at a distance in order to prompt dissenters to give serious consideration to the true religion? Would non-Christians be won over by meekness in mundane dealings, or would they be subtly coerced to attend Christian services to at least give a hearing to the "purity" of Christianity?

I suggest that Locke regards Indians and Africans as not yet capable of consent and thus they cannot be said to be forced.[44] First, they lack a money economy, which he recognizes as a token of consent (*Two Treatises*, II: 86 [367], 184 [438–39]).[45] Second, they do not enclose and develop land as property. Third, even if they are theists, they are not theists in Locke's sense—that is, they do not recognize humans as the sacred property of a divinity who has commanded their unceasing labor and inalienable freedom and equality. Such people would not know the true value of individuals as possessing an inalienable, even sacred, transcendence qua divine property. For Locke property is the basis of consent and justice. Locke, like Hobbes, believed that without personal ownership, there could only be despotism.[46] Nor would they understand the transformative powers of labor, whereby land and resources that are common become property (i.e., the extensions of individuals, who are themselves a form of property). They would not recognize the imperative of protecting property or making it available for trade at a fair price. How could any contracts be made with people who have no shared understanding of value, of property, of what is permissible to be set out to market and what is impermissible to be set out to market?[47] Without a notion of property, they lack the fundamental tools for distinguishing what is inalienable from what is alienable, in other words, for determining absolute and relative value. Consequently, they have not established the means for transactions that will create, sustain, and increase their mutual prosperity into the indefinite future. Without accumulation and inheritance of property—particularly in the form of money, which resists decay—death rules. There can be no religious, cultural, or political project in the midst of such transience.

For Locke the Natives and Africans would have to be taught all this if a political economy was to be established with them. Locke would probably insist that not only has he not violated the imperative of consent, he is preaching the gospel of consent, which makes justice, productivity, futurity, and thus historicity possible![48] Locke's religious doxa is the protection of bodies and properties; hence they can never be justifiably encroached on or hurt for any other reason than their violation of other bodies and properties. Yet such violation includes contagious sloth, the symptoms of which include lack of a money economy, lack of property laws, and begging—all of which indicate the absence of true religion. These are symptomatic of false beliefs and practices that are in danger of infecting the English empire's unwieldy body. There may be no evidence that Locke endorsed and benefited from colonial slavery because he believed the inferiority of Africans to consist in differences of skin color.[49] Race, in this instance—whether that of Africans or Indians (or English, Irish, and French)—pertains to a lack of understanding of the true religion: of a consensual political theology predicated on the sacrality of property.[50] No political contracts could be safely made with such individuals until they had been converted to Locke's political theology.

In this chapter I have sought to illuminate the complexity and tenacity of the relationship between force and religion in Locke. Indeed, what one finds in Locke is that force swings back and forth between the poles of Lockean binaries: from civil to religious, from weapon to speech, and from knowledge to belief. This slippage in the *Letter Concerning Toleration* (and elsewhere in his writings) represents not a contradiction but an implicit recognition of the role of force in making things real, convincing, and efficacious—that is, authoritative. Because Locke is resolute in his rejection of all unmediated sources of authority, such as innate ideas or naked scriptures, power percolates throughout his writings. If knowledge is no longer a given and if it is not predicated on incontestable authority, then it is won, wrested, or wrangled over. It is, in short, the result of force.

Revisiting Locke's regime of secular toleration also challenges us to nuance our understandings of the relationship between force and religion. David Little has recently suggested that the relationship between religion and force is ambivalent because religion is frequently called on to supply the authorization of force despite the repeated insistence on the antithesis of religion and force.[51] But, for Locke religion does more than authorize force; it is a species of force. This is why one must be careful to cultivate some kinds and curb others. Indeed, Locke is surprisingly frank regarding the individuals, opinions, and practices that were intolerable if "toleration" was to succeed. Perhaps we ought to consider the force that is exerted in constituting the secular. So, too, we might reevaluate as pretension the assumption that the secular surpasses parochial religiosities precisely in its extension of a generous toleration and avoidance of all talk of heresy. How might political mobilization and coalition building be affected by the recognition of marginalized or disenfranchised individuals as contemporary *secular heretics*, for example, the poor or nonheterosexuals?

I suggest that focusing on the secular as entailing the sacrality of property, rather than the privacy of religion, illuminates the persistence of certain church-state conflicts in the United States. For instance, Kathleen Sands argues that Locke is the foundational thinker with respect to the sovereign individual whose private, portable religion is analogous to a form of intellectual property, though it is, as she points out, James Madison who first defined religion as a "property of peculiar value."[52] Sands's explicit concern is how this understanding of religion has contributed to state and federal regulation of religion in America to the detriment of Native American claims to cultural preservation, evident, for instance, in the rejection of their attempts to set aside land not as private, not as "property," but as "sacred."⁵³ Taking Locke's logic into account, what I see happening in these cases is not simply the inability of the American legal system to accommodate a religiosity that does not conveniently disappear as "private" but rather the inability of that legal system to recognize sacralities not pegged to considerations of property. Consider, for instance, the dispute between the Apache Nation and the Chicago Field Museum in 2006. The Apache insisted on the return of objects, especially ceremonial masks, from the museum, which had possession of them since 1903. The Apache made their case by labeling the objects as "inalienable cultural patrimony" and thus as rightfully theirs. The museum objected, arguing that the Apache had consented to the transaction and thus that the museum had clear title to the objects and had acted in good faith. The museum's objection was to the claim that the objects were inalienable patrimony; they were willing to return the objects so long as they were categorized as sacred objects, a legal category that permits consensual alienation (whereas the category of cultural patrimony does not). Here we see a logic that bears an uncanny resemblance to that of Locke's political theology: an inalienable "sacred" patrimony enabling a brisk trade in religious objects and fashions.⁵⁴

Locke and Proast's lengthy debates about force at a distance reflect not only the struggle to reimagine and reinstate divine and religious power but also, I suggest, anxieties and uncertainties regarding their placement within an expanding horizon of a far-flung colonial empire and within the increasing density of diverse oral and textual argumentation. Traversing the globe in colonialist travelogues, witnessing the profusion of religious "fashions," and experiencing firsthand precarious employment and political exile, Locke and Proast get down to the business of how, and with what right, one strings together far-flung and proximate (within the span of the hands holding this book) political subjects. I have argued that for Locke a secular public must be leveraged to a shared political theology if the dissentient are to live and prosper together. I have also argued that Locke's political theology excludes or marginalizes some populations, even as it insidiously targets these heretics for continued missionary work. In other words, Locke is not above applying force at a distance to compel some individuals into this regime. In addition to state-mandated proselytization, however, Locke looks to the family to inculcate his political theology. In the next chapter I elaborate on Locke's pedagogy to show that for Locke the quintessence of power is its conveyance before the onset of articulate speech, before the utterance or act of anything that would resemble consent. Indeed, Locke describes this very aspect of power as religious.

5

Secular Family Values

In the previous chapters I have been arguing the case for seeing Locke's project as a multipronged political theology. One of the points of this theology entails reconstructing religion as persuasive speech, text, and fashion so that religious difference and dissent might circulate publicly without injury and so that bodies formerly bound and injured by religion might more freely circulate as well. I have already discussed the concerns that attend the specter of religion as mere opinion and fashion, in particular, the debates surrounding the authority and staying power of a religion that relies on the modern wordish ways of an emergent text culture. Nonetheless, these were not the only anxieties attending what I have referred to as the secularizing of religion. Fears of untethered words were mirrored by fears of untethered bodies. The prospect of freewheeling associations between religious "free agents," especially given the context of European colonialist expansion, generated a significant degree of comment and anxiety. The specter of the secular is of loosed bodies, especially those of women, circulating publicly and indiscriminately and attending only to the vagaries of fashion. This secular does not consist of neat boundaries between soul and body, church and state, public and private; instead, it portends a menacing mixing of genders, races, and nations.

The continued vitality of any religious community depends on regulating the sexual practices of members and guarding against indiscriminate mixing with people who are not members of the same community. Ideally, members marry within the community and produce children who are, in turn, schooled in the customs of that community and who, upon reaching adulthood, marry within the group as well. More extensive commercial enterprises, however, threatened to dissolve established boundaries against intermarriage and conversion. Sixteenth-century Italy enforced nocturnal segregation between Christians and Jews (by keeping Jews confined to the ghetto) to prevent eating, drinking, flirting, and cavorting across religious lines. The city of Venice built a walled compound for Muslim merchants.[1] Quakers, who were subjected to persecution, nonetheless expelled members for marrying outside the group.[2] The sanctity of marriage appeared to trump confessional affiliation, for no Christian confession denied the validity of mixed marriages between Christians. In turn, patriarchal prerogative trumped the sanctity of marriage. In the Lutheran Strasbourg of 1631, a woman who married a Calvinist man lost her citizenship; a man who married a Calvinist woman, however, was assumed to be capable of leading her to the correct path.[3]

Given the tight imbrication of familial and religious reproduction, much of the anxiety surrounding religious intermingling is voiced in the key of fears of sexual promiscuity. Then and now, experiments in religious rearrangements provoked questions about sex and sexuality, just as sexual rearrangements provoked ruminations on religion. One could not promote experimentation in one area without altering the course of the other. These changes seem to promise excitement, even emancipation. But they also portend risk and generate fear. It should come as no surprise, then, that a number of sources from the period in question evidence a good deal of ambivalence about such worldliness. Thus, even as the secular entices individuals to cross various boundaries, to choose their affiliations rather than be confined to inherited ones, to experiment with different pleasures, fashions, and bodily disciplines, its siren song contains discordant notes. Efforts to loosen the hold of patriarchal families give way to their reconstruction and redeployment.

Thus, although Locke untethers religion from the steady reproduction of political and familial patrimony, he reenvisions and redeploys the family as the foundation of his political theology. Lockean political theology thus appears contradictory: Bodies are expressly freed from patriarchal political-religious power only to be quietly imbued with a softer version of this power. This apparent contradiction is not, however, peculiar to Locke. This pattern—whereby patriarchal prerogatives and the steady reproduction of familial lineages are challenged by voluntary religious identifications and promiscuous arrangements of citizens, only to have these arrangements tempered or disciplined by a reinscription of patriarchal marriage—recurs, as I discuss, throughout seventeenth-century English comedies.

In what follows I first contextualize Locke's concerns about promiscuous behaviors by noting a constellation of related anxieties in a number of literary works in seventeenth-century England. I then reconstruct Locke's efforts to enlist family affection and education for the production of secular citizens. Saba Mahmood has remarked that the so-called solution secularism proffers "lies not so much in tolerating difference and diversity but in remaking certain kinds of religious subjectivities."[4] Locke was convinced that effectively remaking religious subjectivities required starting in childhood. Consequently, Locke supplied parents with detailed instructions for fashioning children into the kind of subjects fit for the promiscuous affiliations heralded by his secular. At the same time, the risks posed by these promiscuous affiliations would be tempered by a steady supply of familial affection and parental, especially fatherly, authority.

Whether he is talking about the economy or religious convictions, Locke encourages the circulation and exchange of goods, ideas, and people. Thus, although he insists on the protection of each individual's rights, Locke is also looking to relax boundaries between individuals and nations for their mutual benefit. Whereas all kinds of demarcations (status, class, gender, race, religiosity) work to keep individuals apart, Locke emphasizes consent, and even and especially tacit consent, as the truly significant token of border control. Accordingly, Locke's advocacy of toleration was regarded as part and parcel of his imbibing in unconventional sexual arrangements, exemplified by his living (for the last ten years of his life) with his close friend, Damaris Cudworth Masham, who was married to Sir William Masham.[5] Perhaps it is a bit of defensiveness on his part that prompts Locke to make a point of condemning the promiscuity of Roman toleration and to denounce adultery and promiscuity in the midst of arguing for toleration.[6] (It is hardly surprising, of course, that European colonization should beget comparisons to the Roman empire.)

Locke was also troubled by the immoral behavior of city dwellers; he supported the work of the Society for the Reformation of Manners. They ran neighborhood surveillance teams and supplied the criminal justice system with information about purported offenders of the moral code, especially prostitutes. In the eighteenth century members turned their attention to raids on "molly houses."[7]

A number of supporters of toleration insisted that it contributed to economic growth.[8] At the same time the relaxed boundaries coincident with toleration afforded a wider array of economic and, in some cases, sexual partners.[9] In declaring in favor of indulgence, James II remarked, "Conscience ought not to be constrained, nor people forced in matters of mere religion." Such force "destroys" the "interest of government" by "spoiling trade, depopulating countries and discouraging strangers."[10] This act was criticized as contributing to licentiousness and was followed by a proclamation forbidding debauchery.[11] In promoting toleration, then, one is seen as also implicitly encouraging the following activities: welcoming strangers, exchanging goods and services, and perhaps having sex. Extensive commerce came in myriad forms and threatened to undo European identities and patriarchal family relations. For instance, the Netherlands is widely recognized as having been the most tolerant of European nations and was on its way to becoming the wealthiest in the late seventeenth century. One anonymous seventeenth-century English source queries "whether they [the Dutch] will not tolerate anything rather than hinder their Traffick; and will not stick to entertain the Devil . . . and trade with him should the Fiend assume the habit of a Burgo-master and shew them Merchandize." Dutch toleration is said to be "boundlesse" and the Dutch people to be "without manners," for "they neither respect persons nor apparel." The indiscriminate mixing brought on by Dutch toleration and commerce is claimed to bring on fundamental changes in bodies and familial relationships. The source contends that the Dutch are "heated" by their voyages to the Indies, which results in their bodies being a hybrid of "Christian-European" and "Hellish-Ægyptian." This same source wonders "whether the Father and the Son were not created together, since observation tells us, there is not be found among them any demonstration of Duty or Authority to distinguish them?"[12] Perhaps the Dutch also harbored concerns about the proximity of toleration and scandal; the Netherlands was significantly more repressive of so-called frivolous pleasure (including walks in the country on Sundays) and sexual licentiousness than elsewhere in Europe.[13]

To be tolerant was to reorder one's visceral responses to all kinds of bodies, whose proximity would continue to increase. John Donne (1572–1631) crafts an analogy of religious freedom and wide-ranging sexual appetite. He denounces affection's confinement in marriage and religion's debasement as familial inheritance.[14] Embracing the true religion is akin to finding one's true love. Only in a context in which one's religious and erotic affections are allowed to range freely can one be sure that one's resultant choice is the true one. Consequently, critics consistently denounced advocates of toleration as promoting or engaging in licentious behavior. Polemics were filled with pictures and condemnations of the dangerous and unseemly behaviors of Quakers, Papists, and Familialists. Their lack of appropriate boundaries is conveyed by accusations of their spreading disease, having sex with animals, and giving birth to strange hybrids. Heretics were often lumped together as an indistinguishable mob, vilified by at least one source as "amphibious!"[15] What is apparent in these controversies is a profound sense that roving and voluntary religious appetites and affiliations trampled boundaries and posed a direct threat to the familial unit, headed by the father. Religious desire, curiosity, or fashion, untethered from the reproduction of the family unit and no longer a form of patrimony, was, and is, regarded as deeply threatening.

These linkages between expanded colonial trade, religious toleration and conversion, and sexual promiscuity were not confined to sources debating or denouncing religious toleration. They also appeared in English comedies, both before and after the Restoration. Although I cannot possibly offer an exhaustive account here, I select several episodes to convey the range and spread of attention given to the repercussions of shifting identities, changing fashions, and circulating bodies, particularly those of women. In some cases a domino effect is on display in which one attempted conversion alters the place and identity of everyone else in proximity, necessitating a resolution in which everyone is restored to his or her rightful place by the play's end. The plays seem to be cautionary tales about how far society can afford to go in the direction of allowing individuals to be—or at least appear to be—whomever they wish.

In Thomas Dekker's play *The Honest Whore* (1604, 1630), the character Candido remarks, "Is change strange? 'Tis not the fashion unlesse it alter? Monarkes turn to beggers; beggers creepe in the nests of Princes, Maisters serve their prentises; Ladies their Servingmen, men turne to women.... Ay and women turne to men ... a mad world, a mad world!" (Part I, Scene 12, H2). If everything is ruled by fashion, then everything is subject to inversion: political rule, social hierarchies, and sex. A recurrent character of early-seventeenth-century plays is the supposed virago (also spelled farregoae), or mannish woman. Recurrent features include masquerades, distant historical or geographic settings, and "bed-tricks," in which someone poses as someone else in order to sneak into bed to have sex with the unsuspecting person. If it is all artifice and appearance, if there are no stable identities, then people are continuously subject to deceit and disguise. In a world ruled by alterable fashion, everyone is looking to change places, to affiliate with whomever they will, and to appear to be or not to be whomever they may wish.[16] As one "Spanish-courtesan" in *The Rover* remarks, "England, that Nation of Change and Novelty."

Religion sometimes figures as the one remaining category that is or ought to be resistant to change. *The Honest Whore* suggests the impossibility of religion's being subject to fashion. A character in the play reports that the distinct characteristic of the prostitute is that she welcomes all religions and nations. This appears to be a reference to the implied promiscuity of religious toleration. Nonetheless, the acts of a prostitute are believed to mark and determine the prostitute no less than the various religions her cosmopolitan trade mocks. Indeed, the attempt to convert from the life of a prostitute to that of an honest woman is regarded as a difficult, even impossible, feat, likened to being "newly born" (Part I, Scene 10, G3) and to "altering thy Religion" (Part I, Scene 9, F4). In *The Second Part of the Honest Whore*, prostitution is referred to as a "religion," conversion from which is likened to lightening the skin of a dark man or to changing the spots of a leopard (Act 1, Scene 1, H3). Women may play the prostitute in cavorting with different religions, but changing religion is no more likely than changing skin color. Religion is who we are, one can no more change it than one can undo one's sexual past.

The Virgin Martyr, by Philip Messenger and Thomas Dekker (1622), explores the power of religious conversion to thwart family ties, especially an elite father's arranged betrothal for his daughter. This play also explores modalities of force in religion, similar to Locke and Proast's debate in Chapter 4. Here, the point is that genuine religiosity and affection cannot be forced; forcing religious conversion is portrayed as equivalent to a man ravishing a woman. A similar message is conveyed in William Rowley's *All's Lost by Lust* (1633), which depicts adulterous and unlawful desire as having both religious and political connotations. Such desire is referred to as a "heresy" (Act 2, EA). Rowley appears to be calibrating political force by staging the liabilities of unrestricted choice on the one hand and coercive force in religion and sex on the other. In the first case, allowing daughters to choose their religion or permitting a person to have more than one partner or religion is posed as profoundly unsettling to familial stability and patriarchal prerogative. In the second case, a monarch's act of rape destroys the legitimacy of his rule.

Aphra Behn's popular comedy, *The Rover*, which first appeared in 1677, explores more deeply the gendered aspects governing the anxieties of roving religious and sexual appetites. Such appetites are seen to jeopardize either commitments to entering marriages arranged by fathers and eldest brothers or commitments to entering religious cloisters. The promiscuous Rover, who "must, like cheerfull Birds, sing in all Groves, And perch on every Bough" (62) playfully denounces "willful Fornication" as the "crying Sin of the Nation" (36). The various scenes juxtapose public and private encounters between unmarried men and unmarried women and comments on the larger social context in which unmarried women speaking in public to unmarried men are seen as guilty of fornication or even murder (13). As the play makes clear, men have the prerogative not only of going about in public unaccompanied or unmasked but also of having their roving sexual appetite made public without penalty. The woman who attempts to do the same, however, is severely punished. The changeability of men's sexual fancies parallels the vicissitudes of the women who are at their mercy. The planned marriages at the end of the play do not secure the women's honor but rather highlight its fragility.

For all their exploration of what lies beyond the constraints of the patriarchal household, these plays nonetheless consistently draw attention to the tenuousness of a culture predicated on artifice, whereby marriage (and relatedly religion) becomes subject to the vagaries and voluntarism of fashion. Restoration comedies are populated by male libertines, gallants, and fashionable women on the one hand and by dull husbands and fathers on the other. Plots consist of sexual infidelity, deception, and the fatigue of marital commitment (e.g., William Congreve's 1700 comedy *The Way of the World*). Men and women are portrayed as resorting to deception in order to be able to circulate beyond the confines of traditional domesticity. Desires appear outsized, risky, and reluctant to settle down. For instance, William Wycherley's 1675 comedy, *The Country Wife*, explores the adventures of a man who attempts to pass as a eunuch in order to have unrestricted access to married women. His own desires are matched by the "country wife" longing for fashionable society in the town—a desire that sets her against her husband's desire to keep her literally confined in the country and that drives her to her own forms of deceit. Yet this play, as is the case with the others, ends not with the implosion of marital fidelity but with its reaffirmation.

This same resistance to conventional sexual arrangements appears in the famous, yet anonymous, *Farce of Sodom* (attributed to the Second Earl of Rochester, John Wilmont). The play is a fanciful interpretation of religious indulgence, specifically Charles II's granting of indulgence to Catholics in 1672. Charles's act is satirized as liberty of conscience declaring in favor of sodomy. Members of the court become "proselytes to pagan fuck"; nobles aspire to transcend the parochial nature of exclusive sexual partnerships and to have sex with all nations; and confidantes of the king critique the pleasureless propagative sex of old. Yet the resultant riotous promiscuity yields an epidemic of venereal disease. Thus all are enjoined to revert to the laws of Love and Nature and foreswear sodomy and promiscuity if they wish to be immortal. As in the previous plays, the reproduction of familial, religious, and political order is threatened or undone by fickle and even duplicitous religious identities and sexual attractions. In all these cases the wavering or unraveling of the obligation to faithfully reproduce familial, religious, racial, and national identifications leads to despair, fatigue, insecurity, and barrenness. Who will reproduce the nation if identity is a matter of fashion and if there are no longer obligatory ties between husbands and wives?

As a final literary source, consider Margaret Cavendish's work *The Description of a New World, Called the Blazing-World* (1668). In this utopian fantasy a Lady, abducted by a merchant, finds herself lost in a strange land following a storm, which kills the merchant. She becomes Empress of this so-called Blazing World, where the inhabitants are wealthy yet trade without use of "coin." She soon inquires as to the religion of this world. She learns that in this world there is one God, one religion, and one monarch. The rationale for this arrangement is the need for unity among the people. Moreover, fearing the "promiscuity" brought on by heterosexual men and women in proximity, women are not allowed in the congregations but must pray at home. The Empress despairs the lack of diversity of opinion and forms of worship. She introduces diversity in worship ("women being much delighted with change and variety") and starts her own public "Congregation of Women." Although she is successful at using love and gentle persuasion to convert women to her religion, the Empress comes to regret her initiatives, which, she concludes, yield factions and instability. She then advises the Emperor to return to the state of "one soveraign, one Religion, one Law, and one Language, so that all the World might be as one united Family, without divisions." Cavendish proclaims that her point is to affirm the poetic license to construct worlds, of which women artists might even imagine themselves rulers. Still, her imaginative exercise reveals contemporary anxieties about the dangers that women's fancying of fashion and longing for publicity pose to a religiosity charged with maintaining political unity and social order.[17]

The literary works I have briefly assembled here reflect a recurrent preoccupation with the possibilities and repercussions of identities and social roles becoming increasingly voluntary and subject to refashioning. There is consistent critique of patriarchal and absolutist models of power as well as repudiations of an evoked feminine rule of fashion, which is described as courting dissolution and disorder. The inability to find the alternative to rigid religious and political absolutism on the one hand and dissolution and disorder on the other terminates in rededications to established roles. Thus it seems that no matter how hard seventeenth-century theatrical, literary, and political sources push against and dissemble the arrangements of patriarchal families and religiosities, they always return to its familiar outlines, to its trusty conveyance of "natural" and inexorable power, to its steady demarcations of race, class, gender, and nation. In doing so, they anticipate the sentimentalism and gender conformism that mark cultural productions at the turn of and throughout the eighteenth century.

This same ambivalence about promoting religious diversity and its concomitant promiscuity, this same nostalgia for the unity and affection signaled by the family is evident in Locke. (I have already mentioned Locke's ambivalence about religion as fashion, that is, its trivial and disciplinary qualities.) Nonetheless, Locke prudently returns to the stage of childhood rather than marriage. His return to the family has, for him, two advantages. Given his ambivalence about the power of signs to signify clearly and compellingly and given his repudiation of ritual, pedagogy is the means by which he will ensure the development of secular subjects and the concomitant reproduction of his political theology. Returning to the family, albeit revamped, has the added benefit of cultivating the feeling of dependency that is so prized by Locke. Locke's worldly, promiscuous subjects will nonetheless feel strong emotional bonds for their parental nurturers and their heavenly father.

Although Locke rejected the argument that religion was inherited like property, he was keen to the advantages of cultivating certain predispositions, religious and otherwise, during childhood. Locke insisted that true and tolerant religion made appeal to the understanding, yet in the end Locke was not willing to wait for the understanding to fully develop before unveiling "the light and evidence" that purportedly constitutes his particular brand of theism. (Rousseau criticized Locke for attempting to appeal prematurely to children's "reason.") Already in the *Essay Concerning Human Understanding* Locke points to his future pedagogical project. He wonders whether

> those who have Children, or the charge of their Education, would think it worth their while diligently to watch, and carefully to prevent the undue Connexion of Ideas in the Minds of young People. *This is the time most susceptible of lasting Impressions*, and though those relating to the Health of the Body, are by discreet People minded and fenced against, yet I am apt to doubt, that those which relate more peculiarly to the Mind, and terminate in the Understanding or Passions, have been much less heeded than the thing deserves; nay, those relating purely to the Understanding have, as I suspect, been by most Men wholly over-looked. (2.23.8 [397]; italics added)

Locke is astonished that more parents, for the sake of their children, themselves, and their nation, do not "breed" their children in its "due season," when the mind is "at first . . . most tender, most easy to be bowed" (*Some Thoughts*, 8 [25–26]). Childhood is a short-lived period of leaky margins. Locke advises parents to act quickly to cultivate a lifelong suppleness of mind, to implant those earliest thoughts (before memory) that have the tenacious authority and staying power of the religious.

Locke's influential pedagogy *Some Thoughts Concerning Education* was drawn from letters to his relative Edward Clarke and was published in 1693 and translated into French, Dutch, German, Italian, and Swedish (a fifteenth edition appeared in 1777).[18] Locke's pedagogy is astonishingly detailed. Although the thesis of the early modern "invention" of childhood has been roundly criticized, Locke is credited with contributing to a clear demarcation of childhood as separate from the consensual adult world of politics and law.[19] Moreover, Locke's conviction that adults are 90 percent the product of their early education indicates that he regards childhood as a critical period indeed. Nothing must be overlooked in this formative period, and yet the job is made all that much easier by the purported absence of a possibly resistant will or nature. Childhood is, for Locke, power's opportunity. This is the time at which power gains easy entry into susceptible minds and pliable wills—with no need to solicit and receive a token of consent. As John Tillotson avers, "But the most likely and hopeful Reformation of the World must begin with *Children.* Wholesome *Laws* and good *Sermons* are but slow and late ways."[20]

Children have a peculiar status for Locke. They are not citizens. They are comparable to resident aliens. Locke refers to children as "travelers newly arrived in a strange country, of which they know nothing" (*Some Thoughts*, 120 [94]). Locke refers to the parental cultivation of children as "subjection." It is not, strictly speaking, political subjection; parents do not have power over the life and death of their children. Moreover, insofar as children are without reason, they are without law and hence cannot be said to have a freedom that is curtailed or suspended. Indeed, Locke qualifies his point; it is more correct to say that children have a "priviledge" and parents, a "duty."[21] Locke's analysis of parental authority is illustrious of Hannah Arendt's analysis of authority. Arendt argues that only in "instances of glaring inequality could rule be exerted without seizure of power and the possession of the means of violence... a relationship in which the compelling element lies in the relation itself."[22] Arendt, discussing Plato, refers to the relationships of patient and physician and master and slave. Surely the parent-child relation, as envisioned and exploited by Locke, exemplifies this rule.

Locke repeatedly counsels parents to avoid recourse to the rod or to angry chastisement. He demands, or rather cultivates, parental regard for children's vulnerable bodies and fragile psyches. Moreover, he wants parents to pass on this regard for vulnerable bodies; he insists that parents not expose children to histories that simply recount wars and acts of cruelty. And he recommends that parents provide children with opportunities for the tender care of animals. Nonetheless, there is always the exception in Locke. He suggests whipping for the most obstinate and rebellious of children. The whipping should not be done by parents but by the child's governor and should be done only to the point in which the efficacy of this show of power is evident in signs of submission in the face or voice of the child or when the child is "pliant" and "yielding" (*Some Thoughts*, 83 [59], 87 [62], 112 [84]). Children must be forced to open themselves to the flow of power. (Recall here Jonas Proast's justification for applying "thorns and briars" to the recalcitrant religious dissenter.)

Locke insists that parents educate their children at home and that they delay their travel. He directs that children be made to be in love with the company of their parents and that their parents early on communicate their disapproval (coldness) and approval (affection and friendship) of their children depending on their behavior (*Some Thoughts*, 69 [45]).[23] Locke is adamant that the parents' system of reward and punishment not rely on corporeal pains and pleasures (55–56 [35–36]) but rather on the emotional register of esteem and disgrace (which is, he adds, the "great secret of education," 56 [36]). Locke's approach finds confirmation in Foucault, who argues that "a small penal mechanism" functions at the heart of all disciplinary systems. These punishments may include "coldness, indifference, a question, a humiliation."[24] Parents aid the process of children learning forbearance ("which is the habit of greatest use for health of body and mind too," *Some Thoughts*, 17 [19]), by training the child to delay gratification and to be responsive to the parents' well-timed show of esteem, by easing the child back and forth across the threshold of play and instruction, and, finally, by not conducting strong emotions and shocks to their bodies and minds (115 [87]).

Again and again, Locke insists that the cultivation of children be done in *degrees* or "proceeding by gentle and insensible steps" (*Some Thoughts*, 180 [137]; Tillotson also insists on proceeding by degrees, as does William Falkner). One should always avoid sudden shocks to the body and mind (9–10 [14]); one should not "clog him with too much at once" (169 [129]). For instance, Locke outlines the tiny steps of learning to write: how to hold the pen and paper, to write smaller, to try drawing (160 [119]). Teaching happens by activity that feels effortless, pleasurable, such as the child who finds that he "has played himself into spelling" (151 [115])! Similarly, Tillotson advises that the father "not go against the grain" or proceed by compulsion and force, but rather through pleasure.[25] The orderly, detailed, and peaceful progression of education should take place in the most mundane of activities. Locke recommends that children be roused from their deep sleep (for this is the one activity Locke indulges) tenderly and artfully and in slowly progressing stages (see also *Some Thoughts*, 21 [21], 115 [90], 160 [119], 184 [139]). Locke stresses that everything be done in scarce discernible steps so that everything is kept in motion. Obstacles, clogs, resistance is avoided. No one is to get stuck.

Note that in counseling this gradualism, Locke replicates at a microlevel the gradualism he describes in the second book of the *Two Treatises*. Alongside his argument that political authority consists in consent, Locke notes the historical probability of family members' "scarce avoidable consent" to their father's political rule (II: 75 [360]).[26] If parental power quietly penetrates step by languorous step the porous bodily boundaries of children, then said children would never experience power as coercive or need to explicitly consent to such power. The gradualism of Locke's technique is coupled with reliance on the familiarity of the "mother tongue" as the basis for education. Locke gives careful instruction for raising and educating gentlemen in the correct use of English, primarily by conversation and without burdening them with training in formulating themes or declamations in Latin or Greek.[27] In addition to insisting on the use of English for English children, Locke advocates the use of ordinary language as opposed to esoteric or ornamental language. Locke is intent on aiding the flow of power and thus of words and emotions through bodies.

According to Locke, religious instruction that contributes to the formation of mental and social "clogs" includes anthropomorphic and frightening imagery of God—often instilled by ignorant nurses and servants. Parents must preempt this troublesome instruction, for "there ought very early to be imprinted on his mind a true notion of God" (*Some Thoughts*, 136 [102]). Locke insists that the mind's ideas and images are the invisible powers that govern an individual.[28] And he frequently slips in the adjective *invisible* when describing God. Children are not to make God like themselves. Rather than idolatrously clinging to a particular image of God, children are to lay themselves open to this transcendent, omniscient, albeit benevolent, God. This God is not gazed at (perhaps through the anthropomorphic images Locke claims are supplied by "foolish maids"). Rather, this God gazes at us. Locke writes, "The true ground of morality . . . can only be the will and law of a God, who sees men in the dark."[29] This comment anticipates Foucault's reference to Mettray, the nineteenth-century educational institution for children in which one wall of each child's "cell" contained the inscription in black letters: "God sees you."[30] If Locke's political God models consensual power, his pedagogical God models disciplinary power. According to Foucault, disciplinary power is organized by the criterion of the "normal" and is characterized by the production of various institutions of study and surveillance. Disciplinary power does not call attention to itself. Rather, it is the power enacted by the various institutions or enclosures (and their trained professionals), which continuously create, monitor, survey, and correct subjects, that produces self-monitoring, orderly, and productive subjects.

Locke recommends that children be taught that God is the maker and governor of all things, that he sees and hears everything, and that he "does all manner of good to those that love and obey him" (*Some Thoughts*, 136, [103]). Hence he urges that children be instilled with reverence for God and be kept constantly to acts of devotion. Locke also counsels that children *not* be taught notions of spirits, goblins, or fearful things that will "awe" them. He refers specifically to "*Raw Head* and *Bloody Bones* and such other names as carry with them the ideas of some thing terrible and hurtful which they have reason to be afraid of when alone, especially in the dark" (136 [103], 138 [103]). Indeed, Locke urges that children be taught not to fear the dark and to be secure in God's protection of them. By gentle steps they are to learn not to be afraid of God but rather that God is their "Maker, Preserver and Benefactor" (136 [103]). He further instructs that children learn by heart the Creeds, the Ten Commandments, and the Lord's Prayer. Not only are portions of scripture not suitable for children, but Locke finds it wasteful for a child to read the Bible from one end to the other because it would seem to inculcate an "odd jumble of thoughts" (158 [118]). Certain stories should be selected, for example, David and Goliath, and committed to memory. The fact that Locke places several conditions on the inculcation of this material suggests that he does not want to encourage an overreliance on or literalism regarding scripture. Indeed, he urges that children *listen to* and *not read* scripture. Again, one cannot help but think of Sergeant's critique of textual culture as Protestants' "wordish" ways. Sergeant claims that the truly spiritual and authentic religious tradition is the one that is carried in one's head and learned by heart and not cited in scripture and its endless commentaries.

According to Locke, childhood is not only a window of opportunity for power's easy entry; it is also the time during which ideas take tenacious hold, the very ideas for which one will later die (*Some Thoughts*, 146 [112]).[31] He writes, "[Men] are very tenacious of the opinions that *first possess them*; they are often as fond of their first conceptions as of their first born" (*Of the Conduct*, 26 [202]; italics added; see also 28 [204] and 41 [218]; and *Some Thoughts*, "Dedication," 8). Note that it is as though ideas possess individuals rather than they possessing the ideas (Tillotson also speaks of early education as a "possession" of the mind in his *Six Sermons*, 181; see also 212 and 276). In the *Essay Concerning Human Understanding* Locke comments

that when Men, so instructed, are grown up, and reflect on their own Minds, they cannot find any thing more ancient there, than those Opinions, which were taught them, before their Memory began to keep a Register of their Actions, or date the time, when any new thing appeared to them; and therefore make no scruple to *conclude, That those Propositions, of whose knowledge they can find in themselves no original, were certainly the impress of God and Nature* upon their Minds; and not taught them by any one else. These they entertain and submit to, as many do to their parents, with Veneration; not because it is natural; nor do Children do it, where they are not so taught; but because, having been always so educated, and having no remembrance of the beginning of this Respect, they think it is natural. (1.3.23 [82]; italics in original)

If children's minds are gotten to during these, the "tender and flexible years of life," then the earliest ideas will have an authority *as though* they were from God, *as though* they were natural and innate. Recall Locke's association of certain knowledge with the power of sensory data and belief with the power of personal authority. In his earlier *Essay Concerning Human Understanding* Locke makes it clear that he prefers the first and remains suspicious of the authority of a "Man of credit." Yet here in his pedagogy he is seeking to cultivate deep-seated ideas that are no longer traceable to the authority of individuals. If people cannot trace ideas to particular individuals—if one feels as though those ideas have been there as far back as one can remember—then those ideas will seem to be simply there, traced by the touch of God or nature (*Some Thoughts*, 44 [32]). In other words, for Locke religious power is the epitome of effective power.

The religious analogy recurs again and again in Locke's pedagogy. He counsels: "*Learners must at first be believers*, and, their masters' rules having been once made axioms to them, it is no wonder they should keep that dignity" (*Conduct of the Understanding*, 28 [204]; italics added; see also Tillotson, *Six Sermons*, 278). It is difficult to imagine that this Locke is the same one who had been so leery of the effect of men of credit, who confuse their pupils as to the difference between knowledge and belief. Here, Locke suggests that belief is the foundation of all knowledge. This "early Insinuation" imparted by parent-teachers to their children is referred to as the "Urim and Thummim set up in their Minds immediately by God Himself" and as these "internal Oracles" (*Human Understanding*, 4.20.9 [712]). Here Locke refers to the divinatory tools used by the High Priests as reported in the Hebrew Bible. If we are to see and know clearly, we must be outfitted with built-in oracular devices—the installation of which we will no longer remember.

Because of the religious hold of ideas imparted early in childhood, Locke is particular about the content of those ideas.[32] He speaks of such ideas as "tak[ing] possession of our minds with a kind of authority and will not be kept out or dislodged." These early ideas are like a "sheriff" who "with all the posse" has "seized" the mind. He adds, "Men thus possessed are sometimes as if they were so in the worst sense, and lay under the power of an enchantment" (*Conduct of the Understanding*, 45 [224]). This last quotation reveals that Locke regards this early possession as a tricky undertaking. Religious possession done right makes for sociable and reflective subjects capable of exposure to new ideas and people; religious possession done wrong erodes sociability and is a "tyranny on [the] understanding." Such people "see not what passes before their eyes; hear not the audible discourse of [their] company." They remain locked "in their secret cabinet within wholly taken up with their puppet" (45 [224]). It is as though such a person becomes herself a thing, a puppet. Locke observes: "Who is there . . . whose mind, at some time or other, love or anger, fear or grief, has not so fastened to some clog, that it could not turn itself to any other object? I call it a clog, for it hangs upon the mind so as to hinder its vigor and activity in the pursuit of other contemplations, and advances itself little or not [at] all in the knowledge of the thing which it so closely hugs and constantly pores on" (45 [224]). The shame of such a clog is that it "carries them away from sociability," for the "mind should be always free and ready to turn itself to the variety of objects that occur, and allow them as much consideration" (45 [224]). Rather than clinging to particular pastimes, pleasures, ideas or objects, the critical mind is to be emotionally distanced from each particular object, ready to move on to the next item, ready to engage in comparison and analysis.

Locke compares the force of this early possession to other kinds of forces acting on adults—forces that also jeopardize one's engagements with people and events. In the *Essay Concerning Human Understanding* he lists traumatic events that become insuperable knots of mental association jamming the flow of attention and engagement. He speaks of a man accidentally injured by another and who cannot but think ill of that other; a man who dislikes a room because his friend died there; and a man who cannot bear the sight of the doctor who subjected him to a severe, albeit curative, operation (2.23.11, 12, 14 [398–99]). To these examples he adds another, albeit with sorrowful detail and surprising analogy: "The Death of a Child, that was a daily delight of his Mother's Eyes, and joy of her Soul, rends from her Heart the whole comfort of her Life, and gives her all the torment imaginable; use the Consolations of Reason in this case, and you were as good preach Ease to one on the Rack, and hope to allay, by rational Discourses, the Pain of his Joints tearing asunder" (2.23.13 [398]). Such is the force of passion, traumatic events, and, analogously, ideas absorbed in childhood: that reason is often no use against them. To bring home the hold that such events and ideas have on individuals, Locke reaches for metaphors of a clog, bind, resistance, and enchantment. Sometimes his stage setting is more ominous, populated by figures of coercive power, both ordinary (a sheriff and his posse) and terrible (the rack).

For Locke the stakes of early childhood education are quite high. The risk is the creation of subjects who are wholly unprepared for the brave new world of the secular. Such subjects cannot withstand the flow of information and conviviality. Closed off from each other, such humans are no longer rational, no longer truly alive; their minds and bodies are no longer fertile. They are locked away in cabinets, minds as brittle as mud walls, bodies stretched on the rack; the possessed are impervious to registering the subtle or strong forces of voices, sights, smells, propositions; they are no longer sensitive to the press of objects or to reason's obligatory touch. Locke's description of the person clinging desperately to his or her clog puts one in mind of Augustine's description of the sinner as one who cleaves to the desired object—a clinging that slowly transforms the person into the very thing. Augustine warns his readers that they become what they love. One opens oneself to the infinite and partakes of unceasing bliss, or one loves the finite object and undergoes a slow and painful death.

What Locke wants children to develop is a mental habit, custom, or love for suspending their will and assent. He offers several strategies for laying down this habit. He counsels again and again the practice of self-denial, and he recommends various techniques for disciplining the body: accustoming it to pain and regulating its sleep, exposure, eating, and even defecation. The practice of self-denial is not undertaken to extinguish desire (Locke insists that "where there is no desire, there is no industry") but rather to preempt desire weighed down by a too hasty or habitual attachment to specific foods and toys. The aim is to render a suppleness of mind so that the child is in command of her inclinations rather than getting stuck or hardened by some immediate pleasure or pain. What is desired is a "temper wherein the mind is capable of receiving new information and of admitting into itself . . . impressions" (*Some Thoughts*, 167 [126]). Such a mind is open to considering the evidence, so that it may generate new ideas instead of being possessed by the old, so that it may be productive rather than hard or barren. Locke writes, "For the very end and business of *good breeding* is to supple the natural stiffness and so *soften* men's tempers that they may bend to a compliance and *accommodate themselves to those they have to do with*" (143 [107]; italics added). For Locke individuals should be able to engage with diverse populations and be open to new ideas and practices. The inability to open oneself to differing interpretations and unfamiliar arguments is likened to the atrophying of social skills.

Locke fully intends to exploit the time before memory and implant the lifelong ideas and habits of a rational (read: open-minded and tolerant) person. He wants individuals to feel as though certain ideas are God-given, natural, and sacred. He just wants to make sure that they are the right ones. Thus, although Locke states matter-of-factly in the *Letter Concerning Toleration* that children do not inherit their religion from their parents, Locke counsels the inculcation of a biblically based (but not literalist) transcendent theism "*from their very cradles*" (*Some Thoughts*, 38 [29]; italics in original). The gentlemen and gentlewomen that Locke helps to produce will no doubt regard themselves as critical thinkers who are able to inhabit a distanced view on their own culture—as though they wore it like fashion rather than embodying it—who *have* religious opinions rather than *being* religious, who regard religious scriptures as subject to interpretation, and finally who relish religious debate and exposure to new ideas and practices. With this bundle of assumptions and practices they will never suspect that they are walking embodiments of the secular and thus cannot shake it off like a cloak.

Locke thinks of the gentleman not as one "stiff and insensible" but as supple, pliant, open, indeed tolerant. Power flows easily through the capillaries of such a body. Recall that Proast also scorns people who are impervious to the force of new impressions. Such individuals are "stiff in their Prejudices" (Proast, *Argument of the Letter*, 10), and it is "onely their own Hardness and Insensibility, contracted by the custom of sinning, which render'd them incapable of any impressions from the greatest Evidence that could be given" (Proast, *Third Letter*, 32). Whereas Proast argues that the state is authorized to use force "at a distance" to soften the sinner, Locke's pedagogy is designed to preempt the formation of obdurate individuals. Locke's gentleman is long accustomed to the gaze of an all powerful and male deity and the anxious glances of heavily invested parents—glances indicating alternately censure and praise. If possessing porous boundaries and an internalized critical judge are frequently symptoms of the "feminine," then one might suggest that Locke's "gentleman" has feminine contours.[33]

What Locke imagines his political theology to accomplish is similar to what William James will later say is the necessity of religion for a truly manly and eminently public man. James's project in the *Varieties of Religious Experience* is the construction of a plausible masculinity in the context of both a feminizing American consumer culture and a menacing American imperialism abroad.[34] James's vision is a society in which the hardened boundaries of philistine men would be softened and would enable mutual penetration. For James religious individuals have a "sense of an ideal spectator."[35] This discipline of confident self-correction and humility makes for peaceable relations in the context of a global pluralism. For James "the wider self" bred of religious consciousness will make for productive traffic and trade among strangers. For both Locke and James their understanding of true religion is bound up with their understandings of the Protestant "man" and his project of civilization. Religion and reason are not antithetical; rather, true religion produces amenability to reason: boundaries amenable to exposure to the force of new ideas, experiences, and bodies, without undue clinging to inherited beliefs or traumatic shock at the unfamiliar.

Neither Locke nor James advocates relegating religion to the private sphere. For these two thinkers religion cannot be tucked away into a preexisting privacy or interiority; rather, it is religion that funds an inviolable interiority begotten by one's gradual (Locke) or sudden (James) recognition of one's dependence on or surrender to the higher power that is God. Whereas James imagines the efficacy of religion as consisting in a sudden and sometimes explosive conversion, Locke bets all on a pedagogy of plodding progress. Nonetheless, this process does not create subjects turned in on themselves. Rather, enabled by a transcendent center of gravity, these subjects are able to register and negotiate the force of impressions resulting from frequent traffic with objects, ideas, and individuals. Locke and James are convinced that modernity demands the cultivation of a particular piety. This piety is one that affords congress with all sorts of people and experiences and that is fit to do battle with discordant and dissentient parties. This piety, utterly consonant with reasonableness, consists in a disposition of openness to the world. For these two thinkers religious power is central to the construction of porous subjectivities fit for civil society.

Nonetheless, Locke offsets the risks of his wider, worldly, porous selves by advocating the cultivation of deeply affectionate relationships between parents and children. Locke insists that the parent or teacher of the child "in his whole carriage make the child sensible that he loves him and design nothing but his good, the only way to beget love in the child" (*Some Thoughts*, 167 [125]). Locke turns to the body, not only as habit but also as emotion, as familial love and affection, to offset the liabilities of shifting political and religious allegiances. He chooses neither the fleeting romance of heterosexual love nor the varying palate of aesthetic judgment; instead, he counsels cementing the parent-child bond.[36] In several places Locke asserts that parents' feelings for their children are natural: "because nature for wise ends of her own has made us so that we are delighted with the very being of our children."[37] Locke wants subjection to power to feel natural and positive and thus seeks to exploit parents' purportedly natural care for their children and, in turn, to cultivate the child's desire for the esteem of his parents. The binding force of a fictional, consensual order is not to be had by some verbal formula pronounced at the threshold to a rational adulthood but rather by religious and emotional ties that preexist memory.

Martin Seliger observes that Locke "dispensed far less with fatherly authority inside and beyond the family than his long-winded and vehement polemics with Filmer would lead one to expect." Seliger argues that Locke's taking up the challenge of the paternalists is successful precisely because he "grafts" incorporation by compact onto the paternalists' argument that political society grows out of the (natural) bonds of paternal authority. In doing so, Locke "divests the compact of its fictional character." Moreover, Seliger argues that Locke's account implies a psychological "transference" by which children habituated to obeying their father come to defer and obey the man, who evidencing a preeminent character, becomes by "a kind of natural authority," ruler over them.[38] Although I agree with the gist of Seliger's argument, he ignores the significance of religion in Locke's corpus. Consequently, he fails to notice that Locke constructs and deploys a political theology that both sacralizes and softens paternal authority.[39]

Although Locke critiques Filmer for forgetting that children are under *parental* as opposed to *paternal* authority, his continued invocation of a Father God reveals his retention of the priority of fatherly authority.[40] Locke's God is "a kind and merciful Father" who "hath woven" in parents the same tenderness he showed to the Israelites. Thus Locke retains paternal authority, only softer, more emotional, more modern![41] How progressive Locke sounds when he observes, "The reservedness and distance that fathers keep often deprive their sons of that refuge which would be more advantageous to them than a hundred rebukes and chidings" (*Some Thoughts*, 96 [73]). The power of the father no longer consists in his being progenitor of his children (Locke repudiates Filmer's monogenetic theory), or in his having power to procure their lifelong servitude or freedom, or in his power of life and death over them, but rather in whether he upholds the duty to care for them. Locke is adamant that parental power consists not in punishing power but in parents' capacity as caregivers and educators. Locke specifies that parents' power be "to the Children's good" (*Two Treatises*, II: 55 [346–47], 58 [348–49], 63 [352]). Hence, as soon as the father quits his duty to care, his authority ceases. Locke writes: "Nay, this power so little belongs to the *Father* by any peculiar right of Nature, but only as he is Guardian of his Children, that when *he quits his Care of them, he loses his power over them*" (II: 65 [352]; second set of italics added). Locke downgrades mere procreation in favor of the artificial and labored bonds established by caretakers. As he writes, "It being as impossible for a Governor, if he really means the good of his People, and the preservation of them and their Laws together, not to *make them see and feel it*; as it is for the Father of a Family, not to *let his Children see he loves, and takes care of them*."[42] The analogy is obvious: If the father quits his care and loses power, so, too, the careless governor loses his authority and consequently validates the right to rebel on the part of the people, who, in doing so, make appeal to a caring fatherly God.

The transcendent deity is made intimate, familiar, and dependable through the model of parental love; familial bonds are both sacralized and expanded by reference to the creator of all. If Locke insists that theism is politically necessary insofar as it imparts the dependence that grounds law, it is the parent-child relation that imbues the *sense* of dependence. It is not just that ideas instilled early grab hold but that familial inheritance and influence exert a priority and preeminence that chastises or checks the projects of self-making and reinvention of Locke's free agent. Here Locke seems to anticipate the work of Horace Kallen: "Men may change their clothes, their politics, their wives, their religions, their philosophies, to a greater or lesser extent; they cannot change their grandfathers."[43] Both Kallen and Locke advocate the circulation and conversion of religion among these other exchangeable items; yet both offset the risks of these transactions by insisting on a kind of bedrock of familial inheritance. Kallen goes on to insist: "What we are by heredity and early family influence . . . comes nearest to being inalienable and inalterable."[44]

Eldon Eisenach comments that of the three forms of law in Locke—divine, civil, and opinion—the divine is the "most indeterminate."[45] If, however, divine power seems remote, state power external, and the power of reputation too variable and uncertain, Locke shores up these limitations with a prolonged steeping in parental affection, education, and esteem—a steeping that will produce the dependent or obliged subject, for whom consent to the state will be scarce avoidable. Locke associates tender parental care with a benevolent, albeit ever watchful, divine authority and fuses those together with an accountable magistrate in order to continuously reproduce a *felt* political obligation. Locke is clear that political power is not natural—but that does not mean it should not feel natural.

Indeed, what one sees in Locke is perhaps that strangest of things: a "liberal" version of "family values."[46] Given his oscillation between benevolent patriarchal power, divine and human, and consensual politics, we can perhaps better understand why it is that contemporary liberal regimes continue to accommodate both parental control over their children's education and discrimination based on gender and sexuality in religious communities. Liberalism's accommodation of these two illiberal practices relies on antithetical readings of religion. The accommodation of parental control is predicated on the understanding that religions are generally reproduced through familial lines, whereas the possible negative effects of gender and sexual discrimination in religious organizations is batted away with the declaration that membership in religious bodies is purely voluntary. The tensions apparent in Locke appear to still haunt liberal democratic regimes. This should not be surprising. Individual consent makes for a tenuous foundation. Hence liberal regimes must make a

Faustian deal with illiberal disciplines in order to cultivate citizen loyalties. Liberal political theorists, such as Stephen Macedo, denounce the incivility of religious speech even as they rely on religion's comprehensiveness to supplement liberalism's meager, merely wordish consensus. Contemporary liberalism plays an endless game of denouncing and slyly courting religion. What is insidious about this game is that it defers robust attempts at eliminating all forms of discrimination and building a truly promiscuous public.

In the United States religious entities are permitted to discriminate on the basis of religious identity as well as sexuality and gender. Catholic churches, for instance, are obviously not expected to ordain declared Anglicans; they also do not ordain women or gays. If they wish to maintain their nonprofit status, however, they cannot engage in racial discrimination in ascertaining eligibility for employment or ordination.[47] Why are religious entities penalized for discriminating on the basis of race but not on the basis of gender and sexuality when such employment discrimination is prohibited in all other occupations?[48] Gila Stopler has referred to the contradictory position that liberal regimes take on gender discrimination as "the liberal bind."[49] One cannot help but conclude that perhaps what was true for Locke remains so even today—that is, that the liberal regime of individuals relies on the emotional bonds supplied by heteronormative and patriarchal (with a small *p*) families and religious organizations. Although the secular is typically posed in opposition to all that is purportedly oppressive about religion, including patriarchy and heterosexism, I suggest that we confront the secular as begetting and even courting these practices for the sake of exploiting their purportedly natural and visceral ties.

Macedo is surely right that Locke's program for toleration depends on a certain ordering of the soul, even if, as he says, it is hard to see the explicit mechanisms of that soulcraft in the *Letter Concerning Toleration*. (Macedo does not examine Locke's pedagogy.) And like many readers of Locke, Macedo projects the charged binary of public and private onto Locke. Macedo valorizes the "public"; he frequently pairs the word *public* with *reason*. The public signifies what is common as opposed to what is narrow or parochial. For Macedo religion is to be placed into the private realm and allowed into the public only to the extent that religion is recognized as a narrower concern (as opposed to the shared concerns of peace, security of rights, prosperity, democratic deliberation, and equal individual freedom) and justified by means of publicly available grounds.[50]

Nonetheless, for all Macedo's talk of public reason, he acknowledges that what sustains a commitment to the collective project that is America is not a discursive consensus but affective bonds forged in familial relationships and religious communities, bonds that tie together the particular and the transcendent. In other words, the power that sustains liberalism may not ultimately be the "unforced force of a better argument" but the early insinuation of power, referred to by Locke, as quintessentially religious. Indeed, what is implicit in Macedo yet explicit in Locke is the recognition that for all its value, reason simply cannot generate obligation, and thus political entities will always be dependent on their purportedly irrational or narrow counterparts in religion, family, and perhaps art. (This is a point that Jürgen Habermas and Paul Kahn make as well.) Thus Macedo oscillates between hoping that religious communities might finally become extinct to acknowledging that liberalism needs religion. In my estimation Macedo, by first removing religion from power and then relying on religion to empower liberalism, is confused about where liberalism's power ultimately resides.

Macedo enjoins the *exposure* to pluralism that is in his estimation the hallmark of public education. Moreover, he insists that a pluralistic context requires citizens with multiple allegiances: "Liberal public reason bars governments and political actors from making comprehensive claims to value and meaning; it leaves our allegiances divided."[51] There can be no doubt that Macedo thinks divided allegiances are a good thing for all members of a pluralistic community. His description echoes that of Michael Walzer: "A pluralist, at bottom, is a man with more than one commitment, who may at any moment have to choose among his different obligations."[52] The irony is that despite the fact that religion enables Macedo's brand of liberal toleration, religion cannot actually enjoy the pluralistic promiscuity heralded by secular modernity; it cannot enter the fray of the modern public. For Macedo religion must piously refrain from such promiscuous exposure and helpfully curb its excesses. Religion is somehow necessary to the whole enterprise but must perform its magic out of sight.

In contrast, for Locke political theology opens up the space for a raucous and promiscuous political space, which can accommodate divisive religious claims. In other words, consensus about the truly sacred enables religious dissensus. Locke is explicit and perhaps insistent that the consensus on which religious pluralism pivots is itself religious. Moreover, he augments this fundamental agreement by relying on various other mechanisms for "feeling together"—that is, the consensual ties generated by everyday transactions of communication, labor, money, and trade. He supplements significantly these everyday ties with those generated by familial affection and education, through which children imbibe the right theology and religious disposition from their cradles. Locke's pedagogy is designed to yield religious subjectivities who are not susceptible to injury or offense, who are not brittle and unyielding but open-minded, who can tolerate and even enjoy exposure to the global circulation of religions as ideas, fashions, or commodities.

I have argued that Locke's writings supply a multipronged approach to the problem of intractable and violent religious dissent. Consequently, I see his work as constituting a full-fledged version of the secular and not simply a platform for toleration, a modus vivendi as opposed to a modus operandi, a political theology and not merely a virtue, government advocacy and not neutrality. This is not to say that all the strands of this political theology fit together neatly. (Perhaps the most glaring tension is that between his reading of the significance of Jesus's ministry and his recommendations for punitive action against the poor.) Nor is it to say that Locke is responsible for the production of the secular or even a particular version of the secular. No single source could be. Rather, I see Locke's writings (and those of his interlocutors and various literary sources) as registering subtler shifts in language, body, power, and identity—shifts that impact subject, public, and nation formation as well as notions of sexuality in seventeenth-century colonial England. Reconstructing these clues affords a rubric with which to account for the complexity of the secular and decipher its contemporary conflicts. I turn to these conflicts in the next and final chapter.

6

They're Only Words, But They're Killing Me Softly

In previous chapters I described one of Locke's strategies for dialing down the volatility of religious dissent as the conversion of religion from body (persecution, property, inheritance) to alterable speech act (argument, text, fashion). I referred to this as Locke's secularizing of religion: making religion worldly and thus amenable to the cosmopolitan and promiscuous mixing of individuals. Nonetheless, I also argued that Locke was caught between a sense that religion converted to words might make its battles merely political and a conviction that society was held together by religion, specifically religion that was more than, or perhaps earlier than, words. I think this Locke has more relevance to our contemporary period than the Locke of the public and private, state and church, body and spirit binaries of religious toleration.

Contemporary conflicts are generally attributed to so-called Islamicists or fundamentalists ignoring the divide between state and church, religion and politics, or public and private. In other words, the Lockean legacy I have called into question is repeatedly trotted out to explain religious conflict. Yet just as this rubric proves inadequate for understanding Locke's multipronged approach to religious dissent, I think it fails to capture the complexity and tenacity of contemporary antagonisms. Drawing lessons from my reconstruction of Locke, I suggest, instead, that a predominant feature of contemporary secularism and its discontents is a persistent conflation of speech and body, persuasion and coercion, and politics and war—a conflation that suggests a highly unstable spectrum of force and that admits of no easy solution. Moreover, this is the case despite the nearly universal consensus as to the validity and primacy of human rights.

In what follows I first document the modern attribution of power and violence to words, specifically religious speech designated as "proselytization." I provide a brief sketch of both the international and U.S. contexts. I then turn to a discussion of what these conflicts indicate about contemporary secularity and about the meaning and practice of politics in a secular context. In the third and concluding section of this chapter I discuss an explicit appropriation of Locke: the "overlapping consensus" of John Rawls. I do so in order to suggest affinities between Locke's political theology and contemporary liberalism.

Although he was well aware of the force and possible rough usage of speech, I suspect that Locke would be surprised by the extent to which religious *speech* is currently regarded as capable of inflicting injury, destroying culture, derailing politics, and amounting to a declaration of war. It is perhaps stating the obvious to remark that words cross greater distances and travel at faster speeds than at the time of Locke. Spoken words still journey across slender spans separating bodies, yet printed words increasingly give way to electronic words. Although Locke and Mendelssohn may have doubted the clarity and power of a textual culture, the enchantment and omnipresence of textual media seems inescapable. Circulating words and images continue to accumulate weight, exert force, and orchestrate the attention, comportment, and connectivity of bodies. Yet far from linking us together, words and, specifically, the sharing of religious words appear to be driving us apart.[1] Since the 1990s instances of conflict and legislation (national and international) regarding religious communicative acts have increased. Religious speech has come to be regarded as a formidable force, capable of forcing conversions, imposing regimes, and exacting injuries. In the contemporary secular context religions may be regarded as largely discursive, but these discourses have come to be regarded as a coercive and destabilizing force. How did religious speech become so offensive?

Perhaps the most well-known instance of a recent prohibition of religious signs is the 2004 French law against "ostensible religious signs" in public schools. According to analysts, the controversial religious sign that led to this legislation is the wearing of a veil by Muslim girls and women.² Reasons for the veil ranged from being a fashion statement, to reflecting a burgeoning piety, to signifying a loyalty to the customs of one's home country. Nonetheless, critics contended that the veil violated Republican ideals of mixing (especially of gender), of loosening the hold of particular and communal identities, and of gender equality. For many critics the veil was read as an aggressive attempt to convert others, to declare the superiority of Islam, and to constitute a visual assault. Far from an innocuous fashion choice, the veil was said to exert coercive power over its wearers and its unveiled spectators. Whereas the French state provides ample financial support to religious institutions and personnel that perform "religious" functions in "religious" buildings, it is wary of religious signs and people circulating, handing out pamphlets, knocking on doors, and proselytizing.³

Most Islamic states have long prohibited proselytizing activity by non-Muslims. When the Universal Declaration of Human Rights was ratified in 1948, Saudi Arabia made explicit its objections to the right of religious liberty, regarding the conversion of Muslims to another religion as apostasy and not an exercise of some inherent and inalienable right.⁴ Recent attempts to restrict proselytization are not, however, limited to Islamic states. In addition to France, restrictions have been put in place in Singapore, India, Cambodia, Russia, and Greece.⁵

The words *proselytism* and *proselytize* are derived from the Greek word *proselutos*, meaning "one who has come to a place" or "one who comes over." The proselytizer, according to the Oxford English Dictionary, has the goal of converting or seeking to convert a person from one opinion, religion, or party to another. As is evident from the cases that follow, proselytizing is largely an activity of Christians. Indeed, it can be difficult to distinguish proselytization from Christian conquest. One Christian missionary is surprisingly frank about his ambition: "What is the target? It is the whole world. It is the tribal world, the world of the poor, the world of Islam, the Buddhist world and the Hindu world. . . . It is the world of those people who have never heard the gospel clearly enough to make a decision for Christ."⁶ Proselytization seems antithetical to toleration. After all, people do not seek to alter convictions or behaviors that they find tolerable.⁷ Nonetheless, although proselytism is at odds with toleration (and thus disproves the claim that toleration is a fait accompli),

I suggest that its current prominence is linked to the secularization of religion I have been describing.

Debates about and legislation regarding proselytization are coincident with the increasing influence of the language and instruments of human rights, particularly the right to religious freedom. Article 18 of the 1966 International Covenant on Civil and Political Rights (ICCPR) states: "1. Everyone shall have the right to freedom of thought, conscience and religion. This right shall include freedom to have or to adopt a religion or belief of his choice, and freedom, either individually or in community with others and in public or private, to manifest his religion or belief in worship, observance, practice and teaching. 2. No one shall be subject to coercion which would impair his freedom to have or to adopt a religion or belief of his choice."[8] In addition, the European Court of Human Rights has stated that the freedom to change religion would likely be "a dead letter" if the freedom to manifest religion did not include "the right to try to convince one's neighbour."[9] Can states affirm the freedom to practice religion and yet prohibit proselytism?

Critics of proselytizers argue that proselytizers use inappropriate *force* in attempting to convert others. A 1970 document titled "Common Witness and Proselytism" by the Joint Theological Commission between the Roman Catholic Church and the World Council of Churches describes proselytism as "a perversion of Christian witness." They add that "proselytism embraces whatever violates the right of the human person, Christian or non-Christian, to be free from external coercion in religious matters." Instead of proselytizing, the document recommends "witnessing" through one's exemplary behavior and goodwill. Witnessing is a term that suggests passivity and thus the absence of coercion. But is proselytizing truly coercive or injurious?

To convey its coercive properties, writers associate proselytism with the body (money, food, and sex) rather than with speech (word or teaching). According to the Greek court in the 1993 case *Greece v. Kokkinakis* (in which a Jehovah's Witness was found guilty of proselytization in visiting the home of a cantor's wife), "purely spiritual teaching" is not proselytism. Such "spiritual" teaching may include the demonstration of errors, and it may entail the conversion of individuals away from their previous religious communities. This is perfectly legal insofar as the method used is merely instructional. Spiritual teaching is to be distinguished from enticements that entail "morally reprehensible" means, which apparently constrain the will.[10] (This distinction echoes that of Locke in the *Letter Concerning Toleration*, in which he insists that true religion is addressed to the understanding and not to the will.) The European Court in the *Kokkinakis* case (the case eventually went before the European Court of Human Rights, which overturned the state's conviction) identified such means as "offering material or social advantages."[11] Note that the court presumes that authentic religion is wholly unrelated to one's material or social status and advantages.

Objections to the offer of material and social advantages have motivated recent legislation regarding proselytization in India. In 2006 the western state of Gujarat, India, amended the Freedom of Religion Act (2003) to halt "forced religious conversions."[12] Supporters of the recent legislation say that they worry that members of the lowest caste are in danger of being seduced by low-cost loans and free health care or food. Critics of the law point out that sometimes the only path of social mobility for these people is through conversion. According to the law, if the individuals involved in conversions (promoting them or undergoing them) do not first seek permission from the state and verify that each conversion is genuine and voluntary, they may be penalized by fines ranging from $20 to $1,000 or prison terms ranging from 1 to 3 years. Using similar reasoning, Cambodia passed legislation in June 2007 against Christians proselytizing door to door. Cambodians who are purportedly bribed with food to convert are called Rice Christians. In none of these instances are criteria supplied as to what constitutes a genuine and voluntary conversion. Indeed, what might such criteria be?

Criticisms of Christian conversion efforts in India are long-standing. Recall Gandhi's insistence on the impossibility of religious conversion given that religion is a more integral part of oneself than one's own body. He argued that religion was not like a house or cloak that one could simply exchange. Gandhi also argued that religious conversions created instability and always left "a sore behind" and that, in converting Indians, Christians sought to impose their will as bearers of the religion of the oppressors.[13] As time went on, Gandhi grew even more critical of Christian missionaries, declaring conversion the "deadliest poison."[14]

Even though the 1949 Constitution of India protects the right to propagate religion, Christian missionary efforts continue to meet resistance.[15] In January 1999 then prime minister of India Atal Behari Vajpayee called for a "national debate on conversion."[16] Christianity was said to be intolerant and imperialistic; its adherents' attempts to convert others were condemned as "inherently unethical," a "conscious intrusion into persons," and "violence to humanity" and as attempts to "destroy a people's history," to "semitize Hindus"(!), and to "exterminate all others."[17] Here again attempts at Christian conversion are portrayed as dreadfully potent and violent. No mere missionary speech would have the ability to alter "racial" affiliation from Hindu to Semitic! "Hindu" is not generally proffered as a racial category, but the correlation is telling. The point is to convey the irrevocable character of religious identity by categorizing it as racial. The objection is not, then, to persuasive speech but to what is perceived to be the attempt to uproot and exterminate ways of life and long-established identities, habits, and relationships.

In other cases the destructive force of proselytization is linked to the power of wealth. In 1987 the Church of Jesus Christ of Latter Day Saints opened Brigham Young University's Jerusalem Center for Near Eastern Studies on Mount Scopus. They were able to build this center only by pledging not to proselytize anyone in the state of Israel. Nonetheless, the opening was met by thousands of protesting Orthodox Jews—fearful of the Mormons' industrious missionary efforts. Every year the students who attend the center sign a lengthy pledge that prohibits them not only from proselytizing anyone living in or visiting Israel or the West Bank and Gaza but even from answering any questions about the LDS church.[18] Despite this pledge and despite the apparent continued honoring of these pledges, fears still circulate. In 2007 Mina Fenton, an Orthodox member of the Jerusalem city council warned, "We must remember that the Mormons have a strong belief in missionary work. They have big, big money and they buy things. I call it the money crusade against Jews."[19]

Finally, in some cases the force of proselytism is posed as a matter of seduction or sexual impropriety.[20] One scholar worries that "a grave risk . . . is that the *irresponsible ardor* of fundamentalist preaching may break down that natural resistance, resulting in an irreparable loss of Peru's cultural heritage."[21] For this scholar Peru's cultural heritage is tied to the fact that Catholics have been in Peru for 460 years and make up about three-quarters of the population. Clearly, a claimant to historic Christendom feels threatened by upstart and new-fangled Protestant versions of Christianity.[22] References to the seductive power of proselytization can be rather subtle. In another case the Nepalese government argued that legal provisions against proselytism and conversion "reflect the intent to discourage . . . instances of involuntary religious conversion . . . found to have taken place by means of financial enticement *and other temptations*."[23] In yet another example the High Court of Madhya Pradesh upheld the prohibition of conversion by means of "allurement."[24] In other instances the references to sexual impropriety are blatant. One judge in the *Greece v. Kokkinakis* case argued that proselytism constitutes the "rape of the belief of others."

Note that the conventional secular rubric of public and private does not apply to these cases. Many of those who object to the circulation of religious speech wish to keep public their own talk and practice (even ostensibly religious talk) and eliminate the forms they regard as objectionable. So too in a number of instances the religious speech or practice is private, or at least relatively so, but is nevertheless claimed to be injurious. So how might we respond to these cases? Might we try to prudently raise the threshold of injury? Would we say (in agreement with Locke) that such legislation is much ado about nothing, that no one can *talk* someone into changing his or her religion? Of course, critics of proselytizing would argue that they are not objecting to *mere speech*. They insist that proselytism is distinguished by recourse to social and material incentives that constrain the will. But why presume that genuine religion is unrelated to social and material advantage? And might we be skeptical of the harm committed by individuals *caring* (health care) or *servicing* (lower cost loans) or *feeding* (rice) people in exchange for hearing religious testimony? Would we want to punish or prohibit religious communities that advertised their goods by attending to vulnerable bodies? What is the harm of a bit of rice or cheaper loans? One instructor of future evangelists to Muslims exhorts his audience: "Don't approach them in groups. Don't bring them to your church, because they will misunderstand the singing and clapping as a party. Do invite them home for a meal. Do bring them chocolate chip cookies. Do talk about how, in order to get saved, they must accept Jesus.

Our job is not to make the Muslim a Christian. Our job is to show them the love of Christ."[25] There is a suggestion of vulnerability in the targeting of individuals as opposed to groups, and there are the material inducements of cookies. Should we regard this behavior as almost laughable? As a nuisance? Boorish? Offensive? Illegal?

Jean Bethke Elshtain observes that proselytism's critics tend to blur distinctions between coercion, manipulation, and persuasion. For these critics, "if I change my mind about something after an encounter with you, or after having spent some time in your religious community, the presupposition is that I have been messed with."[26] Elshtain insists that we distinguish persuasion from intimidation, which relies on an implied threat of harm, and from manipulation, which is underhanded and relies on deception. Am I intimidating you if I warn you that you might go to hell? Am I being underhanded if I invite you over to my house, hand you a plate of warm chocolate chip cookies, and then inform you that you need Jesus's redemptive love? Or are both of these instances just attempts at persuasion? Elshtain welcomes ardent attempts at persuasion, for she insists it treats others with respect, that is, as agents. Yet critics of proselytization see victims and not agents. Should we presume that individuals are agents able to withstand subtle and not so subtle pressures? Or should we presume that they are vulnerable and experience injury when informed, albeit ever so politely, that the deity is displeased with their so-called life?

Legislation and debate regarding the force entailed in religious persuasion and/or proselytization likely reflect long-simmering and long-ranging international resentment at Christian persecution and/or colonization as well as Western dominance. Nevertheless, similar concerns have also been voiced in the U.S. domestic context. David Smolin argues that First Amendment jurisprudence creates numerous paradoxes, including "an odd theory of psychic injury that justifies state-enforced censorship to prevent the 'harm' of being exposed to non-threatening religious speech."[27] Consequently, for Smolin the United States provides a striking contrast to other nations. Whereas in America no protection is afforded to religious feelings in relation to hate speech or blasphemy, "American constitutional law is hyper-sensitive toward psychic injury that may be caused by even gently pro religious speech in certain contexts: particularly public schools. Thus, for example, in the 1990s, the United States Supreme

Court held that the prayer of a Rabbi at a junior high graduation created 'psychological coercion.'"[28] The plaintiff in the 2000 (and continuing) *Newdow* case (which made it to the Supreme Court) "claimed that his daughter was *injured* when she was required to watch and listen while her classmates were led in a 'ritual proclaiming that there is a God and that ours is "one nation under God."'"[29] Free speech is nearly a sacred right in America—until that speech refers to God and injures someone's psyche.

Liberal political theorist Stephen Macedo gives voice to the situation Smolin describes. He attributes significant force to the person who speaks about his or her religious convictions. He observes, "Ordinary Americans increasingly seem to be embarrassed not simply about *imposing* their beliefs on other people—which is good—but of advancing any interpersonal moral claims at all."[30] But how can a mere declaration of belief constitute an imposition? To impose is "to establish or apply by authority or bring about as if by force."[31] Frankly, I am dumbfounded by the number of times I have heard my students declare that they just did not want someone else "imposing" his or her beliefs on them. In the context of discussion in a liberal arts college classroom, dining hall, and/or residence hall, no one is able to "impose" one's beliefs. So why do U.S. courts, Macedo, and my students consistently use this rather high-stakes language? Apparently, simply stating one's religious beliefs may prompt in others the discomfort, the outrage, of an attempted political coup!

Ironically, Macedo has also railed against a "solicitude for sensitive psyches," which prompts a conflation of "intellectual disagreement and physical vulnerability" (read: a conflation of speech and body). In this instance, however, it is not a matter of religious speech or individuals seeking to convert others, but religious individuals taking offense at liberal or secular assumptions and speech. Macedo is referring to Stephen Carter's demand that religious individuals qua religious individuals are entitled to respect and not simply toleration. (Extending toleration, Carter argues, reflects, and reinforces an asymmetrical position of power.) Macedo asks Carter to become less sensitive to taking offense at or feeling injured by views with which he disagrees, warning that "in a richly pluralistic society we need to be careful not to encourage offence taking and feelings of vulnerability."[32] Macedo asserts that it "makes all the difference in the world whether someone seeks to 'destroy' a religion through voluntary conversion or force."[33] Just how meaningful is his putting "destroy" in quotation marks and his declared imperative of voluntariness? Macedo concedes, moreover, that he is determined to convert young Americans to the virtues of liberalism: "Profound forms of sameness and convergence should not only be prayed for but planned for without embarrassment."[34] Thus Macedo is okay with destroying religion yet reluctant to allow free reign to religious speech (so that it might "destroy," say, "secularism" or "liberalism"). Yet, even if Macedo is convinced of the righteousness of his cause, he nonetheless retains traces of the liberal disavowal of force of which Stanley Fish has written. For Fish liberalism is simply another guise of force and, despite claiming the mantle of rationality, there are no obvious reasons for preferring governance by liberal principles than, say, Catholic principles. Macedo, however, frequently backs away from overt references to force, declaring that liberal efforts (whether at conversion or even "destruction") are "reasonable." Macedo repudiates the claim that public policies are all decided by political power, clearly disliking the suggestion that there would then be "no good reasons to favor liberal arrangements" and thus public policies would be a matter of "taste and ultimately of political strength."[35] For Macedo liberalism is distinguished by its abiding by "public reason," or at least its appeal to such. (I will revisit public reason in the concluding section of this chapter.)

Of course, opponents of liberalism do not see liberals' attempts at conversion as emblematic of public reason but more akin to a weapon. The evangelical Christian leader of Vision America, Rick Scarborough, titled his 2006 book *Liberalism Kills Kids*. And not just kids are victims of liberalism; we are all at risk, hence J. R. Dunn's 2011 book *Death by Liberalism* and Ann Coulter's 2011 *Demonic: How the Liberal Mob Is Endangering America*. For their part secular liberals have accused conservative Christian parents of the crime of child abuse. Richard Dawkins argues that teaching a child about hell constitutes mental child abuse, more damaging, probably, than their sexual abuse by priests. Brian Barry declares that conservative religious parents "should not be able to get away with cramping [children's] minds in the way that the *Mozert* parents wished." (Barry is referring here to the famous Tennessee case *Mozert v. Hawkins* [1987], in which parents sued the public schools for using reading textbooks that taught principles opposed to their religious convictions and practices.)[36] Barry's remark echoes that of Freud in *The Future of an Illusion* that parents raising their children to be religious is like bandaging their heads; both result in atrophying the brain.[37]

Indeed, the mutual accusations between conservative evangelicals and secular liberals reveals their surprising affinity. Both champion free speech and place tremendous faith in the power of persuasive speech to convert others; both herald the exposure and conversion or reinvention of disembedded selves. Conservative Christians bristle at the "exposure" lauded by so-called secular liberals—the exposure to diverse individuals and materials that is purportedly *not* indoctrination. Yet outside the United States a number of citizens of other nation-states are seeking protection from exposure to the cunning speech, material enticements, and global reach of proselytizing Christians! Liberals ennoble their own efforts at proselytization as "reasonable" while castigating the purported impositions of others. Each side insists that the words of opponents are deleterious, denying the coercive or injurious effects of their own words and claiming to be the sole bearers of "good news."

I suggest that these contemporary hostilities indicate widespread feelings of vulnerability that pose a direct challenge to Charles Taylor's reading of the secular. In his widely read book, *A Secular Age*, Taylor describes the secular self as a "buffered self." The buffered self is in contrast to the purported "pre-modern self," who was porous to random flows of power and influence, both spiritual and demonic.

Modern Westerners have a clear and firm boundary between mind and world, even mind and body. . . . For the modern, buffered self, the possibility exists of taking a distance, disengaging, from everything outside the mind. . . . As a bounded self, I see the boundary as a buffer, such that the things beyond don't need to "get to me," to use the contemporary expression. That's the sense of my use of the term "buffered" here. This self can see itself as invulnerable, as master of the meanings that things have for it.[38]

How are we to reconcile Taylor's reading of the secular with the claims of force and injury that I have cataloged? Taylor's modern secular subjects appear to be able to retreat to the private recesses of the mind (even apart from the body). When the white noise of the world is too loud, Taylor's secular self simply turns down the volume and tunes out. As I pointed out in Chapter 1, Wendy Brown describes liberal tolerance as the *conceit* of inhabiting a critical distance toward cultural, religious, and ethnic embedding. Similarly, Michael Warner speaks of the modern public as constituted in part of a universalizing transcendence, the collective *assumption* (or one might say *imagination*) of a disembodied or abstract self, indifferent to particularities.[39] For Brown and Warner these are the conjectures that enable modern and secular publics (even as they undermine fully inclusive publics). In contrast, for Taylor they are accomplished facts; secular selves *are* buffered selves. Are the buffers of secular selves merely a set of pretensions? The prerogatives of elites? Or the product of widespread access to robust public social welfare programs?[40] Taylor does not consider these possibilities; in his account a buffered self is an attained self-understanding that appears to reflect long-term cultural change that is undifferentiated with regard to class, race, gender, and so on. Taylor might counter that the conflicts I have outlined reflect the fact that some religious selves have yet to become secularized and acquire the necessary buffers. But if it is the case that secular selves are buffered selves, why are so-called liberal (and privileged) secularists so bothered, so imposed-upon, by religious chatter?

Taylor writes in *A Secular Age* that, "living in a disenchanted world, the buffered self is no longer open, vulnerable to a world of spirits and forces which cross the boundary of the mind, indeed, negate the idea of there being a secure boundary" (300). Taylor's description of buffered selves is strained by his own insistence that modernity betrays an "extraordinary confidence to remodel human beings" (121) and his observation as to the "penetration" everywhere of electronic media (423). This remodeling operates through numerous circuits—education, commerce, politics, media—that traffic across a not very secure boundary of the mind and amid a significant amount of indiscriminate mixing of strangers. Being exposed to and penetrated by such powerful currents certainly seems to bespeak unbuffered selves floating in an enchanted world. Thus it seems reasonable to conclude, given the numerous conflicts over the force of religious and liberal speech, that such exposure generates heightened feelings of vulnerability. In a postcolonial world of far-flung and frequent migration and intense and interlocking mediatization—just two instances of the economic and political pressures of global capital—all kinds of individuals are simply *not* impervious to "the world out there."

Indeed, these accusations, conflicts, and legal cases suggest that the brave new world of the secular is inhabited not by the tolerant but by the militant. Indeed, it is not unusual for scholars to see the contemporary situation as one of war. Stanley Fish implores those who wish to censor religious voices to simply let the political games begin. In making this call, he runs together "force, violence, politics" and encourages religious individuals to "shut down" the marketplace of ideas. He defines warfare as "deep conflict over basic and nonnegotiable issues."[41] And even Macedo finally asserts: "Our politics might well come down to holy war."[42] John Witte also makes continual reference to the contemporary situation as one of war.

> Local religious groups resent the participation in the marketplace of ideas that democracy assumes. They resent the toxic waves of materialism and individualism that democracy inflicts. They resent the massive expansion of religious pluralism that democracy encourages. They resent the *extravagant forms of religious speech*, press and assembly that democracy protects. A new war for souls has thus broken out in these regions. It is a war to reclaim the traditional cultural and moral souls of these new societies and a war to retain adherence and adherents to the *indigenous faiths*. In part, this is a theological war, as rival religious communities have begun actively to demonize and defame each other and to gather themselves into ever more dogmatic and fundamentalist stands. . . . In part, this is a legal war, as local religious groups have begun to conspire with their political leaders to adopt statutes and regulations restricting the constitutional rights of their foreign religious rivals.[43]

According to Witte, the catalyst of these wars is not religious individuals' refusal to stay private or even Christianity's alliance with colonialism but rather the surprising and perhaps unwieldy category of democracy. Democracy for Witte signifies the primacy of individualism and the imperative of materialism. I am not convinced that fears of materialism and individualism get at the root of the problem. Witte refers to constitutional rights being restricted, but the legislation of such rights indicates a fundamental recognition of the claims of individuals. So, too, many critics of modernity have nonetheless embraced its technological and entrepreneurial products and venues. Moreover, Witte's points can be co-opted to dismiss these "resentments" as simply antidemocratic.

Rather than tracing these processes to democratization, I submit that both "unbuffered selves" and "holy wars" are symptomatic of the tribulations of the secular. Witte's language is telling in this regard. He refers to resentment toward "extravagant forms of religious speech" and the defense of "indigenous faiths." Whereas the word *extravagant* now usually signifies that which exceeds the bounds with regard to necessity or economy, it also pertains to that which wanders out of bounds, strays, roams, or is vagrant. In contrast, that which is indigenous is inborn, occurs naturally, and is contained within a given environment. I have described a variant of the secular as the worlding of religion. This worlding entails putting into circulation words and bodies. Religion is disembedded from the body as circulating speech or fashion so as to enable the circulation and production of individuals and goods. International efforts to curb proselytization reflect, I suggest, resistance to or perhaps a backlash against a colonial disembedding of cultures, identities, and traditions as so many texts, fashions, or commodities suitable for global circulation, exchange, and conversion.

My reconstruction of Locke's political theology illuminates these more insidious conflicts of the secular, particularly the unstable spectrum of force whereby speech is injury, persuasion is coercion, and politics is war. Nonetheless, I suspect that Locke would regard these contemporary conflicts as indicating the continued relevance of a strategy of disembedding religion from the body, arguing that it is certainly preferable to experience injury in the form of insult, offense, and the conversion of former fellows than in the form of injury to bodies, loss of properties, or exile from one's homeland. Moreover, and related to this first point, Locke would probably regard talk of holy wars as reckless hyperbole.[44] For Locke warfare is not defined by deep political or religious disagreement, as Fish, Macedo, and Witte suggest. According to Locke, a state of war is a "declared design of force upon the person of another, where there is no common superior on earth to appeal to for relief."[45] Where there is a common superior to which citizens and visitors have consented, there can be no state of war, no matter how tumultuous the political and religious dissent. And yet most of those who object to or have drawn up legislation prohibiting proselytization insist that what they oppose is a destructive force. Even Macedo admits that his aim is to "destroy" the opposition, albeit by consent. Locke would most likely insist that such destructive force, albeit designed, is not upon people but upon ideas and arguments. But, of course, it is precisely such a distinction that is being challenged.

Thinking back to Chapter 2, I noted that Locke insisted on the need for explicit consent in the context of profound alienation and suspicion. Surely, a context described as holy wars qualifies as such. Is it the case, then, that reaffirmation of a universal political consensus regarding human rights would ease tensions and return us to merely religious and political dissent? Might this consensus require the sacralization of rights, albeit without reference to God? In other words, does a modified version of Locke's political theology offer a remedy to contemporary holy wars?

The tacit sacrality of human rights is already suggested by the language of international human rights instruments.[46] The United Nations Universal Declaration of Human Rights of 1948 heralds humanity's mysterious endowment of inalienable rights. The preamble to the document reads:

Whereas recognition of the *inherent* dignity and of the equal and *inalienable* rights of all members of the human family is the foundation of freedom, justice and peace in the world, Whereas disregard and contempt for human rights have resulted in *barbarous* acts which have outraged *the conscience of mankind*, and the advent of a world in which human beings shall enjoy freedom of speech and belief and freedom from fear and want has been proclaimed as *the highest aspiration of the common people*, Whereas it is essential, if man is not to be compelled to have recourse, as a last resort, to rebellion against tyranny and oppression, that human rights should be protected by the rule of law.[47]

Human rights appear to be sacralized by standing outside all history and artifice. Eternal or inherent, they come before the law and thus found the rule of law and, moreover, are the purpose and end of law. The civilized part of the human family or the "common people"—those who *share* the "conscience of mankind"—are those who recognize that human rights are the fountain of all good things; the barbarians are those who do not recognize the priority of human rights. "We," the "common people," condemn them.

It is not clear, however, that a renewed consensus on the primacy and sacrality of human rights will soothe the persistent conflicts I have described in this chapter. First, the right to religious freedom has increasingly been articulated as signifying the right to disseminate one's religiosity—a right that has frequently led to conflict and restrictive legislation. The American Convention on Human Rights (1969) explicitly states in Article 12(1) that the right to freedom of religion includes the freedom to "disseminate one's religion or beliefs." The American International Religious Freedom Act of 1998, Sec. 2(a)(4) refers to infringements of religious freedom as including "prohibitions against publishing, distributing . . . religious literature and materials." Moreover, this same act makes it a priority of American foreign policy to promote "religious freedom" around the globe. In turn, this agenda of promoting religious freedom around the globe has recently been adopted by the Tony Blair Faith Foundation and has inspired the Conservative Party of Canada's proposed Department of Religious Freedom. It is difficult to avoid the supposition that the right to religious freedom increasingly serves the secularizing interests I have described. Promoting religious freedom is not so much about encouraging religious diversity but about encouraging culture and religion's disembedding as circulating "free speech," and in turn, freeing up recalcitrant bodies for capitalist investment. As Thomas Farr, director of the Religious Freedom Project at the Berkley Center for Religion, Peace, and World Affairs at Georgetown University, writes: "The foreign affairs establishment routinely acts in a "secularistic" fashion, instinctively removing religion from the policy table. . . . There is, however, a potentially fruitful remedy at hand: *the U.S. policy of promoting international religious freedom.* Properly refurbished and energized, that policy could dramatically increase the capacity of American diplomacy to advance vital U.S. interests abroad and at home."[48] Whereas Farr imagines that a reinvigorated commitment to promoting international religious freedom counteracts an entrenched secularism (understood as ignoring religion in foreign policy), his articulation of this redoubled commitment as fortuitously advancing vital U.S. interests abroad and at home suggests not a project on behalf of religious and cultural diversity but one on behalf of conformism to U.S. interests, which are surely those of stable markets and religiosities subdued by the tonic of consumer choice.

Second, the rights to free speech and to religious freedom exacerbate the individualism of human rights. "Cultural rights" remain controversial;

thus there are no corresponding rights to challenge these individual rights to speech and religion, which are seen to entail the erosion of embedded cultural and religious identities and ways of life.[49] This makes the sacralization of human rights particularly problematic. Michael Ignatieff claims that the sacralization of human rights can tend to make us complacent and can cause us to look to heaven rather than to history. Ignatieff insists that the obliging force of human rights must come from history (particularly massive human suffering and destruction) and not from some fabricated transcendence beyond history.[50] Yet Ignatieff's critique fails to acknowledge the ways in which the individualism of rights is simultaneously a liability. For Ignatieff human rights are the unrivaled achievement of the "solvent of individualism" that has rid the West of the "hold of group identities and the racisms that go with them."[51] Ignatieff's logic here resembles the secularizing logic I have been describing, whereby cultural, religious, and national identities are unmoored from individualized bodies. Furthermore, he argues that a world of "pure individuals" who feel a sense of personal worth and accomplishment would not resort to hoisting markers of difference and intolerance. Yet so long as rights are associated with an attenuated and vulnerable individualism, such rights will be regarded as a threat to communal entities that may supply much needed buffering.

Must we reconcile ourselves to ongoing holy wars? Must we learn to tolerate the clash between rights and restrictions on speech? Must we accustom ourselves to an unstable spectrum of forces? I think so. Moreover, I contend that this is the lesson of Locke's political theology. Locke's goal was not the end of conflict but the transformation of war into political and religious dissent. His vision puts one in mind of Lord Balfour's comment on Walter Bagehot's *English Constitution*: "The whole political machinery presupposes a people so fundamentally at one that they can safely afford to bicker; and so sure of their own moderation that they are not dangerously disturbed by the never-ending din of political conflict."[52] According to Locke, this machinery would be built only if people synchronized their view of God, of what was sacred (human rights), of what power was for and how it was authorized, and, finally, of how they raised their children. In other words, Locke was convinced that political, religious, and cultural dissent was enabled by a substantive theological consensus, that it would take force "at a distance" to keep political force out of religion, and that certain speech acts would have to be prohibited or at least significantly discouraged. In the concluding section of this chapter, I argue for the relevance of this interpretation of Locke's political theology to contemporary liberalism.

John Rawls explicitly connects his project to that of Locke: "the movement of thought that began three centuries ago with the gradual acceptance of the principle of toleration and led to the nonconfessional state and equal liberty of conscience."[53] Rawls argues that the undeniable reality of pluralism means that there can be no consensus on a vision of the good society, that is, what he refers to as a "comprehensive view." Rawls nevertheless insists that liberal democracies must aim for consensus, albeit an "overlapping consensus," which has both internal justification (is freestanding) and can be justified "rationally" by the various comprehensive views. The focus of this overlapping consensus is justice as fairness, which entails the view of humans as reasonable, equal, and free and is addressed to their public reason. Note that Rawls insists that a stable constitutional consensus requires that certain basic rights and liberties be taken off the table. So fundamental are these items that they must be removed, as it were, from contestation.[54] Rawls obviously does not want to make recourse to the transcendent in order to secure his overlapping consensus, but his removal of rights from contestation is equivalent to a tacit sacralization.

Yet neither the tacit sacralization of rights nor a nonconfessional constitutional order dedicated to the protection of those rights appears to be sufficient. For Rawls and many other liberals, liberalism is characterized by an additional duty to advance only those policies that can be justified by appeal to public reason.[55] This duty is incumbent upon individuals when acting in an official governing capacity (the model case is the Supreme Court judge) or in wielding political power, such as voting. In these instances individuals must be able to justify their decisions to others using public values (freedom, equality, fairness, market efficiency, health of the environment or family) and public standards (principles of reasoning that follow rules of evidence and exemplify familiarity with common sense and scientific findings). In other words, one must continually reference what is presumably shared or at least shareable. They grant, however, that in political contexts one may go beyond public reason and reference one's comprehensive doctrine of the good (or dip into what Rawls calls "background culture," which he notes is not "private"). But, Rawls insists, one must be able to translate the contents of this doctrine into public reason.[56] There is, of course, always the possibility that someone acting in an official capacity will simply cite the Bible as a reason for his or her decision. This is no crime. But such an action would be regarded by Rawls (and Macedo) as a breach of civility. Continued breaches of civility would undermine reciprocity predicated on what we have in common, public reason, as opposed to our differences.[57]

Clearly, unlike Locke, Rawls's overlapping consensus does not entail theism. Thus, despite the affinities between their respective projects, Rawls's project may not qualify as a political *theology*. Nevertheless, Rawls's project might be characterized as akin to a civil religion. I suggest that Rawls's recommended orchestration of civil political speech bears more than a faint resemblance to ritual. David Kertzer argues that the particular power of political ritual consists in its efficacy in producing solidarity *despite* the absence of a commonality of beliefs. The elements of ritual that I spy in Rawls are obviously not the civic rituals of flag or military patriotism but, more broadly, the practices that amplify what is shareable, what builds on previously cited and common narratives. Rawls wishes to block out the arbitrary and the subjective. He hears (from behind his famous "veil of ignorance") the cacophony of plural human subjects, and thus he continually attempts to captivate his readers by speaking of reasonableness, of what is shared, as though doing so were a ritual gesture, focusing in on what he wants us to pay attention to and seeking to block out white noise. Switching to vision and thus continuing to set the ritual scene, he speaks of justice as also "seeing" justice done in transparent and reciprocal "public reason." I suggest, however, that it is not so much reason that secures justice but rather a public decorum or civility that will serve as a "focusing lens," magnifying what is common as opposed to contestable.[58] Whereas Locke turns to patriarchalism (divine and familial) to rein in his promiscuous public, Rawls lays down the rules for a proceeding that resembles an agapic gathering.[59]

What these two liberal political theorists imagine and construct, then, are *virtual bodies politic* to supplement, offset, and rein in the unruly public they simultaneously advocate. Locke's shared virtual body is each human linked together as God's property, which is to say God's body or the "Community of Nature." Rawls's shared virtual body is the ritual body speaking a common political language, that is, public reason. Rawls's virtual body calls to mind Kant's "mystical body," which signifies the community of reasonable humans formed by the "free submission of each one to the rule of moral laws."[60] (Of course, Kant's mystical body in turn recalls this same phrase in Catholic eucharistic theology!) These bodies are not identical to the nation-state. Moreover, these virtual bodies *aspire* to transcend divisions of race, class, religion, sexuality, and gender, even as they reinforce them. Locke, for instance, mortgages his vision of a universal, albeit transcendent, sacred body to a soft patriarchalism; his understanding of human rights requires accepting the authority of a divine father who owns property in humans and imparting that authority through heterosexual families. Thus, rather than embrace the risks and pleasures of a truly indiscriminate mixing of ideas and bodies, Locke sought to distinguish the promiscuity he admired (global colonization and trade, mixing in religious fashions and ideas) from the promiscuity he abhorred (sexual partnerships unaccountable to heterosexual reproduction, economic arrangements untethered to the reproduction of private property, and religious convictions uninspired by transcendent, albeit male, monotheism).

Rawls, for his part, implicitly sacralizes rights but also places limits on what qualifies as public reason and thus on what can be admitted into its domains. It is, however, presumptuous to mandate a "public reason." Reason may lay claim to facilitating shareability, but this is not exclusive to reason. Thus a given polity might accordingly permit or encourage whatever aspires to and enriches the shareable. Recall that Locke grants even to the magistrate the freedom to engage in religious persuasion. Rawls might object that Locke can afford to accommodate religious speech in his public sphere because Locke insists on widespread allegiance to a particular conception of the Christian creator god. Rawls cannot afford to be so tolerant, because he cannot expect such a consensus. Moreover, he might point out that Locke's theistic basis of consensus requires censoring the speech of atheists and that only the contingent fact that atheists are still, for better or worse, significantly outnumbered by theists prompts one to say that he appears to constrain speech more than Locke does. Nevertheless, one ought not to lose sight of the fact that both projects are predicated on declaring certain speech acts uncivil: For Locke it is atheism; for Rawls it is comprehensive (religious) visions. Nonetheless, the force they deploy is subtle: no explicit punishments but rather moral denunciation of those who would say what really ought not to be said.

Locke and Rawls agree that a shared vision of the good can no longer be presumed or forced. Their response to this insight is to insist, nonetheless, on what must be shared so that we can get along. In other words, for both political theorists a fairly substantive consensus makes dissensus possible. Thus Locke and Rawls do not espouse neutrality but look to "force at a distance" to stage a substantive consensus. Their version of the secular is not best captured by binary oppositions of religion versus politics, private versus public, or even communalism versus individualism but rather the sometimes awkward oscillation between promiscuous bodies and divine or human fathers, between invitations to "extravagant speech" and restrictions on what can be said, between celebrations of pluralism and the imperative of a shared and incorruptible "public reason."

What is living in Locke's political theology may indeed be the sacrality of human rights. What we can *learn* from his political theology is, however, the inextricability of religion and power, even when, and perhaps especially when, religion has been converted to persuasive speech. Locke acknowledged the power of religion. He did not cordon it off from the public sphere but insisted on its conversion to speech and its authorization by means of consent. But even Locke could not shrug off the temptations of using force at a distance. Consequently, what we must learn to see and feel in the secular is force at a distance become ambient, penetrative, enchanted, injurious. Religious, cultural, and ethnic identities and authorities do not simply become inert in processes of secularization. Rather, their crisscrossing currents of power continue to throw off sparks. What we have to unlearn, then, is the tendency to see eruptions of holy wars as indicating some premodern holdover, for they are generated, I suggest, by the logics and pressures of the secular.

Notes

INTRODUCTION

1. Locke, *Letter Concerning Toleration*, 51–52.
2. Ward, *Locke and Modern Life*, 259.
3. Mahmood, in Asad et al., *Is Critique Secular?* 68–75.
4. Sommerville, *Secularization*, 4, 10. See also W. Brown, "Subjects of Tolerance," 299, 301, 302, 313.
5. See Walsham, *Charitable Hatred*, 5.
6. The secular is not always posed as the opposite of religion. Eldon Eisenach writes that for Locke the protection of biblical Christianity from priestcraft is "secularism as a religious imperative" (Eisenach, *Narrative Power*, 104). Also, John Wilkins, Locke's contemporary, uses the term *secular* in a similarly complementary fashion: "When and where the true religion is publicly professed . . . the profession of religion will be so far from hindring, that it will rather promote a man's secular advantage" (quoted in Rivers, *Reason*, 1: 85; and in Worden, "Question of Secularization," 37).
7. Because to profane means to treat with irreverence, misuse, and disrespect, I am not convinced by Giorgio Agamben's distinction between secularization and profanation. He insists that secularization is repressive in that it simply moves force from one place to another (heaven to earth), whereas an act of profanation entails the neutralization of that force or power. He speaks of profanation as a return to common use, yet the notion or space or category of "common use" cannot be presumed. See Agamben, *Profanations*, 77, 82.
8. See, for instance, C. Smith, *Secular Revolution*, esp. the introduction; and Clark, "Secularization."
9. Locke does not speak of secularization; he used the word *secular* perhaps only once, in a September 1659 letter to Henry Stubbe; see Locke, *Correspondence*, 1: 110.
10. Benjamin J. Kaplan points to security guarantees as the single most important item in maintaining peace in multiconfessional communities in early modern Europe; he does not, however, explain the sanctioning of these guarantees, although he acknowledges the difficulty of distinguishing the secular and

religious in early modern European culture and notes that no value, loyalty, or obedience was without some religious sanction. See Kaplan, *Divided by Faith*, 220.

11. Shagan, *Rule of Moderation*, esp. 288–306.

12. I am also skeptical of the claim that religion's publicness represents a new stage of "deprivatization" or a "resurgence" of religion, which, for some scholars, suggests the onset of the "post-secular." See Casanova, *Public Religions*, chaps. 1 and 8. Nonetheless, Casanova provides a helpful delineation and evaluation of the various strands of secularization theory.

13. This school of thought is heavily indebted to John Dunn. More recently, Jeremy Waldron, in his *God, Locke, and Equality*, wonders whether liberalism must reconnect with the divine to honor the principle of equality; I show that elements of Lockean political theology remain operative in contemporary liberalism. According to John Perry, "Locke forbids atheism not for theological reasons but because it, in some ultimate and indirect sense, threatens rights" (Perry, *Pretense of Loyalty*, 122). I specify the connection between theism and rights that constitutes Locke's political theology and his continued relevance. Moreover, I disagree with Perry's contention that Locke's political theory of human rights establishes "government neutrality." And whereas I agree with Greg Forster (*Locke's Politics of Moral Consensus*) about the significance of consensus (and not just consent) in Locke's liberalism, I argue that his depiction of Locke's understanding of God's power is incongruent with key arguments in Locke's corpus.

14. Mark Goldie writes that "Locke does not advocate just the liberal privatization of religion, but has a doctrine of civil religion" ("Civil Religion," 201). Goldie does not elaborate on this civil religion (declaring the topic fit for a future project), but it apparently does not jeopardize his interpretation that Locke also advocates religion's privatization. Other writers, such as George Windstrup, David McCabe, and Michael Zuckert, have used the term *civil religion* (or *civil theology*) to describe Locke's work. Windstrup and McCabe insist on the public character of Locke's civil religion. I do not, however, agree with McCabe that Locke supports a state church or that only the most minimal conception of a God is necessary. The key to Locke's God is not minimalism but his depiction of divine power as both beholden to and necessary for the recognition and preservation of human individuals. See Zuckert, "Problem of Civil Religion," in his *Launching Liberalism*, 148–68; and McCabe, "Argument Against Strict Separation," 257. Windstrup ("Freedom and Authority") uses the terms "public faith" (251), "religion of liberalism" (254), "civil theology" (256), and "cult of natural rights" (259).

15. Dunn, "What Is Living," esp. 12, 13, 15, 20.

CHAPTER 1

1. Fish, *Trouble with Principle*, 165–67.

2. Interestingly, Michael McConnell suggests that Locke saw his task as dividing public affairs into the categories of sacred and secular; he nonetheless concludes, wrongly in my view, that Locke thought religion was irrelevant to the affairs of this world; see McConnell, "Religious Souls," 131, 132. According to Isaac Kramnick and R. Laurence Moore in *The Godless Constitution*, Locke asserted that religion belongs exclusively to private opinion and has no place in the public sector (96). Timothy Fitzgerald, in his *Discourses on Civility and Barbarity*, also points to Locke's division between the religious and the civil as entailing religion's privatization (22). Fitzgerald offers, however, that this might not be the last word on Locke's position on the religious and the civic.

3. Morris, "Judaism and Pluralism," 180–81.

4. The same line appears in Juergensmeyer's *Religious Nationalism*, 27, and in his *Terror in the Mind of God*, 228.

5. Crockett and Davis, introduction to "The Political and the Infinite," 3; italics added. They also write, "The religious person, according to Locke, should enact her own religion so long as it does not go *beyond her individual conscience*. In a sense, for Locke, religion's force is relegated to the immaterial and spiritual realm of life, and if it passes over from the spiritual to the material world then religion de facto violates its core principle, namely meek tolerance" (1–2).

6. Attila K. Molnár makes a convincing case that "religion" was appropriated from pagan sources and redeployed by early modern thinkers, including Locke, in contrast to the overly individualist sense that Luther had given to "conscience." The appeal of the pagan notion of religion was its intersubjective character, which, in turn, contributed to social and political obligation. See Molnár, "Construction," 48.

7. Locke writes in a September 1659 letter to Henry Stubbe, "You know how easy it is under pretense of spiritual jurisdiction to hook in all secular affairs" (Locke, *Correspondence*, 1: 110).

8. In the *Letter Concerning Toleration* Locke argues that if someone departs from what he regards as the right way to heaven, "it is his own misfortune and *no injury* to thee" (24; italics added). Locke adds that a person may "lawfully kill his calf at home, and burn any part of it that he thinks fit. For *no injury* is thereby done to anyone, no prejudice to another's man's goods" (39; italics added). Locke also writes in "Civil and Ecclesiastical Power" (1674), "Because it is unjust in reference to both *credenda* [matters of faith] and *cultus* [forms of worship], that I should be despoiled of my good things of this world, where I disturb not in the least the enjoyment of others; for my faith or religious worship *hurts not* another man in any concernment of his" (Locke, *Political Essays*, 219; italics added).

9. Jews finally secured the first synagogue in Amsterdam in 1639, although this was denounced by several prominent people. Catholic worship was prohibited into the late eighteenth century. See Marshall, *Locke, Toleration, and Early Enlightenment Culture*, 142, 145. In 1700 there were twenty *Schuilkerk*s, or clandestine Catholic churches, in the Netherlands; see Kaplan, *Divided by Faith*.

10. Locke, *Letter Concerning Toleration*, 31.

11. See Locke, *Letter Concerning Toleration*," 27 and 35; see also "Toleration B" (1676), in Locke, *Political Essays*, 248.

12. Locke, *Letter Concerning Toleration*, 51.

13. "An Essay on Toleration" (1667), in Locke, *Political Essays*, 147; italics added.

14. Whereas I agree with James Block on the significance of self-formation in childhood in Locke (as I elaborate in Chapter 5), I do not agree that this project is "relocated from public space to pre-political childhood" (Block, *Nation of Agents*, 164). Locke's defense of the disciplinary powers of argumentation is perhaps not as thorough as that of John Stuart Mill's *On Liberty*, esp. 31–32.

15. Zaret, *Origins of Democratic Culture*, 175. Zaret critiques Habermas's account of the emergence of the modern public sphere as both late (post-Enlightenment) and flawed in his insistence on its rationality being predicated on its institutional autonomy (a theorization that anticipates its eventual downfall).

16. One petition presented to Charles II in January 1680 garnered as many as 16,000 signatures, including John Locke's; see Knights, "London's Monster Petition."

17. Zaret, *Heavenly Contract*, 66–67.

18. See Lander, *Inventing Polemic*, 20.

19. Lee Ward acknowledges that Locke never asserts the necessity to privatize religion but rather the need to transform religion from "self-justifying moral absolutes into probabilistic claims and contestable premises amenable to discursive engagement" (*John Locke and Modern* Life, 259). Adam Wolfson offers a similar argument in his *Persecution or Toleration*, xv.

20. See Walsham, *Charitable Hatred*, 25, 122–23, 284, 317. See also Marshall, *Locke, Toleration, and Early Enlightenment Culture*, 217–23, 302–11, and ch. 15.

21. Marshall, *Locke, Toleration, and Early Enlightenment Culture*, 323. For more on the depiction of heresy as an infection, see Kaplan, *Divided by Faith*.

22. Locke, *Letter Concerning Toleration*, 26–27.

23. For Martin Luther, as it was for Augustine, the will is central to religion generally and to Christianity specifically. Locke's point here places significant distance between himself and Luther, challenging Richard Ashcraft's assertion that "Locke stands closer to Luther and his world than he does to ours" ("Religion and Lockean Natural Rights," 208).

24. Locke, *Letter Concerning Toleration*, 28.

25. Coke, *Justice Vindicated*, sig. A.2; and Stillingfleet, *Mischief of Separation*, 11; both quoted in Stanton, "Politics and Theology," 88.

26. Barrow, *A Refutation of Mr. Giffard's Reasons* (1590/91) and *A Plaine Refutation* (1591), quoted in Zaret, *Heavenly Contract*, 138 and 139.

27. John Calvin and Ulrich Zwingli defended infant baptism as the seal of the covenant to which infants were entitled.

28. Samuel Smith, *The Ethiopian Eunichs Conversion* (1632), 440, quoted in Zaret, *Heavenly Contract*, 135. Still others argued that although infants could not yet personally bind themselves to God, God bound Godself to the infant in baptism. Furthermore, it was argued that medical remedies are not withheld from infants and children despite the fact that they do not understand their purpose or effect. Hickes [Dean of Worcester], "Infant Baptism," 335, 337.

29. In seventeenth-century New England the major concern of every synod was the criteria of church membership. Those who favored infant baptism as the token of full membership argued that it provided leverage for the church to retain second and third generations who, perhaps in the absence of persecution and the presence of greater social mobility in the colonies, were not so avid in their religiosity. Those who objected to infant baptism as the token of full membership insisted that membership by declared consent (supplied by means of a public conversion narrative) was more consonant with Puritan theology, in which the individual's response to grace was primary. The Halfway Covenant of 1662, which extended church membership to baptized children but not full voting rights, was obviously an attempt to address both of these imperatives. Williston Walker wrote: "The like tryall is to be required from such members of the church, as were born in the same, or received their membership, and were baptized in their infancy, or minority, by vertue of the covenant of their parents, when being grown up [un]to years of discretion, they shall desire to be made partakers of the Lords supper. . . . Yet these church-members that were so born, or received in their childhood, before they are capable of being made partakers of full communion, have many priviledges which others (not church-members) have not: they are in covenant with God . . . are in a more hopefull way of attaining regenerating grace" (Walker, *The Creeds and Platforms of Congregationalism* [New York, 1893], 205–6, 222–24, quoted in Brewer, *By Birth or Consent*, 57).

30. "Some of the Chief Grievances of the present constitution of Virginia, with an Essay towards the Remedies thereof," MS Locke e. 9(a), 159, Locke Archive, Bodleian Library, Oxford University; italics added. For a discussion of Locke's authorship of this document see page 180, note 42.

31. Montaigne, *Essays*, 1213.

32. As Hannah Dawson argues, Locke referred to a common measure of meaning but cautioned that it was wrong to assume semantic uniformity. She then connects his analysis of language to his analysis of coinage, noting that in these instances (as for politicians) the question is whether words and coins mean what they profess. Locke saw intrinsic value in silver and gold and worried about Parliament's alteration of the stamp or face value of coins; see Dawson, *Locke, Language*, 16–17, 234, 238, 263, 275, 288.

33. See the *First Tract on Government*, in Locke, *Political Essays*, 5. See also *On the Conduct of the Understanding*: "They that write . . . to maintain the tenets of a party they are engaged in, cannot be supposed to reject any arms that may help to defend their cause, and therefore such should be read with the greatest caution" (Locke, *Political Essays*, 221).

34. Habermas, *Justification and Application*, 163. For a study of Locke's affirmation of persuasion or rhetoric as force, following a long tradition of Western writing on rhetoric, see Walker, "Force, Metaphor, and Persuasion." Also see the chapter "Force" in Walker, *Literary Criticism*. See also Fish, *Doing What Comes Naturally*.

35. Walker, "Limits," 138. Walker also argues that what Locke should have said is that the difference between state and church is predicated not on force and something else (such as light or speech) but on a "difference between forces." This difference is that of physical force used against the body and persuasive force directed at the mind; see Walker, "Force, Metaphor, and Persuasion," 224.

36. "Toleration B" (1676), in Locke, *Political Essays*, 247.

37. *An Essay on Toleration* (1667), in Locke, *Political Essays*, 138–39. Elsewhere Locke writes that he who "would govern the world well had need consider rather what fashions he makes, than what laws," in "Credit, Disgrace," MS Locke f. 3, fols. 381–82, December 1678, Locke Archive, Bodleian Library, Oxford University. For additional comparisons of religion to fashion, see the *Second Tract on Government*, in Locke, *Political Essays*, 60. See also *An Essay on Toleration* (1667), in Locke, *Political Essays*, 146, 147–48.

38. Fox, *The Priests Fruits*, 1, 5, 2.

39. *Dialogue Between Monmouth-shire and York-shire*, 1–2.

40. The entire quote reads: "In hundreds of classrooms it is being taught daily that the Decalogue is no more sacred than a syllabus; that the home as an institution is doomed; that there are no absolute evils; . . . that the change in one's religion to another is like getting a new hat; that moral precepts are passing shibboleths; that conceptions of right and wrong are as unstable as styles of dress" (Marsden, *Soul of the American University*, 267, quoted in Fish, *Trouble with Principle*, 259). Given the look of *Cosmopolitan* magazine today, this is truly a delicious irony.

41. In critiquing Oprah Winfrey's emphasis on guests representing "modern Muslim women," Kathryn Lofton writes of the honorific title "modern": "Oprah's Muslims are 'just like any other American,' except with different accessories. Religious difference in Oprah's America is a fashion choice rather than a theological commitment, a translatable cultural context rather than an exclusivist worldview" (*Oprah*, 49).

42. Locke, *Letter Concerning Toleration*, 46.

43. "Philanthropy" (1675), in Locke, *Political Essays*, 225; see also "Atlantis," in Locke, *Political Essays*, 259; and "Reputation" (1678), in Locke, *Political Essays*, 272.

44. "Toleration B" (1676), in Locke, *Political Essays*, 248.

45. Bishop Joseph Hall (1574–1656); see his "Fashions of the World" (Sermon XVIII), in Hall, *Works*, 5: 246, 247, 247.

46. *Queries*, 6, 3.

47. Viswanathan, *Outside the Fold*, 145.

48. See Zagorin, *Religious Toleration*, 18.

49. Here I am in agreement with Steve Bruce, who argues, successfully in my view, that the rational choice model cannot explain religious behavior: "We can know the price of cornflakes; it is impossible to know the price of being a Mormon or a Jew. . . . Suffice it to say that in order for us to be free to choose we must be free of loyalties and social constraints. Economistic models work well for cornflakes and cars—products for which there is a very high general demand and little brand loyalty. For those, most people will maximize. It follows that religious behavior will be explained by a rational choice approach only when religion is no longer strongly associated with other important social institutions and identities, when it is removed from the public sphere and reduced to a matter of personal preference, when its focus is not the life of a nation but the privatized sensibilities of the individual. . . . To the extent we are free to choose our religion, religion cannot have the power and authority necessary to make it any more than a private leisure activity" (*Choice and Religion*, 125, 129, 186).

50. W. Brown, *Regulating Aversion*, 152; italics in original. For the distinction between ascriptive (nonliberal) and consensual (liberal) identities, see also R. Smith, *Civic Ideals*.

51. W. Brown "Subjects of Tolerance," 299, 301.

52. Viswanathan, *Outside the Fold*, 231.

53. See Locke, *Letter Concerning Toleration*, and "Toleration B" (1676) in *Political Essays*, 247.

54. Turner, "Religion-Making."

CHAPTER 2

1. Carter, "Evolutionism," 987.
2. P. Kahn, *Liberalism*.
3. Relevant to my point here is Edmund Burke's insistence on property as the material basis of tradition.
4. Armstrong, *Desire*, 33.
5. Canfield, *Word as Bond*.
6. Grotius insists that a linguistic contract about the meaning and right use of language is the precondition of all other contracts; see V. Kahn, *Wayward Contracts*, 34–37.
7. *The Political Works of James I*, ed. by Charles Howard McIlwain (Cambridge, MA: Harvard University Press, 1918), 74, quoted in Kerrigan, *Shakespeare's Promises*, 36.
8. Quoted in Marshall, *Locke, Toleration, and Early Enlightenment Culture*, 80.
9. See Zaret, *Heavenly Contract*, 62–89.
10. A Puritan lecturer in 1632, repeating verbatim a sermon from half a century earlier by John Stockwood; see Zaret, *Heavenly Contract*, 88. On this same page, Zaret also supplies the following from *The Unlawful Practices of Prelates*: "The cutting of preaching . . . is the cutting of the sinews asunder whereby the subjects in all parts of the realm are most strongly knit to their prince."
11. William Paget, in John Strype, *Ecclesiastical Memorials*, 3 vols. (Oxford: Clarendon Press, 1822), II: 1.431, quoted in Zaret, *Heavenly Contract*, 70.
12. *An Humble Motion with Submission unto the . . . Privie Counsell* (1590), 85–86, quoted in Zaret, *Heavenly Contract*, 75; italics added.
13. Locke, *Some Thoughts*, 67 (44); Locke, *Third Letter*, 6: 201.
14. Hence Locke's (and Mendelssohn's) theories of language are subject to Wittgenstein's critique of the split between internal sensation and external sign and the priority accorded the latter; see Wittgenstein, *Philosophical Investigations*, 89–90.
15. See Zuckert's discussion of Locke on language in his "Fools and Knaves: Reflections on Locke's Theory of Philosophical Discourse," in his *Launching Liberalism*.
16. I agree with Vernon that Locke's position is not at bottom an epistemological skepticism. Locke is quite sure that there is a true religion, and he is confident that humans can have access to truth—for the purposes of a humane life. But Locke is equally sure that for humans there is no interpretive authority that could render definitive meanings and make communication a transparent process.

17. Nevertheless, Locke does not endorse Hobbes's solution by which the sovereign decides unilaterally on meanings and enforces this usage. See Hobbes, *Leviathan*, c. xvii (129).

18. See Sergeant, *Sure-Footing in Christianity*; and Tillotson, *Rule of Faith*. Sergeant published replies to his critics, and Tillotson's works were subsequently reprinted in 1676 and 1688.

19. Tillotson, *Rule of Faith*, 5.

20. Sergeant, *Satisfaction in Religion*, 15–16; italics in original.

21. Sergeant, *Groundlessness*, 324, 324, 316, 318.

22. Sergeant, *Groundlessness*, 336; italics in original. Sergeant is responding to Dr. Jeremy Taylor's (Lord Bishop of Down) *Dissuasive from Popery*, which went through five editions between 1664 and 1686.

23. Casaubon, *To J. S.*, 9–10; italics in original.

24. Hughes, *Sure-Footing*, Dedication and B1.

25. Hughes, *Sure-Footing*, 46.

26. Hughes, *Sure-Footing*, 80.

27. Hughes, *Sure-Footing*, 128; italics added.

28. See Murphy, *Conscience*, 152.

29. Falkner, *Answer to Mr. Sergeant*, 416.

30. Sergeant, *Letter to the D. of P.*, 27–28.

31. Whitby, *Answer to Sure-Footing*, 15. Of course, in Whitby's example the patrimony in question is not the bodily inheritance afforded by an unbroken chain of heterosexual reproduction but the spiritual inheritance begotten by the unbroken chain of ordination (laying on of hands) that constitutes apostolic succession.

32. Sergeant, *Groundlessness*, 325.

33. See Mendelssohn, *Jerusalem*, 28.

34. Mendelssohn, *Jerusalem*, 38.

35. Although for Locke Jewish legislation (he calls it a theocracy) is their religion, he argues that this system never entailed required articles of belief or the coercion of those without. See "Toleration C" (1678), in Locke, *Political Essays*, 269. Also: "Amongst so many Captives taken, so many Nations reduced under their Obedience, we find not one man forced into the Jewish Religion, and the Worship of the True God, and punished for Idolatry, tho all of them were certainly guilty of it. If any one indeed, becoming a Proselyte, desired to be made a Denison of their Commonwealth, he was obliged to submit unto their Laws; that is, to embrace their Religion. But this he did willingly, on his own accord, not by constraint" (Locke, *Letter Concerning Toleration*, 45).

36. Mendelssohn's theory resembles, in part, that of William Warburton in *The Divine Legation of Moses*. Other eighteenth-century writers influenced by Locke's rejection of the Adamic theory of language offered a similar evolution of language as proceeding from bodiliness to abstraction. Writers such as Bernard Mandeville (1670–1733), Étienne Bonnot de Condillac (1715–1780), and Jean-Jacques Rousseau (1712–1778) argued that the origin of language consisted in the body, in need and desire, specifically in gestures, cries of pain or passion, and the "language of the eyes." Although these early gestures embody empathy, Mandeville was convinced that humans were fundamentally antisocial and self-interested and that social bonds were formed only by stronger individuals making use of rhetoric to seduce the weaker and to convince them of the worth of imaginary objects. Condillac sees the emergence of abstract and technical language as marking progress, yet he is nostalgic about the loss of poetry, music, and ritual that constitute primitive gesture. Rousseau sought to recover the primal force of gestural communities, of "unmediated transmissions of feeling"; and thus instead of "public speech addressed to calculating reason," he turned to the eye and recommended the use of dress, ornaments, buildings, and ceremonies—in short, what he famously terms civil religion. I take up the topic of civil religion in the concluding section of this chapter. See Hundert, "Thread of Language," 187, 188.

37. Kant, "What Is Enlightenment?" 55.
38. Gottlieb, "Mendelssohn's Metaphysical Defense," 222.
39. Tillotson, *Six Sermons*, 114; italics in original.
40. Tillotson, *Lawfulness*, 23.
41. Wilkins, *Principles and Duties*, 181.

42. Watts seems to have been accused of relying too heavily on Locke (indeed, his language sometimes sounds as though it is lifted from Locke); in a footnote to one of his writings, he is defensive, claiming that for the purposes of that work (*New Essay on Civil Power*, 1739), he consulted only a few articles of Locke's Fundamental Constitutions of Carolina. He rehearses the familiar argument that civil government ought to confine itself to securing the individuals and properties of mankind, that is, the affairs of this world, whereas religion has truly to do with the salvation of souls in another world.

43. Watts, *New Essay on Civil Power*, 58.

44. Watts reports that a justice of the peace told him that the "ignorant people" would swear oaths but "would not be persuaded to assert the same thing boldly with some terrible Imprecation upon themselves, of broken or wither'd Limbs if they did not utter the Truth" (*New Essay on Civil Power*, 16).

45. Watts urges that all those who are not members of the true religion (i.e., Christianity) be not imposed upon but only "allured to unite themselves with

us" (*New Essay on Civil Power*, 23). Ah—what exactly does "allure" mean in this case?! He insists, "good Christians are not made by penalties" (25). Yet he also recommends "small fines and penalties" (35) for those who do not attend the public lectures on natural religion, reasoning that they are "really for the good" (33), and although he is "very cautious in appointing Penalties," he reasons that "Law has but small force without them" (33)!

46. "He also that hath the Idea of an intelligent, but frail and weal being, made by and depending on another, who is eternal, omnipotent, perfectly wise and god, will as certainly know that Man is to honour, fear, and obey GOD, as that the Sun shines when he sees it. . . . Nor can he be surer in a clear Morning that the Sun is risen, if he will but open his Eyes, and turn them that way" (Locke, *Human Understanding*, 4.13.3 [651]).

47. See Locke, *Reasonableness*, 19–20. Locke confides his hope in the eventual conversion of the Jews, Pagans, and Muslims. See his *Second Letter*, 6: 62. This admission, Adam Sutcliffe argues, contradicts Locke's professed support for toleration. See Sutcliffe, *Judaism*, 220. For related comments by Enlightenment writers, see Sutcliffe, *Judaism*, 94–95, 233–40 (for Bayle and Voltaire); Hume, *Natural History*, 175; Kant, *Religion*, 74; and Hegel, *Lectures*, 373n492. Spinoza's argument differs in that he argues that the Jews would have already had to abandon much of the ceremonial law after the first destruction of the temple and city: "We cannot, therefore, doubt that they were no more bound by the law of Moses, after the destruction of their kingdom, than they had been before it had been begun, while they were still living among other peoples" (*Tractatus Theologico-Politicus*, 72). He sees evidence of this already in Jeremiah. Calvin argued that the ceremonial law was directed to the Jews "in their infancy" (Höpfl, *Luther and Calvin*, 67).

48. Locke does not seem to notice that his recommendation that believing in Jesus as the Messiah substitutes for one's inability to fulfill the requirements of a good life comes close to the logic he decries here.

49. In the short work "Pacifick Christians" (MS Locke c. 27, fol. 80, Locke Archive, Bodleian Library, Oxford University), Locke writes: "We hold it to be an indispensable duty of all Christians to maintain love and charity in the diversity of contrary opinions. By which charity we doe not meane an empty sound, but an Actuall forbearance and goodwill carrying men to communion and friendship and mutual assistance one of another in outward as well as spirituall things."

50. See Locke, *Political Essays*, 344–45; italics added.

51. Martin Seliger suggests that Locke's inattention to express consent means that the imperative of consent amounts to the right of *dissent*; see Seliger, *Liberal Politics*. John Dunn writes on this point: "How is it in fact that men *do* incorporate themselves in society; just what sort of a performance *is* an 'express' or 'explicit' consent? There is no very clear answer to this question and it is a

damaging lacuna in Locke's theory that there should be none" ("Consent," 166; italics in original). Theodore Waldman argues that the difference is really a matter of different obligations and recommends that the distinction be cast as that between nonmember consent and member consent ("A Note," 45–50). Charles R. Beitz suggests that Locke is able to make tacit consent, which is really no consent at all, produce obligation only by tying it to property rights; see Beitz, "Tacit Consent." For Julian Franklin the distinction reflects Locke's concern with the territorial integrity of a country and can be understood as follows: "With tacit consent, jurisdiction over persons arises only indirectly from the public's jurisdiction over land, whereas, with express consent, jurisdiction over land arises as an indirect consequence of jurisdiction over people" ("Allegiance," 413–14). For Iain Hampsher-Monk this slip is symptomatic of Locke's (unconscious) patriarchalism insofar as he appears to presume that birth constitutes membership or "Englishness" (if not an explicit political obligation to an English monarch); see Hampsher-Monk, "Tacit Concept," 135–39. Making a similar point, Jacqueline Stevens critiques Locke's lack of attention to the issue of membership and, concomitantly, exclusion; see Stevens, *Reproducing the State*, 71–79.

52. See Locke, *Human Understanding*, 3.2.8 (408).
53. See Waldron, "John Locke."
54. See Scarry, "Consent and the Body," 874–75.
55. Den Hartogh, "Made by Contrivance," 207, 212, 213, 217.
56. Josephson, *Great Art*, 8, 157; see also 268 for discussion of "custom" in Locke.
57. For the interpretation of consent as attitude, see Seliger, *Liberal Politics*, 268, 225; see also 253, 282, and esp. 298. Jonathan Brody Kramnick argues that Locke "locates consent in the mind but then argues that the mind reveals its contents in practice. The result is a kind of dual legacy. Consent is what we bring to relations with other people or abstract institutions and is perceivable in what we do. It lies at once inside and outside the mind" ("Locke, Haywood, and Consent," 454). Kramnick compares Locke's account to the account of consent and agency proffered in Eliza Haywood's novels, *Love in Excess* (1719) and *Fantomina* (1725), whereby "the self is placed in concert with others, a world that shapes the agency misunderstood by Locke to come from within. The move from Locke to Haywood is thus not simply from philosophy to literature; it is also from solitude to worldliness, autonomy to sociability. . . . These two models will over time grow more sharply defined and separate from each other: the one emphasizing the rights a subject brings to a social order, the other emphasizing the social order that constructs and places limits on the subject" (468). Whereas I agree with Kramnick that Locke imagines the subject as bearing rights, and, I would add, as a creature of God, I dispute his claim that Locke locates consent in the mind of an autonomous agent.

58. Unpublished document from 1690 (MS Locke e. 18, Locke Archive, Bodleian Library, Oxford University), reproduced in J. Farr and Roberts, "Glorious Revolution," 395, 397, 398. Farr and Roberts suggest that Locke came to believe that tacit consent was good enough for times of peace, but times of dread, disunity, and war called for express consent (391). See also Den Hartogh, "Express Consent," 105–15.

59. Unpublished document from 1690 (MS Locke e. 18), reproduced in J. Farr and Roberts, "Glorious Revolution," 398.

60. Given Locke's position in 1690, one might speculate that Locke, though a mere secretary to the Lord Proprietors of Carolina, quietly or verbally assented to a number of articles contained in the earlier 1669 Fundamental Constitutions of Carolina. The English colony of Carolina in the 1660s was populated by natives, strangers from different nations, and slaves and masters and would no doubt have its share of estrangement and hostility. Article 95 reads, "No man shall be permitted to be a freeman of Carolina, or to have any estate or habitation within it, that does not acknowledge a God, and that God is publicly and solemnly to be worshipped." Article 101 states that "no person above seventeen years of age shall have any benefit or protection of the law, or be capable of any place of profit or honour, who is not a member of some church or profession, having his name recorded in some one, and but one religion record at once." I suggest that these particular articles entail a public performance of consent. One is recognized as a member or citizen of the colony of Carolina when one makes public record of his affiliation with a religious body. Nonetheless, it is important not to inflate Locke's role in, or conclude his position on, the composition of what Vicki Hsueh argues is a "hybridized creation that grafted strange and even ungainly features of feudalism and paternalism" (*Hybrid Constitutions*, 64).

61. See Lincoln, *Authority*.

62. For Michael Zuckert, Locke proffers Christianity as a truly civil religion insofar as he poses it as broad enough (requiring only belief in Jesus as the Messiah) and as obligatory in the form of the divine or natural law. No doubt Locke proffers a Christianity that he regards as eminently civil, and although Locke nowhere requires belief in Jesus as the foundation of a civil society, he requires adherence to what he understands as the singularity of Jesus's message, that is, the repudiation of theocracy. For Zuckert, despite the fact that Locke sees the necessity for a civil religion, Locke's conviction that it is human reason and labor that will liberate humanity undermines a civil religion founded in biblical Christianity. See Zuckert, *Launching Liberalism* 189. At about the same time as Zuckert's article appeared, Mark Goldie reckoned that Locke's notorious and debated exclusion of Papists was a "doctrine of civil religion"; yet he also left "exploration of Locke's civil religion to another time or author" (Goldie, "Civil Religion," 202, 201).

63. P. Kahn, *Liberalism*.
64. Marvin and Ingle, *Blood Sacrifice*, 1–4.
65. Wilkins, *Principles and Duties*, 182, 184.
66. Tillotson, *A Sermon*, 10, 9, 13.
67. On the latter point, see Sherwood, "God of Abraham," 328.

CHAPTER 3

1. Locke, *Letter Concerning Toleration*, 51; italics added.
2. Recall that the Fundamental Constitutions of Carolina, Article 95, reads, "No man shall be permitted to be a freeman of Carolina, or to have any estate or habitation within it, that does not acknowledge a God, and that God is publicly and solemnly to be worshipped." Article 101 reads, "No person above seventeen years of age shall have any benefit or protection of the law, or be capable of any place of profit or honour, who is not a member of some church or profession, having his name recorded in some one, and but one religion record at once." See page 167, note 60 for discussion of Locke's relationship to this document.
3. In his later *Vindication of the Reasonableness of Christianity*, Locke writes, "But Atheism being a Crime, which for its Madness as well as Guilt, *ought* to shut a Man out of all Sober and Civil Society" (2).
4. Lilla, "The Politics of God," *New York Times*, 19 August 2007, www.nytimes.com (accessed August 20, 2007); adapted from his book, *The Stillborn God: Religion, Politics, and the Modern West*.
5. Euben, *Enemy in the Mirror*, 63; italics in original.
6. Paul Kahn, too, sees an antithesis between liberalism and political theology. See, for instance, his *Political Theology*. C. John Sommerville makes a similar bifurcation in writing "John Locke could assume that society was bound together by agreement on things like property rather than God" (*Secularization*, 143). This comment indicates that Sommerville overlooks or discounts Locke's assertion as to the necessity of God for the maintenance of political society; moreover, it indicates that Sommerville does not see that Locke's theology grounds the primacy of property.
7. Dunn, "What Is Living," 15; McClure, *Judging Rights*, 133.
8. Dunn sees Locke's stress on individualism and duty as evidencing Locke's affinity for the Calvinist doctrine of the calling. Dunn refers to the "belief in the fact of a future life and the steady, simple summons to moral effort which this . . . *made* rational" and to the "grasp of religious duty adequate to secure his salvation" (*Political Thought*, 220, 249). Insofar as Dunn understands Locke to be arguing that salvation is something that can be labored for, then Locke's theology is a radical departure from that of the Calvinist. For

"Latitudinarianism," see Spellman, *John Locke and the Problem of Depravity*, esp. 57–58; and Pearson, "Religion," esp. 245. For the label of Socinianism, see Wallace, "Socianism," 49–66, esp. 56. John Marshall cautions that Locke's writings are not Socinian in a "systematic, dogmatic sense"; see his *Resistance, Religion, and Responsibility*, esp. xx, 121, 131. For the label of Arminian, see Hill, "Covenant Theology," 19. For the characterization of Locke's God as a Manichean and a tyrant, see Schneewind, "Locke's Moral Philosophy," 199 (quoting Thomas Burnet for the "Manichean" label), 225. For the reference to Locke's liberal God, see Forde, "John Locke's Natural Religion," 8. Spellman refers to "Locke's theological independence" (*John Locke*, 59). I differ with Spellman in his insistence on Locke's negative assessment of pro-lapsian human "nature" as opposed to what I would regard as Locke's sometimes negative assessment of human culture and action; see Spellman, *John Locke*, 75–76, and Spellman, *John Locke and the Problem of Depravity*, 103.

9. Waldron, *God, Locke, and Equality*, 228. Waldron's reconstruction of Locke's argument delineates a series of steps: from utilizing the power of abstraction to arrive at belief in God, to recognition of other humans (through their power of abstract thinking), to the conviction of human equality. Of course, one step does not necessarily lead to the next. Atheists may engage in abstraction but do not thereby believe in God (although they may be for equality). Violent criminals are no better than beasts, according to Locke, but they might still be capable of abstraction! So, too, mere assent to the idea of God does not at all entail the premise of human equality—something Waldron also points out. Waldron and John Dunn speculate that the viability of liberalism may depend on theism; see Dunn, *Political Thought*, 100.

10. J. Perry, *Pretense of Loyalty*, 122.

11. McClure, *Judging Rights*, 133. McClure observes that Locke's egalitarian arrangement of individuals is nestled snugly inside a theistic order.

12. McClure overlooks the fact that Locke insists that the existence of God is empirically verifiable and, as I argue later, essential to the legitimacy of the state. McClure assumes that Locke presupposes the legitimacy of the state to which he assigns the power of arbitrating injury. Yet, as his writings on justified rebellion indicate, far from assuming the state's abiding competence to arbitrate injury, Locke recognizes that the state is capable of injuring citizens, in which case, a critical mass of public opinion and an "appeal to God" will justify rebellion. If injuries committed in the name of religion necessitate appeal to the state, injuries committed by the state require community appeal to the Creator. See McClure, "Difference, Diversity."

13. John Dunn claims that "Locke's theory of rights rests foursquare upon this picture of a divinely created universe, of the purposes of its concerned creator, and of the role for which that creator destined human beings. Without that

theoretical frame Locke himself actually did not believe that human beings do possess rights at all" ("What Is Living," 15).

14. On this point, see Brettschneider, *When the State Speaks*, esp. 13.

15. For Locke natural law includes not only promise keeping but also the equality, liberty, sociability, propertyhood in person, and possession of executive (punishing) power of humans; the imperatives of preservation of self and others to the extent the first is not jeopardized; parental care of children and children's duty to responsible parents; and the right of appeal to heaven and that one's labor begets property. See Gough, *Locke's Political Philosophy*, ch. 1. James Tully has an abbreviated list but highlights that this law entails our obligation to God our maker. His list consists of the preservation of self and others, sociability (evidenced by language) and promise keeping, and the duty to praise, honor, and glorify God; see Tully, *Discourse on Property*, ch. 2.

16. Robert Horwitz insists that Locke remains frustratingly elusive regarding the cluster of issues that surround natural law—for example, the relationship between divine and natural law, the status of revelation and of the soul, and the foundations of morality. For Thomas Pangle, Locke is no traditionalist when it comes to natural law; he fails to substantiate the peculiar dignity of humans and makes human happiness rather than human ennoblement the end of natural law. See Horwitz, "Introduction," 19; and Pangle, *Modern Republicanism*, 160, 192.

17. See Locke, *Human Understanding*, 2.17.1 (210) and 2.23.33–35 (314–15).

18. See Locke, *Human Understanding*, 4.10.6 (621). Elsewhere Locke argues that something other, albeit greater, than human beings must have created human beings, because if humans were capable of bringing themselves forth into the world of nature, surely they would have arranged for themselves an eternal rather than temporal life. See *Essays on the Law of Nature*, IV, in Locke, *Political Essays*, 103.

19. Additional contradictions include Locke's assertion that God's creation of us manifests God's goodness, which is contradicted by God's unwillingness to bestow immortality upon humans—a point that suggests God's hostility toward humans. Locke also argues that the inconceivability of something coming from nothing affirms God's existence, whereas he dismisses the same contention as inadequate for questioning how it is that God creates the world. For this last critique, see Bluhm et al., "Locke's Idea of God," 419.

20. Zuckert, *Launching Liberalism*, 193–95.

21. Zuckert, *Launching Liberalism*, 189.

22. Locke, *Two Treatises*, II: 6 (311).

23. Colman argues that God's ownership of humanity extends only to the body and not to the labor of that body or to the actions of individuals; see Colman, *Locke's Moral Philosophy*, 189. See also Locke, *Two Treatises*, II: 6 (311), II: 27 (328).

24. On Locke's contemplation of nontheistic, albeit orderly, societies, see Marshall, *Locke, Toleration, and Early Enlightenment Culture*, 703.

25. *Essays on the Laws of Nature*, IV, in Locke, *Political Essays*, 105.

26. Locke, *Human Understanding*, 4.13.3 (651). Archbishop John Tillotson, whom Locke read and with whom he consulted, states a similar idea: "The Creation is of all other the most sensible and obvious argument of a Deity. Other Considerations may work upon our Reason and Understanding, but this doth as it were *bring God down to our Senses*. . . . Which way soever we turn our eyes, we are encounter'd with plain evidence of a *Superior Being*, which made us and all other things . . . *we cannot avoid the sight of Him if we would*" (*Six Sermons*, 258–59; italics in original).

27. Locke, *Letter Concerning Toleration*, 64.

28. Locke, *Essays on the Law of Nature*, VI, in Locke, *Political Essays*, 117.

29. MS Locke c. 28, para. 10, quoted in King, *Life of John Locke*, 2: 130; see also Locke's "Of Ethic in General" (1686–1688?), in Locke, *Political Essays*, 302.

30. The quotation continues, "If man were independent he could have no law but his own will, no end but himself. He would be a god to himself and the satisfaction of his own will the sole measure and end of all his actions." "Ethica B," MS Locke c. 28, fol. 141, Locke Archive, Bodleian Library, Oxford University; see also *Essays on the Law of Nature*, in Locke, *Political Essays*, 105, 115–16.

31. Gauthier, "Why Ought One Obey God?" 445.

32. Locke, "Second Vindication," in Locke, *Works*, 7: 229; italics added.

33. Schneewind, "Locke's Moral Philosophy," 220. Nicholas Wolterstorff argues that Locke presumes God's "right" without demonstrating it; Wolterstorff, *Ethics of Belief*, 138. See also Harris, *Mind of John Locke*, 271–72, 315.

34. Locke, *Essays on the Law of Nature*, 119. Consider, too, Locke's rather chilling query in the *Essays*: "For who will deny that the clay is subject to the potter's will, and that a piece of pottery can be shattered by the same hand by which it has been formed?" (*Essays on the Law of Nature*, 115).

35. V. Brown, "Figure of God." Brown refers only to *Two Treatises*, II: 166 (424–425), which does not read as an explicit endorsement of God as an "absolute monarch." Furthermore, one should consider Locke's making synonymous "absolute" and "arbitrary" power; see, for instance, Locke, *Two Treatises*, II: 8 (312), 23 (325), 135 (402).

36. Locke's accommodation of the prince's prerogative is not equivalent to Carl Schmitt's understanding of the sovereign as he who decides the exception to the law. For Locke the prince is obligated by natural law regardless of the limitations of state law. See Schmitt, *Political Theology*, 5.

37. Forster, *Locke's Politics of Moral Consensus*, 104–105. Forster has not taken account of texts that would challenge his reading and that I discuss in this book.

38. Representative writers include Francis Oakley, John Colman, J. B. Schneewind, and Greg Forster. Indeed, the evidence for a voluntarist bent in Locke's *Essay Concerning Human Understanding* prompted one of his earliest critics, Thomas Burnet, to charge that Locke seemed to "resolve all into the Will and Power of the Law-Maker" (Burnet, [*First*] *Remarks*, 6); see Oakley, "Locke, Natural Law, and God," 632. Wolfgang von Leyden sees a voluntarism "tempered" by "intellectualist notions"; see his edition of Locke's *Essays on the Law of Nature*, 43, 58. Ian Harris stresses the intellectualist aspects of Locke; see Harris, *Mind of John Locke*, 278. Hans Aarsleff insists that in the context of Locke there is no conflict between a divine "voluntaristic" law and the law of reason, that for Locke "God and his works are rational"; see Aarsleff, "State of Nature," 127, 110n2, 109. Mark Goldie, in his edition of Locke's political essays, somewhat confusingly asserts that Locke chose a middle way between intellectualism and voluntarism but then shortly thereafter claims, "But his fundamental position was voluntarist" (Locke, *Political Essays*, xx).

39. Forster, *Locke's Politics of Moral Consensus*, 105.

40. Journal entry, Sunday, August 1, 1680, MS Locke f. 4, pp. 145–51, Locke Archive, Bodleian Library, Oxford University; see Locke, *Political Essays*, 277. The language in this journal entry suggests that God's power is constrained by goodness. This is suggested in wording elsewhere: "That God himself cannot choose what is not good; the Freedom of the almighty hinders not his being determined by what is best. . . . God almighty himself is under the necessity of being happy; and the more any intelligent Being is so, the nearer is its approach to infinite perfection and happiness" (Locke, *Human Understanding*, 2.21.49–50 [265]). God's justice extends "noe farther than infinite goodnesse shall find it necessary for the preservation of his workes" (Locke, MS Locke f. 4, fols. 145–49; see also Locke, *Political Essays*, 278). "For since God is eternall and perfect in his own being, he can not make use of that power to change his owne being into better or another state, and therefore all the exercise of that power must be in and upon his creatures, which cannot but be imploied for their good and benefit" (MS Locke f. 4, fols. 145–49; see also Locke, *Political Essays*, 277).

41. As John Marshall writes, "Locke upheld both human freedom and God's omniscient omnipotence. He realized the impossibility of both of these tenets. Nonetheless, he resolved to believe both even if he could not understand how both could be true" (*Resistance, Religion, and Responsibility*, 131). Locke, Letter to Molyneux, January 26, 1693; see Dunn, *Political Thought*, 193. Locke writes, "We cannot imagin he hath made any thing with a designe that it should be miserable" (MS Locke f. 4, fol. 142, Locke Archive, Bodleian Library, Oxford University).

42. Indeed, for Locke anyone who attempts to set up fundamental beliefs that all Christians must follow "erects himself presently into God's throne." See

"A Second Vindication of the Reasonableness of Christianity," in Locke, *Works*, 7: 382.

43. See "A Second Vindication," in Locke, *Works*, 7: 382.

44. Locke, *Two Treatises*, I: 6 (178); italics added. Locke repeats this idea in the second book: "No power can exempt them [princes] from the Obligations of that Eternal Law. Those are so great, and so strong, in the case of *Promises*, that Omnipotency it self can be tyed by them. *Grants, Promises* and *Oaths are Bonds that hold the Almighty*" (II: 195 [443]; italics added).

45. See Filmer, *Patriarcha*, 35.

46. Locke, *Two Treatises*, I: 8, 33, 41, 42 (180–82, 200, 205–6).

47. See Locke, *Two Treatises*, I: 57 (218).

48. Berndt Hamm argues that this issue of the self-limitation of God is not about his already being limited by his goodness but rather bespeaks a particular event in which God freely limits God; nonetheless, the divine choice to self-limit in creating the world does not indicate temporality in the, of course, eternal Godhead; see Hamm, *Promissio, Pactum, Ordinatio*, 1–2.

49. *Essays on the Law of Nature*, VII, in Locke, *Political Essays*, 122.

50. Locke, *Political Essays*, 145.

51. Oakley, "Locke, Natural Law, and God," 649, 651.

52. Covenantal theology emphasizes the biblical covenants as indicative of the human and divine relationship. Federal theology is a particular variant of covenantal theology in which Adam is said to have had a political or representative capacity for all humankind when he entered into covenant with God before the Fall. See Weir, *Origins of the Federal Theology*.

53. Miller, *New England Mind*, 379–80; see also 376, 410. Miller notes that the relevant theologians maintained the distinction between God's absolute and ordained power. John Milton 1608–1674) also combines elements of divine transcendence with divine accountability. Milton insists on God's "hidden wayes" but also declares, "God is no covnant breaker, he cannot doe this" (Milton, *Doctrine and Discipline*, 2: 292, 297). Locke owned a collection of all of Milton's works. Although he owned works by representative thinkers such as William Ames and Richard Baxter, the specific works in his library do not deal explicitly with covenant theology. These works are Baxter's *How to Do Good to Many: Or, the Publick Good Is the Christians Life* (London, 1682) and Ames's *Declaration of the Witness of God Manifested in Me from My Youth* (London, 1656). See Harrison and Laslett, *Library of John Locke*, 189, 72, 81. Milton writes, "The hidden wayes of his providence we adore & search not; but the law is his reve[a]led wil, his complete, his evident, and certain will; herein he appears to us as it were in human shape, enters into cov'nant with us, swears to keep it, *binds himself* like a just lawgiver to his own prescriptions, gives himself to be understood by men, judges and is judg'd, measures and is commensurate to right reason" (*Doctrine and Discipline*, 2: 292).

54. Miller, *New England Mind*, 403, quoting William Ames.

55. Christian writers have continued to portray divine sovereign power through scenes of hurt bodies. See, for instance, Augustine of Hippo (354–430), John Calvin (1509–1564), Teresa of Ávila (1515–1582), and Jonathan Edwards (1703–1758). "Since God achieves some good by correcting adults through the suffering and death of children who are dear to them, why shouldn't those things take place?" (Augustine, *Free Choice*, 116). "In times of adversity believers comfort themselves with the solace that they suffer nothing except by God's ordinance and command, for they are under his hand" (Calvin, *Institutes of the Christian Religion*, 1.16.3; from Case-Winters, *God's Power*, 72n18). One could choose many examples from Teresa; here is one: "The pain [of offending God] breaks and grinds the soul to pieces" (*Interior Castle*, 95). "There is no want of *power* in God to cast wicked men into hell at any moment. Men's hands cannot be strong when God rises up. . . . That world of misery, that lake of burning brimstone, is extended abroad under you. There is the dreadful pit of the glowing flames of the wrath of God; there is hell's wide gaping mouth open; and you have nothing to stand upon, nor any thing to take hold of, there is nothing between you and hell but the air; it is only the power and mere pleasure of God that holds you up. . . . The infinite might, and majesty, and terribleness of the omnipotent God shall be magnified upon you" (Edwards, *Sinners*, 5, 12, 20).

56. Miller, *New England Mind*, 389.

57. See Guyatt, *Providence*, esp. 200–12, 229–35.

58. Journal entry for March 20, 1678, MS Locke f. 3, fol. 73, Locke Archive, Bodleian Library, Oxford University. In the same text he writes, "I think god out of his infinite goodness, considering our ignorance and frailty, hath left us a great liberty. Love to god and charity to ourselves and neighbors are no doubt indispensably necessary. But though we keep these thoughts in our heart and sincerely practice them I cannot but think that god allows us in the ordinary actions of our lives a great latitude. That I cannot imagine that god who has compassion on our weaknesse and knows how we are made would put [a] poore man, nay the least of men . . . under always an absolute necessity of sinning perpetually which will almost certainly follow if there is no latitude at all allowed" (fols. 70–71).

59. Locke, *Human Understanding*, 2.28.8 (352), 2.21.70 (281-82); and Locke, *Reasonableness*, para. 183–84, 212, 243, 245.

60. "All obligation binds conscience and lays a bond on the mind itself, so that not fear of punishment, but a rational apprehension of what is right, puts us under an obligation, and conscience passes judgment on morals, and, if we are guilty of a crime, declares that we deserve punishment" (Locke, *Essays on the Law of Nature*, 185).

61. Locke, *Essays on the Law of Nature*, 183–85. John Colman, for instance, argues that moral obligation flows from God's might and right, the latter having to do with God's roles as creator and ongoing preserver of life. Colman, *Locke's Moral Philosophy*, 46.

62. MS Locke f. 27, fol. 248, Locke Archive, Bodleian Library, Oxford University.

63. Locke, *Human Understanding*, 2.28.12 (356–57). Thus I do not think that Locke envisions a punishing God as politically useful; see also Bluhm et al., "Locke's Idea of God."

64. Althusser, *Lenin and Philosophy*, 178, 179; italics in original.

65. Dunn, *Political Thought*, 264.

66. See Stanton, "Politics and Theology."

67. See, for instance, Augustine, *Confessions*, VII: 16 and VIII; Augustine, *City of God*, 609; and Luther, *Bondage of the Will*, 140.

68. Locke's understanding of the relationship of grace and free will comes closer to a Jesuitical understanding of efficacious grace or the Tridentine claims about the possibility of resisting sanctifying grace. As Patrick Riley argues, "Political philosophy since the seventeenth century has been characterized, above all, by voluntarism, by an emphasis on the consent of individuals as the standard of political legitimacy" (*Will and Political Legitimacy*, 1).

69. The entirety of the passage reads: "But if God (which is the point in question) would have men forced to heaven, it must not be by the outward violence of the magistrate on men's bodies, but the inward constraints of his own spirit on their minds, which are not to be wrought on by any human compulsion; *the way to salvation not being any forced exterior performance, but the voluntary and secret choice of the mind*" (Locke, *An Essay Concerning Toleration*, 1667, quoted in Bourne, *Life of John Locke*, pt. 1, 177; italics added). Of course, this comment suggests an echo of Arminianism. Locke and John Milton were agreed in repudiating Restoration Anglican use (by way of Augustine) of the Gospel passages in which Jesus tells a parable of the wealthy man who commands his servants to "go out into the highways and hedges, and compel them [his indifferent invited guests] to come in, that my house may be filled" ("A Treatise of Civil Power in Ecclesiastical Causes," in Milton, *Complete Poems and Major Prose*, 849). On this latter issue, see Goldie, "Religious Intolerance," 337–38.

70. Calvin, *Eternal Predestination*, 138; italics added.

71. MS Locke d. 3, fol. 102, Locke Archive, Bodleian Library, Oxford University.

72. MS Locke d. 3, fol. 104, Locke Archive, Bodleian Library, Oxford University.

73. In MS Locke c. 28, fol. 149 (Locke Archive, Bodleian Library, Oxford University), Locke argues that moral actions are those that flow from a "free agent."

74. The Arminian Remonstrance of 1610 affirms atonement theology. See Hill, "Covenant Theology," 19. Locke's rejection of atonement theology signals an affinity with Socinianism, but he clearly innovates by insisting on the peculiar authority of miraculous power. As was noted by his sometimes harsh critic John Edwards, Locke did not endorse the reading of Jesus's death as a sacrifice. In reply to Edwards, Locke argued that belief in satisfaction (Jesus's redemptive death) is not presented in the Gospels as necessary to being a Christian. Locke countered that belief in Jesus as the Messiah is all that is necessary for one to be considered "Christian." Locke speaks of "attoning the merciful, kind, compassionate Author," not on account of an original sin but of individual failures of duty discernible by reason; see Locke, *Reasonableness*, [253], 140.

75. Locke refers to this "cover" in *Reasonableness*, 134.

76. Locke, *Paraphrase and Notes*, 421.

77. Locke, *Paraphrase and Notes*, 421–22.

78. Locke, *Reasonableness*, 146.

79. Locke, *Reasonableness*, 28.

80. Locke's logic here is the recurrent one in which Christianity is (or aspires to be) the universal religion that triumphs over the more particularistic, even nationalistic or tribalistic, religions, in this case, Judaism. For this view, see Müller, *Science of Religion*, 22–23; Stevens, *Reproducing the State*, 242; Žižek, *Fragile Absolute*, 121; and P. Kahn, *Liberalism*, 79.

81. Locke, *Reasonableness*, 159.

82. Riley, "Finding an Equilibrium," 445, 432.

83. Locke, *Discourse of Miracles*, 80–85.

84. See Locke, *Discourse of Miracles*, 81.

85. See, for instance, Tully, *Approach to Political Philosophy*, 231.

86. Locke, *Reasonableness*, 158.

87. Locke, *Third Letter*, 6: 455 and 6: 372; italics added. Proast is referring, however, to Isaiah 49:23, which reads: "Thus speaks the Lord . . . I beckon to the nations and hoist my signal for the peoples. They will bring back your sons in the cloak, they will take your daughters on their shoulders. Kings will be fosterfathers, their queens your nursing mothers. They will fall prostrate before you, faces to the ground, and lick the dust at your feet. You shall then know that I am [the Lord] and that those who hope in me will not be put to shame" (*Jerusalem Bible*). What is ironic is that earlier, in the second book of his *Two Treatises*, Locke portrays monarchs as nursing fathers: "Paternal affection secured their Property, and Interest under his Care, and the Custom of obeying him, in their Childhood, made it easier to submit to him rather than to any other. . . . And unless they had done so, young Societies could not have subsisted: without *such nursing Fathers tender and carefull* of the publick weale,

all Governments would have sunk under the Weakness and Infirmities of their Infancy; and the Prince and the People had soon perished together" (*Two Treatises*, II: 105, 110 [381, 386]).

88. Locke, *Reasonableness*, 85, 96; Locke, *Letter Concerning Toleration*, 44–45.

89. Harris, *Mind of John Locke*, 323.

90. As Nathan Tarcov tantalizingly muses but does not elaborate, "Divine government seems to have learned something of the limitations of punishment and fear from the art of government taught in the *Thoughts* [Concerning Education]" (*Locke's Education for Liberty*, 187).

91. For studies of the sources of such a theological formulation, see, for instance, Tanner, *Politics of God*; Kaufman, *Face of Mystery*; Botwinick, *Skepticism*; Caputo, *Prayers*; and Coole, *Negativity and Politics*.

92. James I, "Trew Law," 6: 204.

93. The possibility of humans being adopted by God is a recurrent theme in Locke's *Reasonableness* (114, 124) and the *Paraphrase and Notes* (333).

94. Schmitt, *Concept of the Political*, 35, 54, 78.

95. Schmitt, *Concept of the Political*, 61, 64, 65.

96. Pangle, *Spirit of Modern Republicanism*, 271.

CHAPTER 4

1. Locke, *Letter Concerning Toleration*, 33.

2. MS Locke c. 27, fol. 29, Locke Archive, Bodleian Library, Oxford University.

3. This is another factor that challenges Kirstie McClure's argument in "Difference, Diversity."

4. Here Locke betrays echoes of his more conservative position in the earlier *Essay Concerning Toleration*, in Locke, *Political Essays*, esp. 147–48.

5. See, for instance, *An Essay Concerning Toleration*, in Locke, *Political Essays*, 137.

6. Locke, *Reasonableness*, 162.

7. Proast, *Argument*, 5.

8. See, for instance, J. A. Passmore's discussion of the *Essay Concerning Human Understanding* (4.13.2 [650–51]) in his "Ethics of Belief," 191.

9. Proast, *Argument*, 12.

10. See Proast, *Second Letter*, 6.

11. Hickes, "Infant Baptism," 345 (italics added); see also 347.

12. See Walker, *Literary Criticism*, 125.

13. Locke, *Conduct of the Understanding*, 220.

14. Whitby, *Answer to Sure-Footing*, 7.

15. Whitby, *Answer to Sure-Footing*, 9.
16. *An Essay on Toleration*, in Locke, *Political Essays*, 138.
17. J. Farr and Roberts, "Glorious Revolution," 398.
18. J. Farr and Roberts, "Glorious Revolution," 398.
19. Locke, *Second Letter*, 6: 107, 107.
20. Alex Tuckness argues that over the course of their exchange, the gravity of Locke's position falls on this point; that is, for coercion to be legitimate, it must be universalizable "in a world populated by fallible moral agents." For Tuckness this argument is Locke's strongest and the one he eventually emphasizes over the others. See Tuckness, "Main Argument," 136. Proast suggests that coercion is always warranted to save a life, one might add, especially in the context of fallible agents. If the preservation of life is part of the natural law, then coercion toward this end could be construed as lawful.
21. On the frequent use of Augustine as a justification for religious coercion, see Goldie, "Religious Intolerance."
22. Adam Wolfson is the only other scholar to analyze at length Locke's "argument from consent" in these debates with Proast. He argues that Locke mounts two other arguments in this debate: the argument from belief (belief cannot be produced by outward power) and the argument from skepticism (sheer variety of opinions calls into question the possibility of establishing or legislating the truth). I am convinced that only the argument from consent captures a consistent line of argument in Locke. Moreover, I fundamentally disagree with Wolfson's contention that Locke relegates religion to the private sphere and that the "overcoming of the religious worldview" means that religious knowledge or truth must be regarded as matters of opinion only. See Wolfson, *Persecution or Toleration*.
23. Of this lengthy exchange between Locke and Proast, Jeremy Waldron asserts, "Despite the enormous amount of ink that he devoted to his response [to Proast], Locke failed to provide any adequate answer to this point," that is, that force "at a distance" may remove obstacles to truth, such as negligence and prejudice. Waldron acknowledges Locke's points that it is difficult to distinguish the sincere dissenters, who have reflected on the relevant matters, from the lazy ones, who have not, and thus that it would be wrong to use force indiscriminately on all dissenters. He also notes Locke's arguing that the Gospel nowhere advocates the use of force or has God turning to the state to enforce Christianity. But Waldron then boils down Locke's argument to the following: "Force *may* be serviceable, only it is likely to be difficult to tell *in which cases* it will be serviceable" ("Locke, Toleration," 112). Thus Waldron nowhere addresses Locke's insistence on the necessity to consent to be saved.
24. See also Locke, *Letter Concerning Toleration*, 36, 38, 40.
25. "Toleration B" (1676), in Locke, *Political Essays*, 247.

26. James, "Will to Believe," 13; see also 27. James adds, "As a matter of fact, we find ourselves believing, we hardly know how or why" (18).

27. James, *Principles of Psychology*, 948.

28. James, *Varieties*, 45.

29. James, *Varieties*, 177.

30. See, for example, James, *Principles of Psychology*, 1172–73, 928–29, 913, 1169.

31. James, *Varieties*, 108.

32. Vagrant poor children were already a major problem in the sixteenth century. An act of Parliament in 1536 allowed parishes to apprentice begging children, age 5–14. A 1547 act of Parliament allowed wandering, begging children between the ages of 5 and 14 to be taken from their parents "by any manner of person" who promised to keep them occupied up to the age of 20 for women and 24 for men. If a child should run away, he or she was to be captured and put in chains to be used as a "slave." Although permission for slavery was withdrawn two years later, permission for removing children from parents remained. See Pinchbeck and Hewitt, *Children in English Society*, I: 96–97, quoted in Cunningham, *Children*, 95.

33. *A Report to the Board of Trade to the Lords Justices 1697, Respecting the Relief and Unemployment of the Poor* (London, 1789), 115, quoted in Hundert, "Making of *Homo Faber*," 5.

34. Locke's idea was not unique. Workhouses for children were set up in sixteenth- and seventeenth-century England, including Bridewell. There were also the charity schools of the Anglican Society for the Propagation of Christian Knowledge (by 1729 there were 1,419 schools with 22,000 pupils). Although these institutions focused more on schooling, their stated goal was to inure children "to the meanest services." Locke's 1697 recommendations for the Poor Law were reprinted in 1817 because of his emphasis on work. See Cunningham, *Children*, 97–108.

35. If older than 14 (and without a pass and begging) and male, the child would be shipped to another seaport or would work onboard ship; if female, she would be sent to a house of correction. If the child counterfeited a pass, he or she would lose his or her ears.

36. Locke, *Political Essays*, 191–92; italics added.

37. Locke, *Two Treatises*, II: 34, 35 (333–34). See also Olivecrona, "Theory of Appropriation," 228.

38. Tully, *Discourse on Property*, 110.

39. See Dunn, *Political Thought*, 220; see also 249.

40. Poor children were sent to the colonies starting in 1617. In 1627 it was reported that ships to Virginia carried 1,400–1,500 children. See Pinchbeck and

Hewitt, *Children in English Society*, I: 105–107, quoted in Cunningham, *Children*, 98.

41. "Some of the Chief Grievances," MS Locke e. 9(a), Locke Archive, Bodleian Library, Oxford University; this essay was also published as part of Kammen, "Virginia at the Close of the Seventeenth Century," 159; italics added. Because Locke believed that a shortage of labor power was chiefly to blame for holding back England and her colonies from achieving true economic and political power, he was in favor of relaxed immigration and naturalization laws. See "For a General Naturalization," in Locke, *Political Essays*, 322–26.

42. This report starts in Locke's hand but then evidences the hand of S. Brownover, Locke's amanuensis and, later, William Popple's amanuensis. It is included in Locke's papers at the Bodleian Library, MS Locke e. 9. The quotations are from folios 30 and 32. The report is also published in Kammen, "Virginia at the Close of the Seventeenth Century," 166–67. Kammen argues that the text must be the work of Locke and James Blair (first president of the College of William and Mary) and, in fact, resembles Blair's style much more than Locke's. Kammen even suggests that Blair composed the document with "direct encouragement and assistance" from Locke (148). Kammen notes that Jack P. Greene (in *The Quest for Power: The Lower Houses of Assembly in the Southern Royal Colonies, 1689–1776* [Chapel Hill, 1963], 201–2, 345–46) and Philip Long (in *A Summary Catalogue of the Lovelace Collection of the Papers of John Locke*, 40) assert that the document was written by Locke. Richard Ashcraft argues, convincingly, that the document is the work of John Locke; see Ashcraft, "Political Theory," 742–43. He also cites the concurring opinions of Maurice Cranston and Patrick Kelly. The report is also included in Mark Goldie's list of Locke's works in his edition of Locke's *Political Essays*, 383. Certainly, Blair may have had significant input on these matters, especially religious reform. He later composed a document on this very topic; see McCulloch, "James Blair's Plan," 70–86. Yet there is a significant difference between the recommendations of the two documents, suggesting that Blair could not have been the sole author of the 1697 document. For instance, whereas the earlier document recommends the education of Natives in their own language, the later document notes that the retention of their own language in the case of older Negroes makes them "much more indocile" (McCulloch, "James Blair's Plan," 85). Moreover, the later document also gives specifics as to what Negro and Indian children must learn and the penalties (something Locke never offered for religious faults) to be inflicted (taxes) should this not happen (85–86).

43. See J. Farr, "Natural Law," 508. In 1671 Locke drafted a temporary law forbidding the enslavement of Indians; insofar as he refers to their God, Locke may have distinguished between Indians and Africans and found in the Indians' tribal governance indications of a consensual framework.

44. One might speculate that Locke regarded Natives and Africans has having revoked their consent because he regarded them as subdued conquerors (as in his argument in the *Two Treatises*, II: 85 [366]). The problem with relying on this textual argument is that in the same text Locke outlaws the enslavement of the conquerors' heirs, yet he does not offer a formal objection to their enslavement in the English colonial context.

45. Mark A. Michael argues that Locke justifies the appropriation of land in America because he argues that the Americans do not enclose and develop it as property but rather leave it as a wasteland; this argument is anticipated by John Winthrop and John Smith. See Michael, "Locke's *Second Treatise*," esp. 417. Note that James Farr reminds his readers that Locke nowhere uses his just-war theory in the *Two Treatises* to explicitly justify slavery in the colonies. See J. Farr, "Natural Law," 495–522. Locke's discussion in paragraph 102 of book II of the *Two Treatises* suggests that Locke did not regard all colonized peoples as necessarily incapable of consent. In this text he comments on Josephus Acosta's claim that the inhabitants of Peru, Brazil, and Florida had no governments or kings but would band together and declare their captains in war. Locke takes this to indicate their recognition of their equality and power of consent.

46. "For what justice is there where there is no personal property or right of ownership" (*Essays on the Law of Nature*, VIII, in Locke, *Political Essays*, 132).

47. Locke observes, "What would a man value Ten Thousand, or an Hundred Thousand Acres of excellent Land, ready cultivated, and well stocked too with Cattle in the middle of the in-land Parts of America, where he had no hopes of Commerce with other Parts of the World, to draw Money to him by the Sale of the Product?" (*Two Treatises*, II: 48, 343). For a similar argument in relationship to the development of the idea of the fetish, see Pietz, "Problem of the Fetish," pts. 1–3.

48. Jeremy Waldron argues that we should not take Locke's contribution to the Fundamental Constitutions of Carolina ("Every free man of Carolina shall have absolute power and authority over his slaves") and his personal investment in the Royal African Company, which held a monopoly in the slave trade, as nullifying his extensive writings against slavery. Waldron points out that a vulnerable Locke could perhaps not afford a life of scholarly and political integrity. Moreover, Locke's views may have undergone a significant change (if not enough to prompt him to repudiate earlier actions and texts): The Fundamental Constitutions of Carolina was composed in 1669, and Locke bought his shares in the Royal African Company in 1671 (he later sold them at a profit), whereas the *Two Treatises* was first published in 1689 (dated 1690). Maybe they do not nullify his statements, but they surely strain them. One might imagine compromise in political discussions and documents, but investment in the trade poses a much tougher case. Perhaps it is moral queasiness that accounts for the usage of

"Negroes" as opposed to "slaves" in the Virginia report of 1697. Waldron (*God, Locke, and Equality*, 204) is responding to Welchman, "Slavery," who reconstructs Locke's defense of slavery as implicitly applicable to and justificatory of the English enslavement of Africans.

49. See J. Farr, "Natural Law," 510.

50. For an extended argument on race and political theology, see Hickman, "Globalization."

51. Little, "Double-Edged Dilemma," esp. 88–89.

52. Sands, "Property of Peculiar Value," 166, 161.

53. Sands discusses the Supreme Court case *Lyng v. Northwest Indian Cemetery Protective Association*, 485 U.S. 439 (1988). Efforts to pass federal legislation protecting "sacred lands" have consistently failed.

54. See Greg Johnson, "Apache Revelation."

CHAPTER 5

1. Kaplan, *Divided by Faith*, 294–96, 300.
2. See Wiesner-Hanks, *Christianity*.
3. Wiesner-Hanks, *Christianity*.
4. Mahmood, "Secularism," 328.
5. For this accusation (by John Edwards), see Marshall, *Locke, Toleration, and Early Enlightenment Culture*, 461.
6. Locke, *Letter Concerning Toleration*, 42, 54. See also Marshall, *Locke, Toleration, and Early Enlightenment Culture*, 715–16; and Shagan, *Rule of Moderation*, 288–306.
7. See Goldie, "Locke, Proast, and Religious Toleration," 167n81.
8. See Walsham, *Charitable Hatred*, 246; and Knights, "Meer Religion," 58–59.
9. In his painstaking account of the Spanish Inquisition, Stuart B. Schwartz notes that it was a general presumption that dissident attitudes about toleration and fornication went hand in hand. See Schwartz, *All Can Be Saved*, 32.
10. Browning, *English Historical Documents*, 396. In the seventeenth century a similar critique surfaced of the detrimental effect of religious exclusivity on Spain's commercial and diplomatic interests; see Schwartz, *All Can Be Saved*, 213.
11. See Knights, "Meer Religion," 65.
12. *Queries*, all quotes from page 4.
13. Marshall, *Locke, Toleration, and Early Enlightenment Culture*, 178. Marshall also points to the significant limitations of Dutch tolerance; see 162–76.

14. In his poem "Confined Love," Donne writes, "Beasts do no jointures lose / Though they new lovers choose; / But we are made worse than those." In "Love's Usury" he implores, "Love, let my body range." See Greenblatt, *Norton Anthology of English Literature*, 600–602.

15. Marshall, *Locke, Toleration, and Early Enlightenment Culture*, 458; see also 217, 218–19, 308, 363, 375, 389, 399, 412, 450–51, 454, 458, 460–61.

16. In addition to the plays discussed in the text, see James Shirley, *The Wedding* (1629), and Thomas Heywood, *A Woman Kilde with Kindness* (1603).

17. Cavendish, *Description of a New World*; available at http://www.digital.library.upenn.edu/women/newcastle/blazing/blazing.html (accessed July 14, 2010).

18. Locke's text is commented on at length in the widely read early novel *Pamela: or, Virtue Rewarded* (1740), which was also the first novel published in America. See Cunningham, *Children*, 110, 113. Locke's writings on children and education influenced Isaac Watts's bestselling compositions of religious and instructional songs for children (which appeared in 1715 to lure them away from degrading chapbooks) and John Newbery's literature for children, which he began publishing in 1744. See Brewer, *By Birth or Consent*, 97.

19. See, for instance, Ariès, *Centuries of Childhood*; and Cunningham, *Children*.

20. Tillotson, *Six Sermons*, 232; italics in original.

21. Locke, *Two Treatises* II: 67 (355), quoted in Tarcov, *Locke's Education for Liberty*, 74.

22. Arendt, "What Is Authority?" 109.

23. It appears that Locke's model of good parenting was his own father; see Woolhouse, *Locke: A Biography*, 6.

24. Foucault, *Discipline and Punish*, 177; see also 178, 180.

25. Tillotson, *Six Sermons*, 170. Tillotson goes on to state that every temper provides a "*handle* whereby we may take hold of them and steer them more easily" (170).

26. See Jeremy Waldron's discussion of these two arguments in his "John Locke," 3–28.

27. Locke writes that "languages were made not by rules or art, but by accident and the common use of people" and "that he [the child] may understand his own country speech nicely and speak it properly without shocking the ears of those it is addressed to" (*Some Thoughts*, 168 [126 and 128]; see also 168 [127], 170–71 [130], and 189 [142 and 143]).

28. Locke, *Conduct of the Understanding*, 1 (167).

29. Locke, *Human Understanding*, 1.3.6 (69). John Tillotson urges parents to teach children "to be always under a lively sense and apprehension of his pure and allseeing Eye, which beholds us in secret" (*Six Sermons*, 137).

30. Foucault, *Discipline and Punish*, 294.

31. Compare Archbishop John Tillotson's sermon in which the model of the God-fearing, well-instructed, obedient child is Isaac, who is nearly sacrificed by his father, Abraham, in Genesis 22: "What an unexampled instance of the most profound respect and obedience to the Commands of his Father did Isaac give, when without the least murmuring or reluctancy he submitted to be bound and laid upon the Altar, and to have been slain for a Sacrifice" (in Tillotson, *Six Sermons*, 74).

32. Locke is doubly alarmed when such ideas are declared innate by their teachers—a claim that instills the teacher's authority as well. See Locke, *Human Understanding*, 1.4.24 (102). Tillotson, too, declared the Janus face of custom: a tenacious obliging power for both good and bad ends; see Tillotson, *Six Sermons*, 213–14.

33. I disagree, therefore, with Carole Pateman's reading of Locke's individual as traditionally and unqualifiedly "masculine." Her reading is challenged by more extensive consideration of his writings on education and religion. On this point, see Butler, "Early Liberal Roots"; Shanley, "Marriage Contract"; and Severance, "Sex."

34. For a systematic discussion of James's repudiation of colonialism, see Coon, "One Moment."

35. James, *Principles of Psychology*, I: 316.

36. For the early modern use of affectionate and aesthetic (but not parental) models of contract, see V. Kahn, *Wayward Contracts*.

37. See "Pleasure, Pain, the Passions" (1676), in Locke, *Political Essays*, 239.

38. Seliger, *Liberal Politics*, 208, 215, 217, 223, 238; see also 219. Carole Pateman also notices that Locke's talk of trusting the political authority resembles the child's trust of the father; see Pateman, *Political Obligation*, 71.

39. Gordon Schochet also spends little time discussing Locke's God, other than noting how God's creation and ownership of humans serves to limit parental power; he suggests that Locke comes close to sketching an analogy between fatherly concern and that of the magistrate. See Schochet, *Patriarchalism*, 270.

40. As Schochet notes, Locke defaults to referring to "paternal" authority rather than "parental" authority; Schochet, *Patriarchalism*, 249.

41. Hence I disagree with Peter Laslett's comment regarding "Locke's failure to share Filmer's vision of the emotional togetherness implied by all political relationships, the physically, physiologically natural element"; see his introduction to Locke, *Two Treatises*, II: 83.

42. Locke, *Human Understanding*, 2.21.53 (268); Locke, *Two Treatises*, II: 67 (355) (see also II: 170 [428] for Locke's reference to the "tenderness and affection which God hath planted in the breasts of parents"), II: 209 (453), II: 105 (381), II: 110 (386–87); italics added. In *Reasonableness* Locke writes, "God out of

the infiniteness of his Mercy, has dealt with Man as a compassionate and tender Father" (169).

43. Kallen, *Culture and Democracy*, 122, quoted in Macedo, *Diversity and Distrust*, 104.

44. Kallen, *Culture and Democracy*, 61, quoted in Macedo, *Diversity and Distrust*, 105

45. See Eisenach, *Two Worlds*, 91.

46. Anticipating contemporary faith-based initiatives regarding poverty, Locke especially recommends marriage for the poor; see his "Marriage" (1679), in Locke, *Political Essays*, 273. In his unpublished writings Locke goes much further. He declares that only marriage and the begetting of children produce political enfranchisement. Locke considers unmarried men without children minors until the age of 40. Locke also urges benefits for producing children, suggesting that parents of ten children (registered, of course) ought to be exempt from all public taxes. (He even entertained the idea of men having children by plural wives—but scratched this out.) Locke even suggests that a husband can "put away" his wife for adultery (which includes talking to a man in private with whom the husband has forbidden contact in front of two witnesses) or for "barrenness." MS Locke f. 3, fols. 198–201, 15 July 1678, Locke Archive, Bodleian Library, Oxford University; see Locke, *Political Essays*, 255–257; see also 258.

47. In 1971 the Internal Revenue Service (IRS) declared that organizations with policies of racial discrimination may not declare tax-exempt status because such behavior contravenes the purpose of being "charitable." Bob Jones University began to admit African Americans (after the first time that the IRS nullified their tax-exempt status) but prohibited interracial dating. The IRS again rejected their tax-exempt status; the university sued. The Supreme Court ruled in favor of the IRS. Bob Jones University ended this policy in 2000.

48. For those who believe that religious organizations have the right to discriminate in employment, the right of exit is the trump card. This is the argument of Chandran Kukathas. It is also that of Brian Barry. Barry, however, believes that the costs of exit can be high and argues that religious groups should compensate dissenters for their lost assets. See Kukathas, "Are There Any Cultural Rights?" and his "Exit, Freedom, and Gender." Kukathas accords wide, some might say unlimited, latitude to the activities of groups even if they injure vulnerable members—so long as there is a right of exit. See Barry, *Culture and Equality*, ch. 6. For Barry the Amish do not qualify as a voluntary community because the costs of exit are prohibitively high and thus dissenters do not exit (246). Susan Moller Okin suggests that women may be so indoctrinated into their culture that they are incapable of moving toward a better existence. The problem with this contention is that it comes close to the paternalistic claim that others might have false consciousness (which, of course, can be simply turned

around on the accuser); it also calls into serious question the legitimacy of consent. See Okin, "Mistresses."

49. Stopler, "Liberal Bind."
50. Macedo, *Diversity and Distrust*, 34, 222.
51. Macedo, *Diversity and Distrust*, 219.
52. Walzer, "Problem of Citizenship," 205.

CHAPTER 6

1. Alexis de Tocqueville was astonishingly confident with regard to the power of words to form societal and political bonds. He observed, "When no firm and lasting ties any longer unite men, it is impossible to obtain the cooperation of any great number of them unless you can persuade every man whose help is required that he serves his private interests by voluntarily uniting his efforts to those of all the others. That cannot be done habitually and conveniently without the help of a newspaper. . . . So the more equal men become and the more individualism becomes a menace, the more necessary are newspapers. We should underrate their importance if we thought they just guaranteed liberty; they maintain civilization. . . . The newspaper brought them together and continues to be necessary to hold them together" (Tocqueville, *Démocratie en Amérique*, 183; my translation). See Tocqueville, *Democracy in America*, 517–18.
2. See Bowen, *Why the French*, 1.
3. Bowen, *Why the French*, 4–5, 125, 187–88, 193, 197, 211–13.
4. However, Pakistan's former foreign minister, Muhammad Zafrulla Khan, argued that the Declaration's article on religious liberty was consonant with Islam. Khan cited the Quranic injunction that there can be no compulsion in religion. See Kelsay, "Saudi Arabia," 36–37. Nonetheless, because of Saudi Arabia's objections, which garnered explicit support from other Muslim nations as time went on, the explicit endorsements of religious liberty contained in both the 1948 Universal Declaration of Human Rights and the 1966 International Covenant on Civil and Political Rights were not included in the 1981 United Nations Declaration on the Elimination of All Forms of Intolerance and of Discrimination Based on Religion or Belief. For many Muslims the assumption is that one has entered into a binding contract with the deity and community and cannot simply walk away from this commitment. Although the legal basis for punishing apostasy from the Islamic community is disputed, Saudi Arabia, Sudan, and Mauritania expressly prohibit apostasy. Death sentences for apostasy have been delivered in Iran and recently in Afghanistan. Algeria passed a law for imprisoning apostates. In the Declaration on the Rights and Care of the Child in Islam of the Islamic Conference, this prohibition on apostasy is noted in Article 8, which addresses the right to education: "While Islam guarantees Man's freedom

to voluntarily adopt Islam without compulsion, it prohibits apostasy of a Muslim afterwards, in view of the fact that Islam is the Seal of Religions and, therefore, the Islamic society is committed to ensuring that the sons of Muslims preserve their Islamic nature and Creed and to protecting them against attempts to force them to relinquish their religion" (Declaration on the Rights and Care of the Child in Islam, U.N. General Assembly Official Records, 50th Session, Item 28, Annex I: Res. 16/7–C (IS), at 269, U.N. Doc. A/50/85/S/1995/152 [1995]). See Fore, "Shall Weigh," 225; and An-Na'im, "Human Rights in the Muslim World," 13, 23. In its 1957 constitution the Malaysian government prohibited proselytism of Muslims by non-Muslims. In 1988 the U.N. Special Rapporteur alleged that this provision, and the laws enacted pursuant to it, had a negative impact on religious freedom. In response to this allegation the Malaysian government defended the law to maintain social stability in a multireligious state that is nevertheless dominated by a particular religious tradition. See Stahnke, "Proselytism," 307. In Iran evangelical Christians must sign pledges that they will not evangelize Muslims or even allow them into their churches; see U.S. Department of State, *International Religious Freedom*, 6. In Afghanistan in 2001 the Taliban regime arrested eight people for attempting to convert Muslims to Christianity. They were tried for their crime and, while awaiting sentencing, were abandoned in the desert as a result of the presence of American troops. See Davis, "Evolution of Religious Freedom," 218.

5. Singapore banned certain types of religious speech in its Maintenance of Religious Harmony Act in 1990. This act was prompted by actions that the government perceived as threats to religious harmony, including "the mixing of religion and politics" and aggressive and "insensitive" proselytizing. The policies of India, Cambodia, Russia, and Greece are discussed later in this chapter.

6. Luis Bush, "Preface: Working Together Towards 2000," in *Countdown to AD 2000*, ed. Thomas Wang (Pasadena, CA: AD 2000 Movement, 1989), vii, quoted in Kim, *In Search of Identity*, 132.

7. Julia Neuberger writes, "What needs to be taken on board is whether those other religions have equality with one's own or not. If the answer is yes, then proselytizing ceases as of right. If the answer is no, then the limit of tolerance has been reached, and the truth of the matter is that the religion is not tolerant in its true sense ("Religious Toleration in the UK," 131). As Paul Griffiths writes: "Whereas the proselytizer wants to transform the alien into kin by making a proselyte out of him, the practitioner of tolerance wants to let him alone in his error" ("Proselytizing for Tolerance," 32).

8. Article 18 continues: "3. Freedom to manifest one's religion or beliefs may be subject only to such limitations as are prescribed by law and are necessary to protect public safety, order, health, or morals or the fundamental rights and freedoms of others."

9. Stahnke, "Proselytism," 284. Compare *Martin v. City of Struthers*, 319 U.S. 141 (1943), in which the U.S. Supreme Court invalidated a statute that made it unlawful for a person to summon the occupant of a residence to the door for the purpose of distributing a handbill, circular, or advertisement. The Court noted that the freedoms of speech and of the press "embraced the right to distribute literature, and necessarily protected the right to receive it." The Court found that the statute was a "naked restriction of the dissemination of ideas." The homeowner has recourse to the law of trespass that "leaves the decision as to whether distributers of literature may lawfully call at a home where it belongs— with the homeowner himself."

10. Stahnke, "Proselytism," 287–88. In the *Kokkinakis* case of 1993 the European Court examined the conviction of a Jehovah's Witness, Minos Kokkinakis, for a violation of a Greek law criminalizing proselytism. The Greek government argued to the European Court that prohibition was necessary "to protect a person's religious beliefs and dignity from attempts to influence them by immoral and deceitful means." The court ruled that the conviction of Mr. Kokkinakis was in pursuit of the legitimate aim of protecting the rights of others. Furthermore, the court went on to approve of the attempt in the Greek legislation to develop criteria that would separate what it termed "Christian witness" from "improper proselytism." Nonetheless, the court argued that there was no evidence that Mr. Kokkinakis had done anything improper; hence the court determined that his conviction was a violation of Article 9 of the European Convention.

11. Stahnke, "Proselytism," 338.

12. The Freedom of Religion Act is modeled on similar legislation in at least three other Indian states, some of which dates back to the 1960s. The amendment lumps together Hindus, Jains, and Buddhists so that movement between these groups will not be seen as entailing conversion and thus prompt investigation by the state. It is conversions of Hindus to Islam, and especially to Christianity, that has supporters of the law particularly worried. Critics point out that Muslims and Christians constitute such a small percentage of the population (0.5 percent) that worries of mass conversion are unfounded.

13. Critics held up Hinduism as exemplary of tolerance, given its diversity and the absence of conversion activity on the part of Hindus. This was one of the arguments of Mohandas Gandhi. Gandhi, however, echoed points from longstanding debates (from the first part of the nineteenth century between John Muir and Somanatha [among others]) on religious conversion in India. See Kim, *In Search of Identity*, 26.

14. Kim, *In Search of Identity*, 33. Gandhi's increasing rancor may have been attributable in part to his son Harilal's public conversion to Islam in May 1936. His position was also undermined by a paternalistic regard for those he called the Harijans. These were the Dalits, also called the Untouchables, who

were most often the subjects of missionary activity and the ones most frequently converted.

15. Kim argues that the major reason for the Hindu majority agreeing to Article 25 was communal violence, especially over the 1947 partition (*In Search of Identity*, 55). Article 25(1) of the 1949 Constitution of India reads: "Subject to public order, morality and health and to the other provisions of this Part, all persons are equally entitled to freedom of conscience and the right freely to profess, practice and *propagate* religion" (italics added).

16. In 1950 a law was passed whereby *only* Hindu individuals would be considered members of the scheduled castes and tribes and thus eligible for government aid; in the 1950s a series of Hindu personal laws were passed that included the loss of Hindu identity and inheritance and familial rights for Christian converts. In 1954 a critical investigation of a Christian missionary was launched by the Madhya Pradesh government; the findings were published in the Niyogi Report, named after the investigation's leader, retired chief justice Bhawani Shankar Niyogi. Although the investigation was thorough, it did not receive the cooperation of the Catholic Church. The report recommended stricter regulation of missionaries, arguing that this was the priority for Christians. It also argued that most conversions worked on some kind of material inducement and that Christians were motivated by the threat of communism. Their recommendations led to legislation, titled freedom of religion acts, in Orissa (1967) and Madya Pradesh (1968), both of which were upheld by the Indian Supreme Court in 1977.

17. See Kim, *In Search of Identity*, 166–67.

18. The pledge reads: "Brigham Young University, The Church of Jesus Christ of Latter-day Saints, and BYU's Jerusalem Center for Near Eastern Studies, have given assurances and made commitments to the State of Israel to the effect that no member of the Church, nor anyone affiliated with the University or participating in a University-sponsored program will engage in proselyting of any kind within Israel and Palestine (the West Bank and Gaza). It is very important that these assurances and commitments be honored and that those who travel to the Holy Land or have reason to correspond or work with individuals living there be informed of these assurances and commitments and agree to abide by them. Any activities that could be construed as aimed at including, encouraging or leading people in Israel to investigate any religion for possible conversion are strictly contrary to the desires of the government and people of Israel and to the commitments made by BYU, The Jerusalem Center, and The Church. By signing below, you agree to not distribute, either directly or by mail, any materials pertaining to the Church or its doctrines within Israel or Palestine. You will not discuss the Church or its doctrines or answer any questions regarding the Church or its doctrines with individuals who reside in the Holy Land or who may be visiting there. You will not invite guests who are not LDS to attend

Church services held in the Holy Land. You understand the assurances and commitment of the Church, University and the Jerusalem Center not to proselyte within Israel or Palestine and agree to abide by them." *Deseret News*, 12 January 2007, Deseretnews.com (accessed June 7, 2007).

19. Marshall Thompson, "LDS Leaders Find Acceptance in Israel," *Deseret News*, 31 March 2007, Deseretnews.com (accessed June 7, 2007).

20. For an analysis of liberalism's trivialization of seduction, see Talal Asad, "Free Speech, Blasphemy, and Secular Criticism," in Asad et al., *Is Critique Secular*, esp. 43.

21. Adriansén, "Tolerance and Religious Freedom," 782; italics added.

22. In a number of cases attempts to prohibit proselytization are part of a systematic attempt to maintain a dominant cultural and political identity (so that Muslims may proselytize in Muslim-dominated Malaysia but Christians are prohibited from doing so) or to rebuild and preserve a religion or culture in the aftermath of the slow destruction wrought by Christian colonialism and persecution or by communism. As an example of the latter case, in 1997 Russia passed a law restricting the proselytizing efforts of religious groups that could not claim fifteen years' tenure in Russia.

23. Stahnke, "Proselytism," 333.

24. Stahnke, "Proselytism," 318.

25. Laurie Goodstein, "Seeing Islam," *New York Times*, May 23, 2003.

26. Elshtain, "Proselytizing for Tolerance," 37.

27. Smolin, "Exporting the First Amendment?" 689.

28. *Lee v. Weisman*, 505 U.S. 577 (1992); see Smolin, "Exporting the First Amendment?" 696.

29. *Newdow v. U.S. Congress*, 292 F.3d (2002), at 601, quoted in Nahmod, "Pledge," 814; italics added. In 2004 the Supreme Court decided that Michael Newdow, as the noncustodial parent, did not have standing to bring the suit on his daughter's behalf; the Court did not address the constitutional issues of the case.

30. Macedo, *Diversity and Distrust*, 252; italics added.

31. Merriam-Webster, http://search.eb.com/dictionary (accessed September 4, 2006).

32. Macedo, *Diversity and Distrust*, 224, referring to Carter's *Culture of Disbelief*.

33. Macedo, *Diversity and Distrust*, 223.

34. Macedo, *Diversity and Distrust*, 2.

35. Macedo, *Diversity and Distrust*, 225–26; see also 202.

36. The case is analyzed by Stanley Fish in his "Vicki Frost Objects," in *The Trouble with Principle*. See Barry, *Culture and Equality*, ch. 6.

37. Freud, *Future of an Illusion*, 60.

38. Taylor, *Secular Age*, esp. 300–301. Taylor amplifies this point in his contribution to Calhoun et al., *Rethinking Secularism*, 39–42; the quotation is from this second source, 40–41.

39. Warner, *Publics and Counterpublics*, 160, 164.

40. The suggestion that secular selves are buffered selves and that religious selves are vulnerable or needy selves is reflected in the argument of Pippa Norris and Ronald Ingelhart in their book *Sacred and Secular: Religion and Politics Worldwide*. Norris and Ingelhart attribute the persistence of religion in much of the developing world and in the developed United States (and its decline in European states) to its remedying not simply material insecurity but "existential insecurity." What distinguishes the United States from Europe is that America lacks the robust and publicly provided social services and health care of Europe (at least at the time of writing!). This, they argue, instills Americans (and immigrants here and elsewhere) with significantly more anxiety; they turn to religious resources and communities to offset the risks of living and working without a safety net.

41. Fish, *Trouble with Principle*, 207, 250, 259.

42. Macedo, *Diversity and Distrust*, 228.

43. Witte, "Primer," 620–21; italics added.

44. For his part, Carl Schmitt might well remark that the inflated rhetoric of "holy war" evidences liberalism's allergy to politics and that the persistence of conflicts over religion merely confirms the inevitable return of the political. Schmitt would insist that, despite liberalism's attempt to "neutralize" the political by restaging it as intellectual debate and economic competition, the truly political task of distinguishing friend from enemy is indefatigable. Thus the much vaunted legislative enactments of religious toleration were, in Schmitt's estimation, merely "the prelude to another form of conflict" (Tracy B. Strong, foreword to Schmitt, *Concept of the Political*, xxix).

45. Locke, *Two Treatises*, II: 19 (321).

46. As one commentator writes, "Natural law [a reflection of divine law] may have faded from view as the source of people's rights, but the idea of rights, indeed their *enshrinement* as fundamental to civilized society, remains an important part of international political discourse" (Davis, "Evolution of Religious Freedom," 223; italics added). See also Freeman, "Problem of Secularism," esp. 389–90. Michael Perry insists that human rights are sacred; see his *Idea of Human Rights*, 11–41.

47. Italics added. Much of this language is reiterated in the 1966 document (ratified in 1976), titled International Covenant on Civil and Political Rights.

48. See T. Farr, *World of Faith*, 4; italics added.

49. See Kukathas, "Are There Any Cultural Rights?" The United States has signed but has still not ratified the International Covenant on Economic,

Social, and Cultural Rights, which was presented by the U.N. General Assembly in 1966 and went into effect in 1976.

50. See Ignatieff, *Human Rights*, 82–85.

51. Ignatieff, "Nationalism and Toleration," 102; see also 92.

52. Quoted by George Schwab in his introduction to his translation of Schmitt's *Political Theology*, xxiii.

53. Rawls, *Political Liberalism*, 154.

54. See Rawls, *Political Liberalism*, 161.

55. Rawls writes, "Here I shall suppose—perhaps too optimistically—that, except for certain kinds of fundamentalism, all the main historical religions . . . may be seen as reasonable comprehensive doctrines" (*Political Liberalism*, 170). Fundamentalists are clearly not within the domain of the civilized, reasonable, or tolerable. See also Macedo, *Diversity and Distrust*, 172, 219, 222, 225–26, 227. Those who believe that fairness (or relevance) requires that religious individuals not rely on religious reasons in public argumentation include Richard Rorty ("Religion as a Conversation-Stopper," 168–74), John Rawls (see, in particular, "The Idea of Public Reason Revisited"), Amy Gutmann and Dennis Thompson ("Moral Conflict and Political Consensus"; *Democracy and Disagreement*), and Stephen Macedo (*Diversity and Distrust*). The dissent to this is supplied in the following works: Carter, *Culture of Disbelief*; Gamwell, "Religion and Reason"; Greenawalt, *Private Consciences*; Levinson, "Religious Language" (reviewing Michael J. Perry's *Love and Power*); and Thiemann, *Religion in Public Life*. Nicholas Wolterstorff argues against restraints being placed on appeals to religious convictions; see his "Role of Religion." Christopher Eberle, *Religious Convictions*, offers a similar argument. Patrick Riordan, S.J., argues that Catholicism is compatible with John Rawls's theory of public reason despite Eberle's critique of Rawls; see Riordan, "Permission to Speak." Stanley Fish argues that liberals' attempts to restrain religious arguments are not neutral, are contradictory (first is the declaration of the impossibility of consensus on account of irreducible pluralism; second is the attempt to locate just such a principle on which a consensus could be built), and seek to preempt political contestation (for liberalism is fundamentally uncomfortable with conflict and force). See Fish, *Trouble with Principle*, chaps. 9–12. Jeffrey Stout offers a critique of Rawls's attempts to establish a common basis of argumentation for "reasonable persons" as a social contract that amounts to a "poor man's communitarianism. Contractarianism feels compelled to reify a sort of all-purpose, abstract fairness or respect for others because it cannot imagine ethical or political discourse *dialogically*" (Stout, *Democracy and Tradition*, 73–74).

56. See Rawls, *Political Liberalism*, esp. 212–54; 220.

57. Kent Greenawalt describes this duty of public reason as a self-imposed limit, or what he refers to as a principle of self-restraint. He refers to those who

do not abide by the self-restraint of public reason as "dissenters" (one might call them "heretics") who are not "playing by the 'loosely accepted' ground rules for modern political life." One wonders what Greenawalt has in mind with this reference to "loosely accepted." See Greenawalt, *Private Consciences*, 121. See also the lucid discussion by Holmes, "Gag Rules."

58. I am relying here on Jonathan Z. Smith's essay, "The Bare Facts of Ritual," 114.

59. Similarly, Habermas makes a call to allow religion into public debate but quickly reassures his readers that once policy moves from public debate to legislation, religious content will be thoroughly filtered out: "The institutional thresholds between the 'wild life' of the political public sphere and the formal proceedings within political bodies are also a filter [so] that from the Babel of voices in the informal flows of public communication . . . only secular contributions . . . pass through" ("Religion in the Public Sphere," 11). Here again, filtering out religious content requires the application of civic ritual: Habermas salutes parliamentary rules of order that permit the presiding officer to expunge from the record any religious comments.

60. Cardinal Henri de Lubac, *Corpus Mysticium*, 118.

Bibliography

Aarsleff, Hans. "The State of Nature and the Nature of Man in Locke." In *John Locke: Problems and Perspectives*, ed. John W. Yolton, 99–136. Cambridge: Cambridge University Press, 1969.

Adriansén, Carlos Valderrama. "Tolerance and Religious Freedom: The Struggle in Peru to Tolerate Multiple Cultures in Light of Principles of Religious Freedom." *Brigham Young University Law Review* 3 (2007): 775–790.

Agamben, Giorgio. *Profanations*. New York: Zone Books, 2007.

Althusser, Louis. *Lenin and Philosophy and Other Essays*, trans. Ben Brewster. New York: Monthly Review Press, 1971.

An-Na'im, Abdullahi Ahmed. "Human Rights in the Muslim World: Socio-Political Conditions and Scriptural Imperatives—A Preliminary Inquiry." *Harvard Human Rights Journal* 3 (1990): 13–52.

Arendt, Hanna. "What Is Authority?" In her *Between Past and Future: Eight Exercises in Political Thought*, 91–142. New York: Penguin, 1978.

Ariès, Philippe. *Centuries of Childhood: A Social History of Family Life*. New York: Vintage, 1965.

Armstrong, Nancy. *Desire and Domestic Fiction: A Political History of the Novel*. Oxford: Oxford University Press, 1987.

Asad, Talal, Wendy Brown, Judith Butler, and Saba Mahmood. *Is Critique Secular? Blasphemy, Injury, and Free Speech*. Berkeley, CA: Townsend Center for the Humanities, 2009.

Ashcraft, Richard. "Faith and Knowledge in Locke's Philosophy." In *John Locke: Problems and Perspectives*, ed. John W. Yolton, 194–225. Cambridge: Cambridge University Press, 1969.

———. "John Locke, Religious Dissent, and the Origins of Liberalism." In *Restoration, Ideology, and Revolution*, ed. Gordon J. Schochet, 149–68. Washington, DC: Folger Institute, 1990.

———. "Political Theory and Political Reform: John Locke's Essay on Virginia." *Western Political Quarterly* 22.4 (1969): 742–58.

———. "Religion and Lockean Natural Rights." In *Religious Diversity and*

Human Rights, ed. Irene Bloom and J. Paul Martin, 195–212. New York: Columbia University Press, 1996.
Augustine. *City of God*, trans. R. W. Dyson. Cambridge: Cambridge University Press, 1998.
———. *Confessions*, trans. R. S. Pine-Coffin. New York: Penguin, 1961.
———. *On Free Choice of the Will*, trans. Thomas Williams. Indianapolis, IN: Hackett, 1993.
Barry, Brian. *Culture and Equality: An Egalitarian Critique of Multiculturalism*. Cambridge, MA: Harvard University Press, 2001.
Behn, Ann [Aphra]. *The Rover; Or the Banish't Cavaliers*, 2nd ed. London: Richard Wellington, 1697.
Beitz, Charles R. "Tacit Consent and Property Rights." *Political Theory* 8.4 (1980): 487–502.
Block, James E. *Nation of Agents: The American Path to a Modern Self and Society*. Cambridge, MA: Harvard University Press, 2002.
Bluhm, William T., Neil Wintfield, and Stuart H. Teger. "Locke's Idea of God: Rational Truth or Rational Myth?" *Journal of Politics* 42 (May 1980): 414–38.
Botwinick, Aryeh. *Skepticism, Belief, and the Modern*. Ithaca, NY: Cornell University Press, 1997.
Bourne, H. R. Fox. *Life of John Locke*, pt. 1. New York: Harper & Brothers, 1876; reprint, Whitefish, MT: Kessinger, 2003.
Bowen, John R. *Why the French Don't Like Headscarves: Islam, the State, and Public Space*. Princeton, NJ: Princeton University Press, 2007.
Brettschneider, Corey. *When the State Speaks, What Should It Say? How Democracies Can Protect Expression and Promote Equality*. Princeton, NJ: Princeton University Press, 2012.
Brewer, Holly. *By Birth or Consent: Children, Law, and the Anglo-American Revolution in Authority*. Chapel Hill: University of North Carolina Press, 2005.
Brown, Vivienne. "The 'Figure' of God and Limits to Liberalism: A Rereading of Locke's *Essay* and *Two Treatises*." *Journal of the History of Ideas* 60.1 (1999): 83–100.
Brown, Wendy. *Regulating Aversion: Tolerance in the Age of Identity and Empire*. Princeton, NJ: Princeton University Press, 2008.
———. "Subjects of Tolerance: Why We Are Civilized and They Are the Barbarians." In *Political Theologies: Public Religions in a Post-Secular World*, ed. Hent de Vries and Lawrence E. Sullivan, 298–317. New York: Fordham University Press, 2006.
Browning, Andrew, ed. *English Historical Documents*, 8 vols. London: Routledge, 1953.
Bruce, Steve. *Choice and Religion*. Oxford: Oxford University Press, 1999.

Burnet, Thomas. *Remarks upon An Essay Concerning Humane Understanding.* London: M. Wotton, 1697.
Butler, Melissa. "Early Liberal Roots of Feminism: John Locke and the Attack on Patriarchy." *American Political Science Review* 72 (1978): 135–50.
Calhoun, Craig, Mark Juergensmeyer, and Jonathan VanAntwerpen, eds. *Rethinking Secularism.* Oxford: Oxford University Press, 2011.
Calvin, John. *Concerning the Eternal Predestination of God*, trans. J. K. S. Reid. London: James Clarke, 1961.
Canfield, J. Douglas. *Word as Bond in English Literature from the Middle Ages to the Restoration.* Philadelphia: University of Pennsylvania Press, 1989.
Caputo, John D. *The Prayers and Tears of Jacques Derrida: Religion Without Religion.* Bloomington: Indiana University Press, 1997.
Carter, Stephen L. *The Culture of Disbelief.* New York: Random House, 1994.
———. "Evolutionism, Creationism, and Treating Religion as a Hobby." *Duke Law Journal* 36 (December 1987): 977–96.
Casanova, José. *Public Religions in the Modern World.* Chicago: University of Chicago Press, 1994.
Casaubon, Méric. *To J. S. (The Author of Sure-Footing) His Letter: Lately Published the Answer of Meric Casaubon.* London: Timothy Garthwait, 1665.
Case-Winters, Anna. *God's Power.* Louisville: Westminster/John Knox Press, 1990.
Cassinelli, C. W. "The Consent of the Governed." *Western Political Quarterly* 12.2 (1959): 391–409.
Cavendish, Margaret. *The Description of a New World, Called the Blazing-World.* London: A. Maxwell, 1668.
Chen, Selina. "Locke's Political Arguments for Toleration." *History of Political Thought* 19.2 (1998): 167–85.
Clark, J. C. D. "Secularization and Modernization: The Failure of a 'Grand Narrative.'" *Historical Journal* 55.1 (2012): 161–94.
Coke, Roger. *Justice Vindicated from the False Focus Put Upon It, by Thomas White Gent, Mr. Thomas Hobbs and Hugo Grotius.* London: Bedell and Collins, 1660.
Colman, John. *John Locke's Moral Philosophy.* Edinburgh: Edinburgh University Press, 1983.
Congreve, William. *The Way of the World.* London: Jacob Tonson, 1700.
Coole, Diana. *Negativity and Politics.* New York: Routledge, 2000.
Coon, Deborah. "'One Moment in the World's Salvation': Anarchism and the Radicalization of William James." *Journal of American History* 83 (June 1996): 70–99.
Cragg, G. R. *From Puritanism to the Age of Reason.* Cambridge: Cambridge University Press, 1966.
Crockett, Clayton, and Creston Davis. Introduction to "The Political and the

Infinite: Theology and Radical Politics." *Angelaki: Journal of the Theoretical Humanities* 12.1 (2007): 1–10.

Cunningham, Hugh. *Children and Childhood in Western Society Since 1500*, 2nd ed. New York: Pearson Longman, 2005.

Danchin, Peter G. "Of Prophets and Proselytes: Freedom of Religion and the Conflict of Rights in International Law." *Harvard International Law Journal* 49 (summer 2008): 249–321.

Davis, Derek H. "The Evolution of Religious Freedom as a Universal Human Right: Examining the Role of the 1981 United Nations Declaration on the Elimination of All Forms of Intolerance and of Discrimination Based on Religion or Belief." *Brigham Young University Law Review* 217 (2002): 217–36.

Dawson, Hannah. *Locke, Language, and Early Modern Philosophy*. Cambridge: Cambridge University Press, 2007.

Dekker, Thomas. *The Honest Whore*. London: Valentine Simmes for John Hodgets, 1604.

———. *The Second Part of the Honest Whore*. London: Nathaniel Butter, 1630.

de Lubac, Henri, Cardinal. *Corpus Mysticium*, trans. Gemma Simmonds with Richard Price and Christopher Stephens. Notre Dame, IN: University of Notre Dame, 2006.

Den Hartogh, Govert. "Express Consent and Full Membership in Locke." *Political Studies* 38.1 (1990): 105–15.

———. "Made by Contrivance and the Consent of Men: Abstract Principle and Historical Fact in Locke's Political Philosophy." *Interpretation* 17.2 (1989–1990): 193–221.

A Dialogue Between Monmouth-shire and York-shire About Cutting Religion According to Fashion. London: W. R., 1681.

Dunn, John. "The Claim to Freedom of Conscience: Freedom of Speech, Freedom of Thought, Freedom of Worship?" In *From Persecution to Toleration: The Glorious Revolution and Religion in England*, ed. Ole Peter Grell, Jonathan I. Israel, and Nicholas Tyacke, 171–98. Oxford: Clarendon Press, 1991.

———. "Consent in the Political Theory of John Locke." *Historical Journal* 10.2 (1967): 153–82.

———. *The Political Thought of John Locke: An Historical Account of the Argument of the "Two Treatises of Government."* Cambridge: Cambridge University Press, 1969.

———. "What Is Living and What Is Dead in the Political Theory of John Locke." In *Interpreting Political Responsibility: Essays, 1981–1989*, ed. John Dunn, 9–25. Oxford: Polity Press, 1990.

Durst, David C. "The Limits of Toleration in John Locke's Liberal Thought." *Res Publica* 7 (2001): 39–55.

Eberle, Christopher. *Religious Convictions in Liberal Politics.* Cambridge: Cambridge University Press, 2002.
Edwards, Jonathan. *Sinners in the Hands of an Angry God: A Sermon Preached at Enfield, July 8, 1741.* Boston: S. Kneeland & T. Green, 1741.
Eisenach, Eldon J. *Narrative Power and Liberal Truth.* Lanham, MD: Rowman & Littlefield, 2002.
———. *Two Worlds of Liberalism: Religion and Politics in Hobbes, Locke, and Mill.* Chicago: Chicago University Press, 1981.
Ellis, Stephen, and Gerrie ter Haar. *Worlds of Power.* Oxford: Oxford University Press, 2004.
Elshtain, Jean Bethke. "Proselytizing for Tolerance," pt. 2. *First Things* 127 (November 2002): 34–36.
Euben, Roxanne. *Enemy in the Mirror: Islamic Fundamentalism and the Limits of Modern Rationalism.* Princeton, NJ: Princeton University Press, 1999.
Falkner, William. *An Answer to Mr. Sergeant's Discourse Intitled Sure-Footing in Christianity.* London: R. Chiswell, 1684.
The Farce of Sodom, or the Quintessence of Debauchery. 1684.
Farr, James. "Locke, Natural Law, and New World Slavery." *Political Theory* 36.4 (2008): 495–522.
Farr, James, and Clayton Roberts. "John Locke on the Glorious Revolution: A Rediscovered Document." *Historical Journal* 28.2 (1985): 385–98.
Farr, Thomas. *World of Faith and Freedom: Why International Religious Liberty Is Vital to American National Security.* New York: Oxford University Press, 2008.
Filmer, Robert. *Patriarcha and Other Political Works*, ed. Peter Laslett. Oxford: Basil Blackwell, 1949.
Fish, Stanley. *Doing What Comes Naturally.* Durham, NC: Duke University Press, 1989.
———. *The Trouble with Principle.* Cambridge, MA: Harvard University Press, 1999.
Fitzgerald, Timothy. *Discourses on Civility and Barbarity.* Oxford: Oxford University Press, 2007.
Forde, Steven. "John Locke's Natural Religion." Paper presented at the 100th annual meeting of the American Political Science Association, Chicago, 2004. http://citation.allacademic.com/meta/p61841_index.html.
———. "Natural Law, Theology, and Morality in Locke." *American Journal of Political Science* 45.2 (2001): 396–409.
Fore, Matthew L. "Shall Weigh Your God and You: Assessing the Imperialistic Implications of the International Religious Freedom Act in Muslim Countries." *Duke Law Journal* 52 (November 2002): 423–53.
Forster, Greg. *John Locke's Politics of Moral Consensus.* Cambridge: Cambridge University Press, 2005.

Foster, David. "Taming the Father: John Locke's Critique of Patriarchal Fatherhood." *Review of Politics* 56.4 (1994): 641–70.
Foucault, Michel. *Discipline and Punish: The Birth of the Prison*, trans. Alan Sheridan. New York: Pantheon, 1977.
Fox, George. *The Priests Fruits Made Manifest and the Vanity of the World Discovered. Who are Given up to Their Hearts Lust, to Run Out of One Fashion into Another*. London: Thomas Simmons, 1657.
Franklin, Julian. "Allegiance and Jurisdiction in Locke's Doctrine of Tacit Consent." *Political Theory* 24.3 (1996): 407–22.
Freeman, Michael. "The Problem of Secularism in Human Rights Theory." *Human Rights Quarterly* 26 (2004): 375–400.
Freud, Sigmund. *The Future of an Illusion*, trans. and ed. James Strachey. New York: Norton, 1961.
Gamwell, Franklin. "Religion and Reason in American Politics." *Journal of Law and Religion* 2.2 (1984): 325–42.
Gauthier, David. "Why Ought One Obey God? Reflections on Hobbes and Locke." *Canadian Journal of Philosophy* 7.3 (1977): 425–46.
Goldie, Mark. "The Civil Religion of James Harrington." In *The Languages of Political Theory in Early Modern Europe*, ed. Anthony Pagden, 197–224. Cambridge: Cambridge University Press, 1987.
———. "John Locke and Royal Anglicanism." *Political Studies* 31 (1983): 61–85.
———. "John Locke, Jonas Proast, and Religious Toleration, 1688–1692." In *The Church of England, c. 1689–c. 1833: From Toleration to Tractarianism*, ed. John Walsh, Colin Haydon, and Stephen Taylor, 143–71. Cambridge: Cambridge University Press, 1993.
———. "The Theory of Religious Intolerance in Restoration England." In *From Persecution to Toleration: The Glorious Revolution and Religion in England*, ed. Ole Peter Grell, Jonathan I. Israel, and Nicholas Tyacke, 331–68. Oxford: Clarendon Press, 1991.
Gottlieb, Micah. "Mendelssohn's Metaphysical Defense of Religious Pluralism." *Journal of Religion* 86.2 (2006): 205–25.
Gough, J. W. *Locke's Political Philosophy*. Oxford: Oxford University Press, 1956.
Greenawalt, Kent. *Private Consciences and Public Reasons*. New York: Oxford University Press, 1995.
Greenblatt, Stephen. *The Norton Anthology of English Literature*, 8th ed. New York: Norton, 2006.
Griffiths, Paul J. "Proselytizing for Tolerance," pt. 1. *First Things* 127 (November 2002): 30–34.

Gutmann, Amy, and Dennis Thompson. *Democracy and Disagreement.* Cambridge, MA: Harvard University Press, 1996.
———. "Moral Conflict and Political Consensus." *Ethics* 101.1 (1990): 64–88.
Guyatt, Nicholas. *Providence and the Invention of the United States, 1607–1876.* Cambridge: Cambridge University Press, 2007.
Habermas, Jürgen. *Justification and Application,* trans. C. P. Cronin. Cambridge, MA: MIT Press, 1993.
———. "Religion in the Public Sphere." *Journal of European Philosophy* 14.1 (2006): 2–25.
Hall, Bishop Joseph. *The Works of Bishop Joseph Hall,* ed. Josiah Pratt, 10 vols. London: Whittingham, 1808.
Hamm, Berndt. *Promissio, Pactum, Ordinatio: Freiheit und Selbstbindung Gottes in der scholastischen Gnadenlehre.* Tübingen, Germany: J. C. B. Mohr, 1977.
Hampsher-Monk, Iain. "Tacit Concept of Consent in Locke's *Two Treatises of Government*: A Note on Citizens, Travellers, and Patriarchalism." *Journal of the History of Ideas* 40.1 (1979): 135–39.
Harris, Ian. *The Mind of John Locke.* Cambridge: Cambridge University Press, 1994.
Harrison, John, and Peter Laslett. *The Library of John Locke,* 2nd ed. Oxford: Clarendon Press, 1971.
Hegel, Georg Wilhelm Friedrich. *Lectures on the Philosophy of Religion,* ed. Peter Hodgson. Berkeley: University of California Press, 1988.
Herzog, Don. *Happy Slaves: A Critique of Consent Theory.* Chicago: University of Chicago Press, 1989.
Heywood, Thomas. *A Woman Kilde with Kindnesse.* London: William Iaggard, 1607.
Hickes, George. "The Case of Infant Baptism." In *A Collection of Cases and Other Discourses Lately Written to Recover Dissenters to the Communion of the Church of England,* 2nd ed. London: T. Basset et al., 1694.
Hickman, Jared. "Globalization and the Gods, or the Political Theology of 'Race.'" *Early American Literature* 45:1 (2010): 145–82.
Hill, Christopher. "Covenant Theology and the Concept of 'A Public Person.'" In *Powers, Possessions, and Freedom: Essays in Honour of C. W. Macpherson,* ed. Alkis Kontos, 3–22. Toronto: University of Toronto Press, 1979.
Hobbes, Thomas. *Leviathan,* ed. Michael Oakeshott. New York: Macmillan, Collier Books, 1969.
Holmes, Stephen. "Gag Rules or the Politics of Omission." In *Constitutionalism and Democracy,* ed. Jon Elster and Rune Slagstad, 19–58. Cambridge: Cambridge University Press, 1993.
Höpfl, Harro, ed. and trans. *Luther and Calvin on Secular Authority.* Cambridge: Cambridge University Press, 1991.

Horton, John. "The *Satanic Verses* Controversy: A Brief Introduction." In *Liberalism, Multiculturalism, and Toleration*, ed. John Horton, 104–13. New York: St. Martin's Press, 1993.

Horwitz, Robert. Introduction to *John Locke: Questions Concerning the Law of Nature*, ed. Diskin Clay; trans. Robert Horwitz and Jenny Strauss Clay, 1–62. Ithaca, NY: Cornell University Press, 1990.

Houston, Alan, and Steve Pincus, eds. *A Nation Transformed: England After the Restoration*. Cambridge: Cambridge University Press, 2001.

Hsueh, Vicki. *Hybrid Constitutions: Challenging Legacies of Law, Privilege, and Culture in Colonial America*. Durham, NC: Duke University Press, 2010.

Hughes, George. *Sure-Footing in Christianity Examined*. London: Abisha Brocas, 1668.

Hume, David. *The Natural History of Religion* in *Writings on Religion*, ed. Anthony Flew. La Salle, IL: Open Court, 1992.

Hundert, E. J. "The Making of *Homo Faber*: John Locke Between Ideology and History." *Journal of the History of Ideas* 33.1 (1972): 3–22.

———. "The Thread of Language and the Web of Dominion: Mandeville to Rousseau and Back." *Eighteenth Century Studies* 21.2 (1987–1988): 3–22.

Ignatieff, Michael. *Human Rights as Politics and Idolatry*. Princeton, NJ: Princeton University Press, 2001.

———. "Nationalism and Toleration." In *The Politics of Toleration in Modern Life*, ed. Susan Mendus, 77–105. Edinburgh: Edinburgh University Press, 1999.

Jakobsen, Janet, and Ann Pellegrini. "World Secularisms at the Millennium: Introduction." *Social Text* 18.3 (2000): 1–27.

James I. "The Trew Law of Free Monarchies: or the Reciprock and Mutuall Duetie Betwixt a Free King and His Naturall Subjects." In *Early Modern Europe: Crisis of Authority*, ed. Eric Cochrane, Charles M. Gray, and Mark A. Kishlansky, 201–221. Chicago: University of Chicago Press, 1987.

James, William. *Principles of Psychology*. Cambridge, MA: Harvard University Press, 1981.

———. *Varieties of Religious Experience*. New York: Macmillan, 1961.

———. "The Will to Believe." In *The Will to Believe and Other Essays in Popular Philosophy*, 1–31. New York: Longmans Green, 1896.

The Jerusalem Bible. Garden City, NY: Doubleday, 1966.

Johnson, Greg. "Apache Revelation: Making Indigenous Religion in the Legal Sphere." In *Secularism* and *Religion-Making*, ed. Markus Dressler and Arvind-Pal S. Mandair, 170–86. New York: Oxford University Press, 2011.

Josephson, Peter. *The Great Art of Government: Locke's Use of Consent*. Lawrence: University of Kansas Press, 2002.

Juergensmeyer, Mark. *Religious Nationalism Confronts the Secular State.* Oxford: Oxford University Press, 1994.
———. *Terror in the Mind of God: The Global Rise of Religious Violence*, 3rd ed. Berkeley: University of California Press, 2003.
Kahn, Paul. *Political Theology: Four New Chapters on the Concept of Sovereignty.* New York: Columbia University Press, 2011.
———. *Putting Liberalism in Its Place.* Princeton, NJ: Princeton University Press, 2005.
Kahn, Victoria. *Wayward Contracts: The Crisis of Political Obligation in England, 1640–1674.* Princeton, NJ: Princeton University Press, 2004.
Kallen, Horace. *Culture and Democracy in the United States: Studies in the Group Psychology of the American People.* New York: Boni & Liveright, 1924.
Kammen, Michael G. "Virginia at the Close of the Seventeenth Century: An Appraisal by James Blair and John Locke." *Virginia Magazine* 74 (April 1966): 141–69.
Kant, Immanuel. "An Answer to the Question: 'What Is Enlightenment?'" In *Kant's Political Writings*, trans. H. B. Nisbet; ed. Hans Reiss, 54–60. Cambridge: Cambridge University Press, 1970.
———. *Religion Within the Limits of Reason Alone*, trans. Theodore M. Greene and Hoyt H. Hudson. New York: Harper & Row, 1960.
Kaplan, Benjamin J. *Divided by Faith: Religious Conflict and the Practice of Toleration in Early Modern Europe.* Cambridge, MA: Harvard University Press, 2007.
Kaufman, Gordon. *In Face of Mystery.* Cambridge, MA: Harvard University Press, 1993.
Kelsay, John. "Saudi Arabia, Pakistan, and the Universal Declaration of Human Rights." In *Human Rights and the Conflict of Cultures: Western and Islamic Perspectives on Religious Liberty*, ed. David Little, John Kelsay, and Abdulaziz A. Sachedina, 33–52. Columbia: University of South Carolina Press, 1988.
Kerrigan, William. *Shakespeare's Promises.* Baltimore: Johns Hopkins University Press, 1999.
Kim, Sebastian C. H. *In Search of Identity: Debates on Religious Conversion in India.* New York: Oxford University Press, 2003.
King, Peter. *The Life of John Locke*, 2 vols. London: Henry Colburn & Richard Bentley, 1830.
Knights, Mark. "London's Monster Petition of 1680." *Historical Journal* 36.1 (1993): 39–67.
———. "'Meer Religion' and 'Church-State' of Restoration England: The Impact and Ideology of James II's Declarations of Indulgence." In *A Nation Transformed*, ed. Alan Houston and Steve Pincus, 41–70. Cambridge: Cambridge University Press, 2001.

Kramnick, Isaac, and R. Laurence Moore. *The Godless Constitution: A Moral Defense of the Secular State*. New York: Norton, 2005.
Kramnick, Jonathan Brody. "Locke, Haywood, and Consent." *ELH: English Literary History* 72 (2005): 453–70.
Kraynak, Robert P. "John Locke: From Absolutism to Toleration." *American Political Science Review* 74.1 (1980): 53–69.
Kukathas, Chandran. "Are There Any Cultural Rights?" *Political Theory* 20.1 (1992): 105–39.
———. "Exit, Freedom, and Gender." In *On Exit*, ed. Dagmar Borchers and Annamari Vitikainen, 34–56. Berlin: de Gruyter, 2012.
Kymlicka, Will. *Liberalism, Community, and Culture*. Oxford: Clarendon Press, 1989.
Lander, Jesse. *Inventing Polemic*. Cambridge: Cambridge University Press, 2006.
Laslett, Peter. Introduction to Locke's *Two Treatises of Government*, 3–152. Cambridge: Cambridge University Press, 1960.
Levinson, Sanford. "Constituting Communities Through Words That Bind: Reflections on Loyalty Oaths." *Michigan Law Review* 84.7 (1986): 1440–70.
———. "Religious Language in the Public Square." *Harvard Law Review* 105.8 (1992): 2061–79.
Levy, Leonard W. *Blasphemy*. New York: Knopf, 1993.
Lilla, Mark. *The Stillborn God: Religion, Politics, and the Modern West*. New York: Knopf, 2007.
Lincoln, Bruce. *Authority: Construction and Corrosion*. Chicago: University of Chicago Press, 1994.
Little, David. "A Double-Edged Dilemma." *Harvard Divinity Bulletin* 35.4 (2007): 87–95.
Locke, John. *The Correspondence of John Locke*, ed. E. S. DeBeer, 8 vols. Oxford: Clarendon, 1976.
———. *A Discourse of Miracles*. In *The Reasonableness of Christianity with A Discourse of Miracles*, ed. I. T. Ramsey. Stanford, CA: Stanford University Press, 1958.
———. *An Essay Concerning Human Understanding*. Oxford: Oxford University Press, 1975.
———. *Essays on the Law of Nature*, ed. W. von Leyden. Oxford: Clarendon Press, 1958.
———. *A Fourth Letter for Toleration*. In *The Works of John Locke*, 6: 547–74. London: Thomas Tegg, et al., 1823.
———. *A Letter Concerning Toleration*. Indianapolis, IN: Hackett, 1983.
———. *A Paraphrase and Notes on the Epistles of Saint Paul*. In *The Works of John Locke*, v. 8. London: Thomas Tegg et al., 1823.

---. *Political Essays*, ed. Mark Goldie. Cambridge: Cambridge University Press, 1997.
---. *The Reasonableness of Christianity*, ed. John C. Higgins-Biddle. Oxford: Clarendon Press, 1999.
---. *A Second Letter for Toleration*. In *The Works of John Locke*, 6: 59–137. London: Thomas Tegg et al., 1823.
---. *Some Thoughts Concerning Education* and *Of the Conduct of the Understanding*. ed. Ruth Grant and Nathan Tarcov. Indianapolis, IN: Hackett, 1996.
---. *A Third Letter for Toleration*. In *The Works of John Locke*, 6: 139–546. London: Thomas Tegg et al., 1823.
---. *Two Treatises of Government*. Cambridge: Cambridge University Press, 1960.
---. *A Vindication of the Reasonableness of Christianity*. London: Awnsham & Churchil, 1695.
---. *Works*, 18 vols. Oxford: Clarendon Press, 1976–2012.
Lofton, Kathryn. *Oprah: The Gospel of an Icon*. Berkeley: University of California Press, 2011.
Luther, Martin. *On the Bondage of the Will*. In *Luther and Erasmus: Free Will and Salvation*, ed. E. Gordon Rupp and Philip S. Watson, 101–334. Philadelphia: Westminster Press, 1969.
Macedo, Stephen. *Diversity and Distrust: Civic Education in a Multicultural Democracy*. Cambridge, MA: Harvard University Press, 2000.
Macpherson, Crawford Brough. *The Political Theory of Possessive Individualism: Hobbes to Locke*. Oxford: Clarendon Press, 1962.
Mahmood, Saba. "Secularism, Hermeneutics, and Empire: The Politics of Islamic Reformation." *Public Culture* 18.2 (2006): 323–47.
Marsden, George. *The Soul of the American University*. New York: Oxford University Press, 1994.
Marshall, John. *John Locke: Resistance, Religion, and Responsibility*. Cambridge: Cambridge University Press, 1994.
---. "John Locke's Religious, Educational, and Moral Thought." *Historical Journal* 33.4 (1990): 993–1001.
---. *John Locke, Toleration, and Early Enlightenment Culture*. Cambridge: Cambridge University Press, 2006.
Marvin, Carolyn, and David W. Ingle. *Blood Sacrifice and the Nation: Totem Rituals and the American Flag*. Cambridge: Cambridge University Press, 1999.
McCabe, David. "John Locke and the Argument Against Strict Separation." *Review of Politics* 59.2 (1997): 233–58.
McClure, Kirstie M. "Difference, Diversity, and the Limits of Toleration." *Political Theory* 18.3 (1990): 361–91.

———. *Judging Rights: Lockean Politics and the Limits of Consent.* Ithaca, NY: Cornell University Press, 1996.

McConnell, Michael. "Religious Souls and the Body Politic." *Public Interest* 155 (spring 2004): 126–42.

McCulloch, Samuel Clyde. "James Blair's Plan of 1699 to Reform the Clergy of Virginia." *William and Mary Quarterly,* 4.1 (1947): 70–86.

Mehta, Uday Singh. *The Anxiety of Freedom: Imagination and Individuality in Locke's Political Thought.* Ithaca, NY: Cornell University Press, 1992.

———. *Liberalism and Empire.* Chicago: University of Chicago Press, 1999.

Mendelssohn, Moses. *Jerusalem: Or on Religious Power and Judaism,* trans. Allan Arkush. Hanover, NH: University Press of New England, 1983.

Messenger, Philip, and Thomas Dekker. *The Virgin Martyr.* London: Thomas Jones, 1631.

Michael, Mark A. "Locke, Religious Toleration, and the Limits of Social Contract Theory." *History of Philosophy Quarterly* 20.1 (2003): 21–40.

———. "Locke's *Second Treatise* and the Literature of Colonization." *Interpretation* 25.3 (1998): 407–27.

Mill, John Stuart. *On Liberty.* Indianapolis, IN: Hackett, 1978.

Miller, Perry. *The New England Mind: The Seventeenth Century.* Cambridge, MA: Harvard University Press, 1954.

Milton, John. *The Doctrine and Discipline of Divorce.* In *Complete Prose Works of John Milton,* ed. Don M. Wolfe, 2: 220–356. New Haven, CT: Yale University Press, 1959.

———. *John Milton: Complete Poems and Major Prose,* ed. Merritt Y. Hughes. Indianapolis, IN: Odyssey, 1957.

Mitchell, Joshua. "John Locke and the Theological Foundation of Liberal Toleration: A Christian Dialectic of History." *Review of Politics* 52.1 (1990): 64–83.

———. *Not by Reason Alone: Religion, History, and Identity in Early Modern Thought.* Chicago: University of Chicago Press, 1993.

Molnár, Attila K. "The Construction of the Notion of Religion in Early Modern Europe." *Method and Theory in the Study of Religion* 14 (2002): 47–60.

Montaigne, Michele de. *Essays,* trans. Michael Screech. London: Penguin, 1993.

Morris, Paul. "Judaism and Pluralism: The Price of 'Religious Freedom.'" In *Religious Pluralism and Unbelief,* ed. Ian Hamnett, 179–201. London: Routledge, 1990.

Müller, F. Max. *Lectures on the Science of Religion.* New York: Scribner, Armstrong, 1874.

Murphy, Andrew R. *Conscience and Community: Revisiting Toleration and Religious Dissent in Early Modern England and America.* University Park, PA: Penn State University Press, 2001.

Nahmod, Sheldon N. "The Pledge as Sacred Political Ritual." *William and Mary Bill of Rights Journal* 13 (February 2005): 797–819.

Neuberger, Julia. "Religious Toleration in the UK." In *Politics of Toleration in Modern Life*, ed. Susan Mendus, 119–32. Edinburgh: Edinburgh University Press, 1999.
Norris, Pippa, and Ronald Ingelhart. *Sacred and Secular: Religion and Politics Worldwide*. Cambridge: Cambridge University Press, 2004.
Oakley, Francis. "Locke, Natural Law, and God—Again." *History of Political Thought* 18.4 (1997): 624–51.
Okin, Susan Moller. "'Mistresses of Their Own Destiny': Group Rights, Gender, and Realistic Rights of Exit." *Ethics* 112.2 (2002): 205–30.
Olivecrona, Karl. "Locke's Theory of Appropriation." *Philosophical Quarterly* 24.96 (1974): 220–34.
Pangle, Thomas. *The Spirit of Modern Republicanism: The Moral Vision of the American Founders and the Philosophy of Locke*. Chicago: University of Chicago Press, 1988.
Parry, Geraint. "Individuality, Politics, and the Critique of Paternalism in John Locke." *Political Studies* 12.2 (1964): 163–77.
Passmore, J. A. "Locke and the Ethics of Belief." *Proceedings of the British Academy* 64 (1979): 185–208.
Pateman, Carol. *The Problem of Political Obligation*. New York: Wiley, 1979.
———. *The Sexual Contract*. Stanford, CA: Stanford University Press, 1988.
Pearson, Samuel C. "The Religion of John Locke and the Character of His Thought." *Journal of Religion* 58 (July 1978): 244–62.
Perry, John. *The Pretense of Loyalty: Locke, Liberal Theory, and American Political Theology*. Oxford: Oxford University Press, 2011.
Perry, Michael J. *The Idea of Human Rights*. Oxford: Oxford University Press, 1998.
———. *Love and Power: The Role of Religion and Morality in American Politics*. New York: Oxford University Press, 1991.
Pietz, William. "The Problem of the Fetish." Pt. 1, *RES: Anthropology and Aesthetics* 9 (1985): 5–17; pt. 2, *RES: Anthropology and Aesthetics* 13 (1987): 23–45; pt. 3, *RES: Anthropology and Aesthetics* 16 (1988): 105–23.
Pinchbeck, Ivy, and Margaret Hewitt. *Children in English Society*, 2 vols. London: Routledge & Kegan Paul, 1969.
Polin, Raymond. *La Politique Morale de John Locke*. New York: Garland, 1984.
Polinska, Wioleta. "Faith and Reason in John Locke." *Philosophy and Theology* 11.2 (1999), 287–309.
Proast, Jonas. *The Argument of the Letter Concerning Toleration, Briefly Consider'd and Answer'd*. Oxford: George West & Henry Clements, 1690.
———. *A Second Letter to the Author of the Three Letters for Toleration from the Author of the Argument of the Letter Concerning Toleration, Briefly Consider'd and Answer'd and of the Defense of It*. Oxford: L. Lichfield, 1704.

———. *A Third Letter Concerning Toleration: In Defense of The Argument of the Letter Concerning Toleration, Briefly Consider'd and Answer'd*. Oxford: L. Lichfield, 1691.

Queries: Or a Dish of Pickled-Herring Shread, Cut and Prepared According to the Dutch Fashion. For the Squeamish Consciences of English Phanaticks, Who Pray for the New-Building of Their Old Babell. London, 1665.

Rabieh, Michael S. "The Reasonableness of Locke or the Questionableness of Christianity." *Journal of Politics* 53.4 (1991): 933–57.

Rawls, John. "The Idea of Public Reason Revisited." *University of Chicago Law Review* 64.3 (1997): 765–807.

———. *Political Liberalism*. New York: Columbia University Press, 1993.

Raz, Joseph. "Authority and Consent." *Virginia Law Review* 67 (1981): 103–31.

Riley, Patrick. "On Finding an Equilibrium Between Consent and Natural Law in Locke's Political Philosophy." *Political Studies* 22.4 (1974): 432–52.

———. *Will and Political Legitimacy: A Critical Exposition of Social Contract Theory in Hobbes, Locke, Rousseau, Kant, and Hegel*. Cambridge, MA: Harvard University Press, 1982.

Riordan, Patrick, S.J. "Permission to Speak: Religious Arguments in Public Reason." *Heythrop Journal* 45 (2004): 178–96.

Rivers, Isabel. *Reason, Grace, and Sentiment: A Study of the Language of Religion and Ethics in England, 1660–1780*, v. 1, *Whichcote to Wesley*. Cambridge: Cambridge University Press, 1991.

Rorty, Richard. "Religion as a Conversation-Stopper." In his *Philosophy and Social Hope*, 168–74. London: Penguin, 1999.

Rowley, William. *All's Lost by Lust*. London: Thomas Harper, 1633.

Roy, Olivier. *Holy Ignorance: When Religion and Culture Part Ways*. New York: Columbia University Press, 2010.

Russell, Paul. "Locke on Express and Tacit Consent: Misinterpretations and Inconsistencies." *Political Theory* 14.2 (1986): 291–306.

Sample, Ruth. "Locke on Political Authority and Conjugal Authority." *Locke Newsletter* 31 (2000): 115–46.

Sandoz, Ellis. "The Civil Theology of Liberal Democracy: Locke and His Predecessors." *Journal of Politics* 34 (1972): 2–36.

Sands, Kathleen. "A Property of Peculiar Value: Land, Religion and the Constitution." *Culture and Religion* 6.1 (2005): 161–80.

Scarry, Elaine. *The Body in Pain*. New York: Oxford University Press, 1987.

———. "Consent and the Body: Injury, Departure, and Desire." *New Literary History* 21 (autumn 1990): 867–96.

Schmitt, Carl. *The Concept of the Political*, trans. George Schwab. Chicago: University of Chicago Press, 2007.

———. *Political Theology: Four Chapters on the Concept of Sovereignty*, trans. George Schwab. Chicago: University of Chicago Press, 2006.
Schneewind, J. B. "Locke's Moral Philosophy." In *The Cambridge Companion to Locke*, ed. Vere Chappell, 199–225. Cambridge: Cambridge University Press, 1994.
Schochet, Gordon. *Patriarchalism in Political Thought*. New York: Basic Books, 1975.
———. "Toleration, Revolution, and Judgment in the Development of Locke's Thought." *Political Science* 40.1 (1988): 84–96.
Schwartz, Stuart B. *All Can Be Saved: Religious Tolerance and Salvation in the Iberian Atlantic World*. New Haven, CT: Yale University Press, 2008.
Schwartzman, Micah. "The Relevance of Locke's Religious Arguments for Toleration." *Political Theory* 33.5 (2005): 678–705.
Seliger, Martin. *The Liberal Politics of John Locke*. New York: Praeger, 1969.
Sergeant, John. *A Discovery of the Groundlessness and Insincerity of My Lord of Down's Dissuasive Being the Fourth Appendix to Sure-Footing with a Letter to Dr. Casaubon and Another to His Answerer*. London, 1665.
———. *A Letter to the D. of P. [Dean of St. Paul's, Dr. Stillingfleet] in Answer to the Arguing Part of His First Letter to Mr. G.* London: Henry Hills, 1687.
———. *The Method to Arrive at Satisfaction in Religion*. London, 1671.
———. *Sure-Footing in Christianity*. London, 1665.
Severance, Mary. "Sex and the Social Contract." *ELH: English Literary History* 67 (2000): 453–513.
Shagan, Ethan. *The Rule of Moderation: Violence, Religion, and the Politics of Restraint in Early Modern England*. Cambridge: Cambridge University Press, 2011.
Shanley, Mary. "Marriage Contract and Social Contract in Seventeenth Century English Political Thought." *Western Political Quarterly* 32.1 (1979): 79–91.
Sherwood, Yvonne. "The God of Abraham and Exceptional States, or The Early Modern Rise of the Whig/Liberal Bible." *Journal of the American Academy of Religion* 76.2 (2008): 312–43.
Shirley, James. *The Wedding*. London: John Groue, 1629.
Smith, Christian, ed. *The Secular Revolution: Power, Interests, and Conflict in the Secularization of American Public Life*. Berkeley: University of California Press, 2003.
Smith, Jonathan Z. "The Bare Facts of Ritual." *History of Religions* 20.1–2 (1980): 112–27.
Smith, Rogers M. *Civic Ideals: Conflicting Ideals of Citizenship in U.S. History*. New Haven, CT: Yale University Press, 1999.
Smolin, David. "Exporting the First Amendment? Evangelism, Proselytism, and

the International Religious Freedom Act." *Cumberland Law Review* 31 (2001): 686–708.

Sommerville, C. John. *The Secularization of Early Modern England*. New York: Oxford University Press, 1992.

Snyder, David. "Faith and Reason in Locke's Essay." *Journal of the History of Ideas* 47.2 (1986): 197–213.

———. "Locke on Natural Law and Property Rights." *Canadian Journal of Philosophy* 16.4 (1986): 723–50.

Spellman, W. M. *John Locke*. New York: St. Martin's Press, 1997.

———. *John Locke and the Problem of Depravity*. Oxford: Clarendon, 1988.

Spinoza, Baruch. *Tractatus Theologico-Politicus*, trans. R. H. M. Elwes. New York: Dover, 1951.

Stahnke, Tad. "Proselytism and the Freedom to Change Religion in International Human Rights Law." *Brigham Young University Law Review* 251 (1999): 251–354.

Stanton, Timothy. "Locke and the Politics and Theology of Toleration." *Political Studies* 54 (2006): 84–102.

Stevens, Jacqueline. *Reproducing the State*. Princeton, NJ: Princeton University Press, 1999.

Stillingfleet, Edward. *The Mischief of Separation*. London, 1687.

Stopler, Gila. "The Liberal Bind: The Conflicts Between Women's Rights and Patriarchal Religions in the Liberal State." *Social Theory and Practice* 31.2 (2005): 191–231.

Stout, Jeffrey. *Democracy and Tradition*. Princeton, NJ: Princeton University Press, 2004.

Sutcliffe, Adam. *Judaism and Enlightenment*. Cambridge: Cambridge University Press, 2003.

Tanner, Kathryn. *The Politics of God*. Minneapolis: Augsburg Fortress Press, 1992.

Tarcov, Nathan. *Locke's Education for Liberty*. Chicago: University of Chicago Press, 1984.

Taylor, Charles. *A Secular Age*. Cambridge, MA: Harvard University Press, 2007.

Teresa of Ávila. *The Interior Castle*. Mahwah, NJ: Paulist Press, 1979.

Thiemann, Ronald. *Religion in Public Life: A Dilemma for Democracy*. Washington, DC: Georgetown University Press, 1996.

Tillotson, John. *"The Lawfulness and Obligation of Oaths": A Sermon Preached at the Assises Held at Kingston upon Thames, July 21, 1681*. London: B. Aylmer, 1681.

———. *The Rule of Faith, Or, An Answer to the Treatise of Mr. J. S.* London: Gellibrand, 1666.

———. *"A Sermon Concerning the Sacrifice and Satisfaction of Christ," Preached Before the Queen at Whitehall, April 9, 1693*. London: 1693.

———. *Six Sermons*. London: Aylmer & Rogers, 1694.
Tocqueville, Alexis de. *De la Démocratie en Amérique*. Paris: Michel Lévy, 1864.
———. *Democracy in America*, trans. George Lawrence. Garden City, NY: Doubleday, 1969.
Tuck, Richard. "Scepticism and Toleration in the Seventeenth Century." In *Justifying Toleration*, ed. Susan Mendus, 21–36. Cambridge: Cambridge University Press, 2009.
Tuckness, Alex. *Locke and the Legislative Point of View*. Princeton, NJ: Princeton University Press, 2002.
———. "Locke's Main Argument for Toleration." In *Toleration and Its Limits*, ed. Jeremy Waldron and Melissa S. Williams, 114–38. New York: New York University Press, 2008.
Tully, James. *An Approach to Political Philosophy: Locke in Contexts*. Cambridge: Cambridge University Press, 1993.
———. *A Discourse on Property: John Locke and His Adversaries*. Cambridge: Cambridge University Press, 1980.
Turner, Alicia. "Religion-Making and Its Failures: Turning Monasteries into Schools and Buddhism into a Religion in Colonial Burma." In *Secularism and Religion-Making*, ed. Markus Dressler and Arvind-Pal S. Mandair, 226–42. New York: Oxford University Press, 2011.
U.S. Department of State. *International Religious Freedom Report*, 2004. Washington, DC: U.S. Department of State, Bureau of Democracy, Human Rights and Labor, 2004.
Viswanathan, Gauri. *Outside the Fold: Conversion, Modernity, and Belief*. Princeton, NJ: Princeton University Press, 1998.
Waldman, Theodore. "A Note on John Locke's Concept of Consent." *Ethics* 68.1 (1957): 45–50.
Waldron, Jeremy. *God, Locke, and Equality: Christian Foundations in Locke's Political Thought*. Cambridge: Cambridge University Press, 2002.
———. "John Locke: Social Contract Versus Political Anthropology." *Review of Politics* 51.1 (1989): 3–28.
———. "Locke, Toleration, and the Rationality of Persecution." In his *Liberal Rights: Collected Papers, 1981–1991*, 88–114. Cambridge: Cambridge University Press, 1993.
Walker, William. "Force, Metaphor, and Persuasion in Locke's *A Letter Concerning Toleration*." In *Difference and Dissent: Theories of Toleration in Medieval and Modern Europe*, ed. Cary J. Nederman and John Christian Laursen, 205–29. Lanham, MD: Rowman & Littlefield, 1996.
———. "The Limits of Locke's Toleration." *Studies on Voltaire and the Eighteenth Century* 332 (1995): 133–54.

———. *Locke, Literary Criticism, and Philosophy*. Cambridge: Cambridge University Press, 1994.

Wallace, Dewey D. "Socianism, Justification by Faith, and the Sources of John Locke's *The Reasonableness of Christianity*." *Journal of the History of Ideas* 45 (spring 1984): 49–66.

Walsham, Alexandra. *Charitable Hatred: Tolerance and Intolerance in England, 1500–1700*. Manchester: Manchester University Press, 2006.

Walzer, Michael. "The Problem of Citizenship." In his *Obligations: Essays on Disobedience, War, and Citizenship*, 203–25. Cambridge, MA: Harvard University Press, 1970.

Warburton, William. *The Divine Legation of Moses*. London: Cadell & Davies, 1811.

Ward, Lee. *John Locke and Modern Life*. Cambridge: Cambridge University Press, 2010.

Warner, Michael. *Publics and Counterpublics*. New York: Zone Books, 2005.

Watts, Isaac. *A New Essay on Civil Power in Things Sacred, Or an Enquiry After and Established Religion Consistent with the Just Liberties of Mankind and Practicable Under Every Form of Civil Government*. London: M. Steen, 1739.

Weir, David A. *The Origins of the Federal Theology in Sixteenth-Century Reformation Thought*. Oxford: Clarendon Press, 1990.

Welchman, Jennifer. "Locke on Slavery and Inalienable Rights." *Canadian Journal of Philosophy* 25.1 (1995): 67–81.

Whitby, Daniel. *An Answer to Sure-Footing*. Oxford: R. Davis, 1666.

Wiesner-Hanks, Merry. *Christianity and Sexuality in the Early Modern World: Regulating Desire, Reforming Practice, 1500–1750*. New York: Routledge, 2000.

Wilkins, John. *Of the Principles and Duties of Natural Religion*. London: T. Basset, H. Brome, R. Chiswell, 1675.

Windstrup, George. "Freedom and Authority: The Ancient Faith of Locke's 'Letter on Toleration.'" *Review of Politics* 44.2 (1982): 242–65.

Witte, John. "A Primer on the Rights and Wrongs of Proselytism." *Cumberland Law Review* 31 (2000): 619–29.

Wittgenstein, Ludwig. *Philosophical Investigations*, trans. G. E. M. Anscombe. New York: Macmillan, 1953.

Wolfson, Adam. *Persecution or Toleration: An Explication of the Locke-Proast Quarrel, 1689–1707*. Blue Ridge Summit, PA: Lexington Press, 2010.

Wolterstorff, Nicholas. *John Locke and the Ethics of Belief*. Cambridge: Cambridge University Press, 1996.

———. "The Role of Religion in Decision and Discussion of Political Issues." In *Religion in the Public Square*, by Nicholas Wolterstorff and Robert Audi, 67–118. Lanham, MD: Rowman & Littlefield, 1997.

Woolhouse, Roger. *Locke: A Biography.* Cambridge: Cambridge University Press, 2007.
Worden, Blair. "The Question of Secularization." In *A Nation Transformed: England After the Restoration*, ed. Alan Houston and Steve Pincus, 20–40. Cambridge: Cambridge University Press, 2001.
Wycherley, William. *The Country-Wife.* London: Samuel Briscoe, 1695.
Zagorin, Perez. *How the Idea of Religious Toleration Came to the West.* Princeton, NJ: Princeton University Press, 2003.
Zaret, David. *The Heavenly Contract: Ideology and Organization in Pre-Revolutionary Puritanism.* Chicago: University of Chicago Press, 1985.
———. *Origins of Democratic Culture: Printing, Petitions, and the Public Sphere in Early-Modern England.* Princeton, NJ: Princeton University Press, 2000.
Žižek, Slavoj. *The Fragile Absolute.* London: Verso, 2000.
Zuckert, Michael P. *Launching Liberalism: On Lockean Political Philosophy.* Lawrence: University Press of Kansas, 2002.

Index

Aarsleff, Hans, 172n38
absolute rulers, 72, 77–79, 176–77n87
Acosta, Josephus, 181n45
Adorno, Theodor W., 8
Afghanistan, proselytization in, 186–87n4
African slaves, coercive treatment of, 99, 101–3, 180–81n42–44
Agamben, Giorgio, 155n7
All's Lost by Lust (Rowley, 1633), 113
Althusser, Louis, 72
ambassadorial credentials, miracles as, 76
Ambedkar, Bhimrao Ramji, 33
America in Locke's time. *See* early America
American Convention on Human Rights (1969), 148
American International Religious Freedom Act of 1998, 148
American natives: contemporary property and religious conflicts, 104–5, 182n53; Locke on coercive treatment of, 99, 101–3, 180–81n42–44
Ames, William, 173–74n53–54
Amish, 185n48
Anglican Church, 77, 87, 94, 130, 175n69, 179n34
Apache Nation, 105
appropriation of land in America, Locke's justification of, 181n45
Arendt, Hannah, 117–18
The Argument of the Letter Concerning Toleration, Briefly Consider'd and Answer'd (Proast, 1690). *See* Proast, Jonas
Aristotle, 42
Arminianism, 60, 74, 89, 169n8, 175n69, 176n74
Asad, Talal, 10, 30
Ashcraft, Richard, 158n23, 180n42
atheists: lack of toleration for, 7, 28–29, 59, 85, 98, 99, 168n3; oaths and promises, inability to keep, 64; unreasonableness of, 63–64
atonement theology, Locke's rejection of, 74–76, 79, 176n74
Augustine of Hippo, 21, 67–68, 95, 124, 158n23, 174n55, 175n67, 175n69, 177n6, 178n21
authority of God, 78

Bagehot, Walter, 149
Balfour, Lord, 149
Barrow, Henry, 21
Barry, Brian, 142–43, 185n48
Baxter, Richard, 173n53
Behn, Aphra, *The Rover* (1677), 112, 113
Beitz, Charles R., 166n51
Bellah, Robert, 56
Bible. *See* Scripture
Blair, James, 180n42
Block, James, 158n14
Bob Jones University, 185n47
bodies and religion: contemporary religious conflict and, 13, 141, 146, 152; discursive and textual culture,

emergence of, 37, 39, 52–53, 57; family in Locke's political theology and, 107–9, 118, 127; fashions and persuasions, religion converted into, 11, 16, 20, 32, 33; force in religion and, 84, 93, 99; secularization as religion placed into circulation, 3–4; theism of Locke and, 6, 8, 77; toleration, anxieties associated with, 107–11
The Body in Pain (Scarry, 1987), 70
Boyle, Robert, 18
Brown, Vivienne, 65–66, 171n35
Brown, Wendy, 31–32, 144
Brownover, S., 180n42
Bruce, Steve, 31, 161n49
Buddhism, 33–34, 135, 188n12
buffered selves, 143, 144, 191n40
Burke, Edmund, 162n3
Burmese Buddhist monastery education, 33–34
Burnet, Thomas, 169n8, 172n38

Calvin, John, 20, 73, 159n27, 165n47, 174n55
Calvinism, 60, 108, 168n8
Cambodia, proselytization in, 137
capitalist logic. *See* colonialist and capitalist logic
Carter, Stephen, 36, 141
Casaubon, Méric, 43–44
Catholics and Catholicism: discursive and textual culture, emergence of, 38, 41–46, 57, 167n62, 168n66; fashions and persuasions, reconstruction of religion as, 16, 19, 26–27, 158n9; force in religion and, 90, 98; Glorious Revolution, 38, 54–55, 93–94; indulgence of 1672, 114; proselytism and, 136, 139; public reason and, 192n55; theism of Locke and, 72; toleration, anxieties concerning, 111
Cavendish, Margaret, 114–15
Charles II (king of England), 114
Chicago Field Museum, American Indian objects in, 105
children. *See* family in Locke's political theology
choice, religion as, 30–32
Christianity: atonement theology, Locke's rejection of, 74–76, 79, 176n74; civil religion and, 56–58, 167n62; Locke's secularism and, 10–11; proselytization in contemporary culture and, 135–40. *See also specific denominations*
Church of Jesus Christ of Latter Day Saints in Israel, 138, 189–90n18
Cicero, 38
civic ritual, 37, 49–53, 56–58
"Civil and Ecclesiastical Power" (Locke, 1674), 157n8
civil religion, concept of, 10, 37, 56–57, 151, 156n14, 167n62
Clarke, Edward, 117
Cleaver, Robert, 21
Clinton, Bill, 59
coercion. *See* force in religion
coinage, Locke's analysis of, 160n32
Coke, Roger, 21
collective effervescence, 49
Colman, John, 170n23, 175n61
colonialist and capitalist logic: appropriation of land in America, Locke's justification of, 181n45; economic growth and toleration, 110–11; James, William, repudiation of colonialism by, 126, 184n34; of Locke's reconstruction of religion, 32–34; of Locke's treatment of poor, African slaves, and American natives, 100–103, 179n40; proselytization, resistance to, 137–38, 140
commodification of religion, 9, 26, 32, 36
"Common Witness and Proselytism" (Joint Theological Commission), 136
Condillac, Étienne Bonnot de, 164n36
"Confined Love" (Donne), 183n14

Congreve, William, 114
consent: border control and, 109; explicit and tacit, 53–56; family in Locke's political theology and, 117, 119, 129; force in religion and, 95–99, 102, 103, 105, 106
Conservative Party of Canada, proposed Department of Religious Freedom, 148
contemporary religious conflict and Lockean theory, 13, 133–53; American natives, 104–5, 182n53; attribution of power and violence to words, 134–43; bodies and religion, 13, 141, 146, 152; democracy, results of, 145–46; discrimination in religious communities, 129–30, 185–86n47–48; explicit consent, instances of necessity of, 54–55; free speech and religious speech, 140–41, 148–49; holy war, specter of, 145–47, 191n44; human rights, sacrality of, 147–49, 150, 152, 191n46; implications for modern secularity, 143–50; liberal or secular speech and religious conservatives, 141–43; proselytization, 135–40; public reason, concept of, 131, 142, 150–53, 192–93n57, 192n55; Rawlsian "overlapping consensus" and, 13, 134, 150–53; transformation of war into political and religious dissent, 149–50; veil, French banning of, 134–35
Contractarianism, 192n55
Cosmopolitan magazine, 27–28, 160–61n40
Coulter, Ann, 142
The Country Wife (Wycherley, 1675), 114
covenantal theology, 69–71, 78, 173n52
Cranston, Maurice, 180n42
"Credit, Disgrace" (Locke, 1678), 160n37
Crocket, Clayton, 15, 157n5
Cromwell, Oliver, 27
cultural/personal authority, force of, 89–90, 122

cultural rights, 148–49, 191–92n49

Dalits (Untouchables), 33–34, 188–89n14
Davis, Creston, 15, 157n5
Davis, Derek H., 191n46
Dawkins, Richard, 142
Dawson, Hannah, 160n32
Death by Liberalism (Dunn, 2011), 142
debauchery and religious freedom, anxieties about, 9, 107–11, 138–39
Dekker, Thomas, 112–13
democracy, results of, 145–46
Demonic: How the Liberal Mob Is Endangering America (Coulter, 2011), 142
Den Hartogh, Govert, 54
The Description of a New World, Called the Blazing-World (Cavendish, 1668), 114–15
Dialectic of Enlightenment (Horkheimer and Adorno, 1944), 8
discrimination in religious communities, contemporary accommodation of, 129–30, 185–86n47–48
discursive and textual culture, emergence of, 11, 36–58; ambiguity of Enlightenment responses to, 37–39; argumentation, religion viewed as species of, 19–24; bodies and religion, 37, 39, 52–53, 57; civic ritual and, 37, 49–53, 56–58; civil religion, concept of, 10, 37, 56–57, 151, 156n14, 167n62; language, theories of origins of, 47, 164n36; Locke's own doubts about, 37, 39–41; Mendelssohn's critique of Locke and, 11, 37, 46–51; oaths, 38, 50–52; preaching, power of, 39, 43–44; publishing revolution of 17th century and, 18–19; religious power as persuasive power, 17, 20, 23–24, 47; Sergeant on debate over tradition versus Scripture, 11, 41–46, 49, 51; tacit and explicit consent, Locke on, 53–56; Tillotson and, 11,

218   Index

41–42, 50, 57, 171n26; Watts and, 11, 50–51, 164–65n44–45, 164n42
divine power. *See* theism of Locke
Donne, John, 111, 183n14
"Don't ask, don't tell" policy, 59
Dunn, J. R., 142
Dunn, John, 11, 60, 72, 100, 156n13, 165–66n51, 168n8, 169–70n13, 169n9
Durkheim, Émile, 49

early America: African slaves, coercive treatment of, 99, 101–3, 180–81n42–44; appropriation of land, Locke's justification of, 181n45; coercive treatment of American natives, 99, 101–3, 180–81n42–44; "Fundamental Constitutions of Carolina" (Locke, 1669), 101–2, 164n42, 167n60, 168n2, 181–82n48; "Some of the Chief Grievances of the present constitution of Virginia, with an Essay towards the Remedies thereof" (Locke), 101, 159n30, 180n41
Eberle, Christopher, 192n55
economic growth and toleration, 110–11
Edwards, John, 176n74
Edwards, Jonathan, 174n55
Eisenach, Eldon, 129, 155n6
Elshtain, Jean Bethke, 140
English Constitution (Bagehot, 1867), 149
enthusiasm, Locke's dislike of, 90
epistemology and force in religion, 87–91, 104
Essay Concerning Human Understanding (Locke, 1690): discursive and textual culture, emergence of, 39–40, 41, 51, 165n46; family in Locke's political theology and, 116, 121, 122, 123; fashions and persuasions, religion reconstructed as, 22, 23, 24, 28, 29; force in religion and, 86, 88, 89, 90, 93; Sergeant on, 41; theism of Locke and, 65, 71, 172n40
An Essay Concerning Toleration (Locke, 1667), 69, 160n37, 175n69

"Essay on the Poor Law" (Locke, 1697), 99, 179n34
Essays on the Law of Nature (Locke, c. 1663–1664), 71, 78, 86, 174n60
"Ethica B" (Locke, c. 1693), 171n30
Euben, Roxanne, 60
European Court of Human Rights, 136, 137
explicit and tacit consent, 53–56

Falkner, William, 45–46, 119
Familialists, 111
family in Locke's political theology, 12, 107–32; affectionate relationships between parents and children, 127; bodies and religion, 107–9, 118, 127; consent in, 117, 119, 129; crucial importance of early childhood, 117; governmentality, rise of rule of, 8; gradualism of Lockean pedagogy, 119; influence of Locke's writings on, 117, 183n18; intermarriage anxieties and religious freedom, 107–8; liberalism and, 129–31; literary sources contextualizing, 111–16, 183n16; literature for children, 183n18; marriage, Locke's ideas about, 185n46; mental habits of flexibility and openness, inculcation of, 124–27; parental cultivation of children, 116–21; paternal authority and the Fatherly God, 127–29; poor children, treatment of, 99–100, 179n32, 179n34–35, 179n40; reenvisioned and redeployed, 108–9; religion uncoupled from familial ties and inheritance, 20–21, 116, 125; religious instruction of children, 120–21; sexual promiscuity, anxieties about, 107–11; tacit consent, children's inheritance of parental property as instance of, 53; tenacity of ideas inculcated in early childhood, 121–24
Fantomina (Haywood, 1725), 166n57
Farce of Sodom (attrib. Wilmont, 1672), 114

Farr, James, 181n45
Farr, Thomas, 148
fashions and persuasions, religion converted into, 11, 14–35; argumentation, religion viewed as species of, 19–24; bodies and religion, 11, 16, 20, 32, 33; capitalist and colonialist logic of, 32–34; choice, religion as, 30–32; comparison of religious difference to matters of fashion, 24–30; in contemporary conflicts over religion, 9; dangers of private practice of religion, 17–18; disciplinary aspects of fashion, 28–29; discursive and textual culture, emergence of, 11; force, Locke's use of metaphors of, 23–24; privatization of religion, Locke's political theology wrongly understood as, 1–4, 14–19, 126; publishing revolution in 17th-century England and, 18–19; religious power as persuasive power, 17, 20, 23–24, 47; secularization as religion placed into circulation, 1–4, 15–16
federal theology, 173n52
feminization. *See* gender
Fenton, Mina, 138
Filmer, Sir Robert, 67–68, 71, 127–28, 184n41
Fish, Stanley, 14, 142, 145, 146, 192n55
Fitzgerald, Timothy, 157n2
"For a General Naturalization" (Locke, 1693), 159n30
force in religion, 12, 83–106; African slaves and American natives, 99, 101–3, 180–81n42–44; bodies and religion, 84, 93, 99; consent, Locke's insistence on, 95–99, 102, 103, 105, 106; epistemology and, 87–91, 104; Glorious Revolution and, 93–94; Locke's three intolerables and, 84–85, 98–99; metaphors of force used for persuasive religious speech, 23–24;

miracles, Locke on, 91, 94; personal/cultural authority, force of, 89–90, 122; the poor and, 99–101, 132; Proast and Locke, dispute between, 12, 86–88, 91–96, 102, 105, 178n20, 178n23; science and demonstration versus faith and opinion, 88–90; separation of church and state, permeability of, 84–86; toleration principle and, 84–85, 98–99, 104; usefulness/efficacy of force, 93–95
Forster, Greg, 66–67, 156n13, 171n37
Foucault, Michel, 8, 70, 71, 118, 120
A Fourth Letter for Toleration (Locke, 1704), 88
Fox, George, 25–26
Foxe, John, 19
France, law against ostensible religious signs in, 134–35
Franklin, Julian, 166n51
free speech and religious speech, 140–41, 148–49
free will, grace, and Lockean theism, 72–74, 172n41, 175n68
Freedom of Religion Act (India, 2003), 137, 188n12
Freud, Sigmund, 143
"Fundamental Constitutions of Carolina" (Locke, 1669), 101–2, 164n42, 167n60, 168n2, 181–82n48
fundamentalism, 133, 138, 145, 192n55
The Future of an Illusion (Freud, 1927), 143

Gandhi, Harilal, 188n14
Gandhi, Mohandas, 32–33, 34, 137, 188–89n13–14
Gauthier, David, 65
gender: anxieties associated with secularization of religion and untethered bodies of, 107; contemporary accommodation of discrimination in religious communities, 129–30, 185–86n47–48; intermarriage, anxieties about,

107–8; James's construction of masculinity, 126; religion as fashion and, 24, 27–28; rhetoric characterized as woman, 40; Sergeant on "feminine seat" of mind, 41
Glorious Revolution, 38, 54–55, 93–94
God. *See* theism of Locke
Goldie, Mark, 56, 156n14, 167n62, 172n38, 180n42
goodness of God, 67, 71, 80, 170n19, 172n40, 173n48, 174n58
Gottlieb, Micah, 48
governmentality, rise of rule of, 8
grace, free will, and Lockean theism, 72–74, 172n41, 175n68
Greece v. Kokkinakis (Greece/European Court, 1993), 136–37, 139, 188n10
Greenawalt, Kent, 192–93n57
Griffiths, Paul, 187n7
Grotius, Hugo, 38, 162n6

Habermas, Jürgen, 24, 31, 131, 158n15, 193n59
Halfway Covenant (1662), 159n29
Hall, Joseph, 29
Hamm, Berndt, 173n48
Hampsher-Monk, Iain, 166n51
Harris, Ian, 78
Haywood, Eliza, 166n57
Hegel, Georg Wilhelm Friedrich, 52, 73, 165n47
Heywood, Thomas, 183n16
Hickes, George, 87, 159n28
Hindus and Hinduism, 33, 135, 138, 188–89n12–16
Hobbes, Thomas, 73, 74, 102, 163n17
holy war, contemporary concerns about, 145–47, 191n44
The Honest Whore (Dekker, 1604, 1630), 112
Horkheimer, Max, 8
Horwitz, Robert, 170n16
"Hounslow-Heath 1686" (poem), 38
Hsueh, Vicki, 167n60

Hughes, George, 44–45
human and divine power. *See* theism of Locke
human rights. *See* rights
Hume, David, 61, 76, 165n47

identity and religion, relationship between, 3–4, 19–21, 30–32, 137–38
idolatry and concept of universal faith, 48–49
Ignatieff, Michael, 149
India, religious identity in, 32–33, 137–38, 188–89n12–16
Indians, American. *See* American natives
individualism of human rights, 148–49
infant baptism, 21, 159n27–29
Ingelhart, Ronald, 191n40
Ingle, David W., 56–57
intelligent design, 61
intermarriage, anxieties about, 107–8
International Covenant on Civil and Political Rights (ICCPR, 1966), 136, 191n47
International Covenant on Economic, Social, and Cultural Rights (ICESCR, 1966), 191–92n49
Iran, proselytization in, 187n4
Islam: contemporary religious conflicts and, 133, 134–35, 139–40, 161n41, 186–87n4, 188n12, 190n22; equality and religion in, 60; Locke's three intolerables and, 98; Venetian walled compound for Muslim merchants, 108
Israel, Church of Jesus Christ of Latter Day Saints in, 138, 189–90n18

James I (king of England), 38, 78
James II (king of England), 38, 110
James, William, 12, 97–98, 126–27, 184n34
Jerusalem (Mendelssohn), 46, 47, 49, 50, 51
Jews and Judaism: discursive and

textual culture, emergence of, 46–47, 57, 58, 163n35, 165n47; family in Locke's political theology and, 108; fashions and persuasions, religion converted into, 16–17, 158n9; in "Fundamental Constitutions of Carolina" (Locke, 1669), 102; Israel, Church of Jesus Christ of Latter Day Saints in, 138, 189–90n18; theism of Locke and, 75
Joint Theological Commission, 136
Josephson, Peter, 54
Juergensmeyer, Mark, 14–15
just-war theory, 181n45

Kahn, Paul, 36, 56, 131, 168n6
Kallen, Horace, 129
Kammen, Michael G., 180n42
Kant, Immanuel, 31, 152, 165n47
Kaplan, Benjamin J., 155–56n10
Kelly, Patrick, 180n42
Kertzer, David, 151
Khan, Zafrulla, 186n4
Kramnick, Isaac, 157n2
Kramnick, Jonathan Brody, 166n57
Kukathas, Chandras, 185n48

language origin theories, 39–40, 47, 164n36
Laslett, Peter, 184n41
Latitudinarianism, 28, 60, 169n8
Letter Concerning Toleration (Locke, 1689): discursive and textual culture, emergence of, 163n35; family in Locke's political theology and, 125, 130; fashions and persuasions, religion reconstructed as, 17, 21–22, 23, 25, 157n8; force in religion and, 84, 85–86, 92, 93, 95, 98, 101, 104; on spiritual teaching, 137; Watts's admiration of, 50
Leyden, Wolfgang von, 172n38
liberalism and Locke's theism, 61, 79–82
liberalism, contemporary: Lockean political theology and, 14–15, 31, 36, 129–31, 156n13; Rawlsian "overlapping consensus," 13, 134, 150–53; religious conservatives and, 141–43
Liberalism Kills Kids (Scarborough, 2006), 142
licentiousness and religious freedom, anxieties about, 9, 107–11, 138–39
Lilla, Mark, 59–60
Lincoln, Abraham, 56
Lincoln, Bruce, 55–56
Little, David, 104
Locke, John. political theology of. *See* political theology of John Locke
Locke, John, works of: "Civil and Ecclesiastical Power" (1674), 157n8; "Credit, Disgrace" (1678), 160n37; *An Essay Concerning Toleration* (1667), 69, 160n37, 175n69; "Essay on the Poor Law" (1697), 99, 179n34; *Essays on the Law of Nature* (c. 1663-1664), 71, 78, 86, 174n60; "Ethica B" (c. 1693), 171n30; "For a General Naturalization" (1693), 159n30; *A Fourth Letter for Toleration* (1704), 88; "Fundamental Constitutions of Carolina" (1669), 101–2, 164n42, 167n60, 168n2, 181–82n48; *On the Conduct of the Understanding* (1706), 121, 122, 160n33; "Pacifick Christians" (1688), 165n49; *Paraphrase and Notes* (1703), 177n93; *The Reasonableness of Christianity* (1695), 52, 86, 165n47, 177n93, 184–85n42; "Sacerdos" (1698), 52; *A Second Letter for Toleration* (1690), 86, 87, 94, 95, 165n47; *Second Tract on Government* (1667), 160n37; "A Second Vindication of the Reasonableness of Christianity" (1695), 172–73n42; "Some of the Chief Grievances of the present constitution of Virginia, with an Essay towards the Remedies thereof" (1697), 101, 159n30, 180n41; *Some Thoughts Concerning Education* (1693), 92, 117–22, 124, 125, 127, 128,

183n27; *A Third Letter for Toleration* (1692), 86, 91, 92, 94; *Vindication of the Reasonableness of Christianity* (1695), 168n3. *See also Essay Concerning Human Understanding; Letter Concerning Toleration; Two Treatises*
Lofron, Kathryn, 161n41
Love in Excess (Haywood, 1719), 166n57
Luther, Martin, 157n6, 158n23, 175n67
Lutherans, 90, 108
Lyng v. Northwest Indian Cemetery Protective Association (US, 1988), 182n53

Macedo, Stephen, 12, 130–31, 141–42, 145, 146–47
Madison, James, 104
Mahmood, Saba, 3, 109
Maintenance of Religious Harmony Act (Singapore, 1990), 187n5
Malaysia, proselytization in, 187n4, 190n22
Mandeville, Bernard, 164n36
Manicheanism, 60, 169n8
Maoris, New Zealand, 31
marriage: intermarriage, anxieties about, 107–8; Locke on, 185n46
Marshall, John, 169n8, 172n41, 182n13
Martin v. City of Struthers (US, 1943), 188n9
Marvin, Carolyn, 56–57
Masham, Damaris Cudworth, 109
Masham, Sir William, 109
McCabe, David, 156n14
McClure, Kirstie, 60, 169n11–12
McConnell, Michael, 157n2
Mendelssohn, Moses, 11, 37, 46–51, 134, 164n36
Messenger, Philip, 112–13
Michael, Mark A., 181n45
Mill, John Stuart, 31, 158n14
Miller, Perry, 69, 70–71, 173n53
Milton, John, 173n53, 175n69
mind, Locke on, 88

miracles, Locke on, 10, 52, 75–77, 91, 94
molly houses, 110
Molnár, Attila K., 157n6
Monmouth-shire (Protestant) and York-shire (Catholic), debate between, 26–27
Montaigne, Michel de, 22
Moore, R. Laurence, 157n2
Mormons in Israel, 138, 189–90n18
Morris, Paul, 14
Mozert v. Hawkins (US, 1987), 142–43
Muir, John, 188n13
Muslim Brotherhood, 60

Native Americans. *See* American natives
natural law, Locke's understanding of, 61, 64, 170n15
Nepal, on proselytism, 139
Netherlands: broadsheet (1165) on toleration in, 29–30; Catholics and Jews forbidden public houses of worship in, 16; economic growth and toleration in, 110–11
Neuberger, Julia, 187n7
A New Essay on Civil Power in Things Sacred (Watts, 1739), 50–51, 164–65n44–45, 164n42
New Zealand, Maoris in, 31
Newbery, John, 183n18
Newdow v. U.S. Congress (US, 2002), 141, 190n29
Niyogi, Bhawani Shankar, 189n16
Norris, Pippa, 191n40

Oakley, Francis, 68–69
oaths and promises, 38, 50–52, 64, 68, 173n44
Okin, Susan Moller, 185n48
omnipotence of God, 67–69, 73–74, 172n41
On the Conduct of the Understanding (Locke, 1706), 121, 122, 160n33
original sin, Locke's rejection of, 10, 68, 72, 74, 79, 83, 176n74

"overlapping consensus" of John Rawls, 13, 134, 150–53

"Pacifick Christians" (Locke, 1688), 165n49
Paget, William, 162n11
Pakistan, on Universal Declaration of Human Rights, 186n4
Pamela: or, Virtue Rewarded (Richardson, 1740), 183n18
Pangle, Thomas, 81, 170n16
Paraphrase and Notes (Locke, 1703), 177n93
Pateman, Carole, 184n33, 184n38
paternal authority and the Fatherly God, 127–29
Patriarcha (Filmer, 1680), 67–68, 71, 127–28, 184n41
Patrimony of Christian Children (Cleaver, 1624), 21
pedagogy. *See* family in Locke's political theology
Perry, John, 60, 156n13
Perry, Michael, 191n46
personal/cultural authority, force of, 89–90, 122
persuasion, religion as. *See* fashions and persuasions, religion converted into
Peru: Acosta on, 181n45; fundamentalism in, 138–39; Locke on Peruvian parents eating their children, 68
Pierre d'Ailly, 68
plantation labor, 100–101, 179n40
Plato, 118
pluralism: contemporary religious conflicts and, 141, 145, 150, 153, 192n55; discursive and textual culture, emergence of, 39; family in Locke's political theology and, 126, 131–32; theism of Locke and, 59, 66, 67
political theology of John Locke, 1–13; bodies and religion (*See* bodies and religion); contemporary religious conflict and, 13, 133–53 (*See also* contemporary religious conflict and Lockean theory); contemporary religious conflicts and, 9; in corpus of Locke's work, 9–10; divine and human power, relationship between, 6–8; family in, 12, 107–32 (*See also* family in Locke's political theology); fashions and persuasions, religion converted into, 11, 14–35 (*See also* fashions and persuasions, religion converted into); force in religion and, 12, 83–106 (*See also* force in religion); Protestant Christianity and secularism, collusion between, 10–11; secularization as religion placed into circulation, 1–6; term *secular*, Locke's use of, 5, 16, 155n9; textual culture and, 11, 36–58 (*See also* discursive and textual culture, emergence of); theism, 12, 59–82 (*See also* theism of Locke); toleration in, 4, 8–9 (*See also* toleration); worldly, secular defined as, 4–5, 26
poor, the: coercive treatment of, 99–101, 132; marriage for, 185n46
Popple, William, 180n42
power, divine and human. *See* theism of Locke
power, forceful. *See* force in religion
preaching, 39, 43–44
privatization of religion: contemporary concerns about proselytism and, 139; Locke's political theology wrongly understood as, 1–4, 14–19, 126
Proast, Jonas: on absolute rulers, 77, 176–77n87; on force in religion, 12, 86–88, 91–96, 102, 105, 178n20, 178n23; Locke on family and, 113, 118, 125; Locke's debates with, 10, 86, 105, 113, 178n22
profanation and secularization, 4, 5, 155n7
promises and oaths, 38, 50–52, 64, 68, 173n44
proofs of existence of God, 61–62, 87, 170n19

property: appropriation of land in America, Locke's justification of, 181n45; as basis of consent and justice, 102–3; religion as form of, 104–5
proselytization in contemporary culture, 135–40
prostitution, 110, 112
Protestants and Protestantism: in contemporary religious conflicts, 139; discursive and textual culture, emergence of, 43, 45, 46, 57; family in Locke's political theology and, 121, 126; fashions and persuasions, religion converted into, 26–27, 34; force in religion and, 90, 100; Locke's secularism and, 10–11; theism of Locke and, 72
public and private, Locke's political theology wrongly understood as division of, 1–5
public reason, 131, 142, 150–53, 192–93n57, 192n55
publishing revolution in 17th-century England, 18–19
Puritans, 19, 27, 39, 43–44, 159n29, 162n10

Quakers, 16, 24, 25, 51, 108, 111
Qut'b, Sayyid, 60

Rawls, John, 13, 31, 134, 150–53, 192n55
The Reasonableness of Christianity (Locke, 1695), 52, 86, 165n47, 177n93, 184–85n42
religion in Locke's political theology. *See* political theology of John Locke
Restoration plays contextualizing anxieties associated with toleration, 111–16, 183n16
rhetoric, Locke's misgivings concerning, 40
Rice Christians, 137
Richardson, Samuel, *Pamela* (1740), 183n18

rights: contemporary sacrality of, 147–49, 150, 152, 191n46; cultural rights, 148–49, 191–92n49; individualism of, 148–49; natural law and, 61; theism, grounded in, 60–61
Riley, Patrick, 75–76, 175n68
Riordan, Patrick, 192n55
ritual, civic, 37, 49–53, 56–58
Roman Catholicism. *See* Catholics and Catholicism
Rorty, Richard, 192n55
Rousseau, Jean-Jacques, 16n36, 56, 116
The Rover (Aphra Behn, 1677), 112, 113
Rowley, William, 113

"Sacerdos" (Locke, 1698), 52
sacrifice and civil religion, 56–58
Sands, Kathleen, 104
Saudi Arabia, religious liberty in, 135, 186n4
Scarborough, Rick, 142
Scarry, Elaine, 54, 70
Schmitt, Carl, 12, 65, 76, 79–81, 171n36, 191n44
Schneewind, J. B., 65, 66
Schochet, Gordon, 184n39–40
Schwartz, Stuart B., 182n9
science, assent compelled by, 88–89
Scripture: divine power in, 70; preaching of, 39; religious education of children and, 121; tradition versus, 42–46
A Second Letter for Toleration (Locke, 1690), 86, 87, 94, 95, 165n47
Second Tract on Government (Locke, 1667), 160n37
"A Second Vindication of the Reasonableness of Christianity" (Locke, 1695), 172–73n42
A Secular Age (Taylor), 143, 144
secularism in Locke's political theology. *See* political theology of John Locke
Seliger, Martin, 127, 165n51, 165n57
separation of church and state, permeability of, 84–86

Sergeant, John, 11, 41–46, 49, 51, 121
sexual promiscuity and religious freedom, anxieties about, 9, 107–11, 138–39
Shagan, Ethan, 8
Shirley, James, 183n16
signs: in contemporary religious conflicts, 134, 135; discursive and textual culture, emergence of, 36–37, 39, 47, 48, 50, 51–52, 58; family in Locke's political theology and, 116, 118; fashions and persuasions, religion converted into, 16, 19, 21, 26, 35; force in religion and, 83; theism of Locke and, 76, 78
Singapore, proselytization in, 187n5
Six Sermons (Tillotson), 121, 122, 183n25, 183n29, 184n31–32
slavery: African slaves, coercive treatment of, 99, 101–3, 180–81n42–44; Locke's views on, 103, 181–82n48, 181n44
Smith, Samuel, 159n28
Smolin, David, 140–41
Society for the Reformation of Manners, 110
Socinianism, 16, 60, 169n8, 176n74
Somanatha, 188n13
"Some of the Chief Grievances of the present constitution of Virginia, with an Essay towards the Remedies thereof" (Locke, 1697), 101, 159n30, 180n41
Some Thoughts Concerning Education (Locke, 1693), 92, 117–22, 124, 125, 127, 128, 183n27
Sommerville, C. John, 3, 10, 168n6
speech and religion: free speech and religious speech, 140–41, 148–49; modern attribution of power and violence to words, 134–43; power to form societal and political bonds, 134, 186n1. *See also* discursive and textual culture, emergence of; fashions and persuasions, religion converted into

Spellman, W. M., 169n8
Spinoza, Baruch, 73, 74, 165n47
Stanton, Timothy, 72
Stevens, Jacqueline, 166n51
Stillingfleet, Edward, 21
Stopler, Gila, 130
Stout, Jeffrey, 192n55
Stubbe, Henry, 157n7
Sure-Footing in Christianity (Sergeant, 1665), 42
Sutcliffe, Adam, 165n47

tacit and explicit consent, 53–56
Tarcov, Nathan, 177n90
Taylor, Charles, 2, 143, 144, 191n38
Taylor, Jeremy, 163n22
Teresa of Avila, 174n55
textual culture. *See* discursive and textual culture, emergence of
theism of Locke, 12, 59–82; atonement theology rejected, 74–76, 79, 176n74; authority of God, 78; contemporary critiques of, 65–67; covenantal theology and, 69–71, 78, 173n52; eternal torment and other divine sanctions rejected, 72, 174n55; Filmer's *Patriarcha*, Locke's objections to, 67–68, 71; free will and grace, 72–74, 172n41, 175n68; goodness of God, 67, 71, 80, 170n19, 172n40, 173n48, 174n58; human sacrality extending from, 6–8, 62–63, 78–79; liberalism and, 61, 79–82; in Locke's corpus of work, 10; miracles, 10, 52, 75–77, 91, 94; natural law and, 61, 64, 170n15; omnipotence of God, 67–69, 73–74, 172n41; original sin rejected, 10, 68, 72, 74, 79, 83, 176n74; paternal authority and the Fatherly God, 127–29; power of God, 6–8, 64–72; proofs of existence of God, 61–62, 87, 170n19; relationship between divine and human power, 6–8; rights grounded in, 60–61; Schmitt's

political theology and, 12, 65, 76, 79–81, 171n36; secularization of religion and, 15–16; transcendence of God, 78–79. *See also* atheists

A Third Letter for Toleration (Locke, 1692), 86, 91, 92, 94

Tillotson, John: on creation as proof of existence of God, 171n26; discursive and textual culture, emergence of, 11, 41–42, 50, 57; family in Locke's political theology and, 117, 119, 121, 122, 183n25, 183n29, 184n31–32

Tocqueville, Alexis de, 186n1

toleration, 4, 8–9; atheists, lack of toleration for, 7, 28–29, 59, 85, 98, 99, 168n3; discursive and textual culture, emergence of, 77, 165n47; economic growth and, 110–11; fashions and persuasions, religion converted into, 21–22, 30; force in religion and, 84–85, 98–99, 104; literary sources contextualizing anxieties associated with, 111–16, 183n16; Locke's three intolerables, 84–85, 98–99; proselytization in contemporary culture and, 135–40, 187n7; sexual promiscuity and religious freedom, anxieties about, 107–11

Tony Blair Faith Foundation, 148

tradition versus Scripture, 42–46

transcendence of God, 78–79

Tuckness, Alex, 178n20

Tully, James, 170n15

Turner, Alicia, 34

Two Treatises (Locke, 1689): discursive and textual culture, emergence of, 53, 62, 65–66; family in Locke's political theology and, 119, 128; force in religion and, 102, 181n44, 181n48; theism of Locke and, 171n35, 173n44

understanding, Locke's association of religion with, 20, 98, 116

Universal Declaration of Human Rights (1948), 135, 147, 186n4

universal faith, 48–49, 176n80

The Unlawful Practices of Prelates, 162n10

Untouchables (Dalits), 33–34, 188–89n14

Vajpayee, Atal Behari, 138

The Varieties of Religious Experience (James, 1901-1902), 97, 126

veil, French banning of, 134–35

Vernon, Richard, 40, 162n16

Vindication of the Reasonableness of Christianity (Locke, 1695), 168n3

The Virgin Martyr (Messenger and Dekker, 1622), 112–13

Vision America, 142

Viswanathan, Gauri, 30

voluntarism, 66–69, 78, 97, 113–14, 172n38, 175n68

Waldman, Theodore, 166n51

Waldron, Jeremy, 60, 64, 91, 156n13, 169n9, 178n23, 181–82n48

Walker, William, 24, 160n35

Walker, Williston, 159n29

Walsham, Alexandra, 4

Walzer, Michael, 131

Warburton, William, 164n36

Ward, Lee, 2, 158n19

Warner, Michael, 144

Watts, Isaac, 11, 50–51, 164–65n44–45, 164n42, 183n18

The Way of the World (Congreve, 1700), 114

The Wedding (Shirley, 1629), 183n16

Whitby, Daniel, 46, 89, 163n31

Wilkins, John, 50, 57, 155n6

will: free will and Lockean theism, 72–74; Locke's use of consent and, 97; uncoupling of religion from, 20–21, 30, 85

"The Will to Believe" (James), 97

William III of Orange (king of England), 54–55

William Ockham, 68

Williams, John, 50

Wilmont, John, 2nd Earl of Rochester, 114

Windstrup, George, 156n14
Winfrey, Oprah, 161n41
Witte, John, 145–46
Wittgenstein, Ludwig, 162n14
Wolfson, Adam, 158n19, 178n22
Wolterstorff, Nicholas, 171n33, 192n55
A Woman Kilde with Kindness (Heywood, 1603), 183n16
women. *See* gender
words, culture of. *See* discursive and textual culture, emergence of

World Council of Churches, 136
worldly, secular defined as, 4–5, 26
Wycherly, William, 114

York-shire (Catholic) and Monmouth-shire (Protestant), debate between, 26–27

Zaret, David, 18, 158n15
Zuckert, Michael, 56, 62, 156n14, 167n62
Zwingli, Ulrich, 159n27

Cultural Memory in the Present

Ankhi Mukherjee, *What Is a Classic? Postcolonial Rewriting and Invention of the Canon*
Jean-Pierre Dupuy, *The Mark of the Sacred*
Henri Atlan, *Fraud: The World of Ona'ah*
Niklas Luhmann, *Theory of Society, Volume 2*
Ilit Ferber, *Philosophy and Melancholy: Benjamin's Early Reflections on Theater and Language*
Alexandre Lefebvre, *Human Rights as a Way of Life: On Bergson's Political Philosophy*
Theodore W. Jennings, Jr., *Outlaw Justice: The Messianic Politics of Paul*
Alexander Etkind, *Warped Mourning: Stories of the Undead in the Land of the Unburied*
Denis Guénoun, *About Europe: Philosophical Hypotheses*
Maria Boletsi, *Barbarism and its Discontents*
Sigrid Weigel, *Walter Benjamin: Images, the Creaturely, and the Holy*
Roberto Esposito, *Living Thought: The Origins and Actuality of Italian Philosophy*
Henri Atlan, *The Sparks of Randomness, Volume 2: The Atheism of Scripture*
Rüdiger Campe, *The Game of Probability: Literature and Calculation from Pascal to Kleist*
Niklas Luhmann, *A Systems Theory of Religion*
Jean-Luc Marion, *In the Self's Place: The Approach of Saint Augustine*
Rodolphe Gasché, *Georges Bataille: Phenomenology and Phantasmatology*
Niklas Luhmann, *Theory of Society, Volume 1*
Alessia Ricciardi, *After* La Dolce Vita*: A Cultural Prehistory of Berlusconi's Italy*
Daniel Innerarity, *The Future and Its Enemies: In Defense of Political Hope*
Patricia Pisters, *The Neuro-Image: A Deleuzian Film-Philosophy of Digital Screen Culture*
François-David Sebbah, *Testing the Limit: Derrida, Henry, Levinas, and the Phenomenological Tradition*
Erik Peterson, *Theological Tractates*, edited by Michael J. Hollerich
Feisal G. Mohamed, *Milton and the Post-Secular Present: Ethics, Politics, Terrorism*

Pierre Hadot, *The Present Alone Is Our Happiness, Second Edition: Conversations with Jeannie Carlier and Arnold I. Davidson*
Yasco Horsman, *Theaters of Justice: Judging, Staging, and Working Through in Arendt, Brecht, and Delbo*
Jacques Derrida, *Parages*, edited by John P. Leavey
Henri Atlan, *The Sparks of Randomness, Volume 1: Spermatic Knowledge*
Rebecca Comay, *Mourning Sickness: Hegel and the French Revolution*
Djelal Kadir, *Memos from the Besieged City: Lifelines for Cultural Sustainability*
Stanley Cavell, *Little Did I Know: Excerpts from Memory*
Jeffrey Mehlman, *Adventures in the French Trade: Fragments Toward a Life*
Jacob Rogozinski, *The Ego and the Flesh: An Introduction to Egoanalysis*
Marcel Hénaff, *The Price of Truth: Gift, Money, and Philosophy*
Paul Patton, *Deleuzian Concepts: Philosophy, Colonialization, Politics*
Michael Fagenblat, *A Covenant of Creatures: Levinas's Philosophy of Judaism*
Stefanos Geroulanos, *An Atheism That Is Not Humanist Emerges in French Thought*
Andrew Herscher, *Violence Taking Place: The Architecture of the Kosovo Conflict*
Hans-Jörg Rheinberger, *On Historicizing Epistemology: An Essay*
Jacob Taubes, *From Cult to Culture*, edited by Charlotte Fonrobert and Amir Engel
Peter Hitchcock, *The Long Space: Transnationalism and Postcolonial Form*
Lambert Wiesing, *Artificial Presence: Philosophical Studies in Image Theory*
Jacob Taubes, *Occidental Eschatology*
Freddie Rokem, *Philosophers and Thespians: Thinking Performance*
Roberto Esposito, *Communitas: The Origin and Destiny of Community*
Vilashini Cooppan, *Worlds Within: National Narratives and Global Connections in Postcolonial Writing*
Josef Früchtl, *The Impertinent Self: A Heroic History of Modernity*
Frank Ankersmit, Ewa Domanska, and Hans Kellner, eds., *Re-Figuring Hayden White*
Michael Rothberg, *Multidirectional Memory: Remembering the Holocaust in the Age of Decolonization*
Jean-François Lyotard, *Enthusiasm: The Kantian Critique of History*
Ernst van Alphen, Mieke Bal, and Carel Smith, eds., *The Rhetoric of Sincerity*
Stéphane Mosès, *The Angel of History: Rosenzweig, Benjamin, Scholem*
Pierre Hadot, *The Present Alone Is Our Happiness: Conversations with Jeannie Carlier and Arnold I. Davidson*
Alexandre Lefebvre, *The Image of the Law: Deleuze, Bergson, Spinoza*
Samira Haj, *Reconfiguring Islamic Tradition: Reform, Rationality, and Modernity*
Diane Perpich, *The Ethics of Emmanuel Levinas*
Marcel Detienne, *Comparing the Incomparable*
François Delaporte, *Anatomy of the Passions*
René Girard, *Mimesis and Theory: Essays on Literature and Criticism, 1959–2005*

Richard Baxstrom, *Houses in Motion: The Experience of Place and the Problem of Belief in Urban Malaysia*
Jennifer L. Culbert, *Dead Certainty: The Death Penalty and the Problem of Judgment*
Samantha Frost, *Lessons from a Materialist Thinker: Hobbesian Reflections on Ethics and Politics*
Regina Mara Schwartz, *Sacramental Poetics at the Dawn of Secularism: When God Left the World*
Gil Anidjar, *Semites: Race, Religion, Literature*
Ranjana Khanna, *Algeria Cuts: Women and Representation, 1830 to the Present*
Esther Peeren, *Intersubjectivities and Popular Culture: Bakhtin and Beyond*
Eyal Peretz, *Becoming Visionary: Brian De Palma's Cinematic Education of the Senses*
Diana Sorensen, *A Turbulent Decade Remembered: Scenes from the Latin American Sixties*
Hubert Damisch, *A Childhood Memory by Piero della Francesca*
José van Dijck, *Mediated Memories in the Digital Age*
Dana Hollander, *Exemplarity and Chosenness: Rosenzweig and Derrida on the Nation of Philosophy*
Asja Szafraniec, *Beckett, Derrida, and the Event of Literature*
Sara Guyer, *Romanticism After Auschwitz*
Alison Ross, *The Aesthetic Paths of Philosophy: Presentation in Kant, Heidegger, Lacoue-Labarthe, and Nancy*
Gerhard Richter, *Thought-Images: Frankfurt School Writers' Reflections from Damaged Life*
Bella Brodzki, *Can These Bones Live? Translation, Survival, and Cultural Memory*
Rodolphe Gasché, *The Honor of Thinking: Critique, Theory, Philosophy*
Brigitte Peucker, *The Material Image: Art and the Real in Film*
Natalie Melas, *All the Difference in the World: Postcoloniality and the Ends of Comparison*
Jonathan Culler, *The Literary in Theory*
Michael G. Levine, *The Belated Witness: Literature, Testimony, and the Question of Holocaust Survival*
Jennifer A. Jordan, *Structures of Memory: Understanding German Change in Berlin and Beyond*
Christoph Menke, *Reflections of Equality*
Marlène Zarader, *The Unthought Debt: Heidegger and the Hebraic Heritage*
Jan Assmann, *Religion and Cultural Memory: Ten Studies*
David Scott and Charles Hirschkind, *Powers of the Secular Modern: Talal Asad and His Interlocutors*
Gyanendra Pandey, *Routine Violence: Nations, Fragments, Histories*
James Siegel, *Naming the Witch*

J. M. Bernstein, *Against Voluptuous Bodies: Late Modernism and the Meaning
    of Painting*
Theodore W. Jennings Jr., *Reading Derrida / Thinking Paul: On Justice*
Richard Rorty and Eduardo Mendieta, *Take Care of Freedom and Truth Will
    Take Care of Itself: Interviews with Richard Rorty*
Jacques Derrida, *Paper Machine*
Renaud Barbaras, *Desire and Distance: Introduction to a Phenomenology
    of Perception*
Jill Bennett, *Empathic Vision: Affect, Trauma, and Contemporary Art*
Ban Wang, *Illuminations from the Past: Trauma, Memory, and History
    in Modern China*
James Phillips, *Heidegger's Volk: Between National Socialism and Poetry*
Frank Ankersmit, *Sublime Historical Experience*
István Rév, *Retroactive Justice: Prehistory of Post-Communism*
Paola Marrati, *Genesis and Trace: Derrida Reading Husserl and Heidegger*
Krzysztof Ziarek, *The Force of Art*
Marie-José Mondzain, *Image, Icon, Economy: The Byzantine Origins
    of the Contemporary Imaginary*
Cecilia Sjöholm, *The Antigone Complex: Ethics and the Invention
    of Feminine Desire*
Jacques Derrida and Elisabeth Roudinesco, *For What Tomorrow . . . :
    A Dialogue*
Elisabeth Weber, *Questioning Judaism: Interviews by Elisabeth Weber*
Jacques Derrida and Catherine Malabou, *Counterpath: Traveling
    with Jacques Derrida*
Martin Seel, *Aesthetics of Appearing*
Nanette Salomon, *Shifting Priorities: Gender and Genre in Seventeenth-Century
    Dutch Painting*
Jacob Taubes, *The Political Theology of Paul*
Jean-Luc Marion, *The Crossing of the Visible*
Eric Michaud, *The Cult of Art in Nazi Germany*
Anne Freadman, *The Machinery of Talk: Charles Peirce and the Sign Hypothesis*
Stanley Cavell, *Emerson's Transcendental Etudes*
Stuart McLean, *The Event and Its Terrors: Ireland, Famine, Modernity*
Beate Rössler, ed., *Privacies: Philosophical Evaluations*
Bernard Faure, *Double Exposure: Cutting Across Buddhist and Western Discourses*
Alessia Ricciardi, *The Ends of Mourning: Psychoanalysis, Literature, Film*
Alain Badiou, *Saint Paul: The Foundation of Universalism*
Gil Anidjar, *The Jew, the Arab: A History of the Enemy*
Jonathan Culler and Kevin Lamb, eds., *Just Being Difficult? Academic Writing
    in the Public Arena*
Jean-Luc Nancy, *A Finite Thinking*, edited by Simon Sparks
Theodor W. Adorno, *Can One Live after Auschwitz? A Philosophical Reader*,
    edited by Rolf Tiedemann

Patricia Pisters, *The Matrix of Visual Culture: Working with Deleuze in Film Theory*
Andreas Huyssen, *Present Pasts: Urban Palimpsests and the Politics of Memory*
Talal Asad, *Formations of the Secular: Christianity, Islam, Modernity*
Dorothea von Mücke, *The Rise of the Fantastic Tale*
Marc Redfield, *The Politics of Aesthetics: Nationalism, Gender, Romanticism*
Emmanuel Levinas, *On Escape*
Dan Zahavi, *Husserl's Phenomenology*
Rodolphe Gasché, *The Idea of Form: Rethinking Kant's Aesthetics*
Michael Naas, *Taking on the Tradition: Jacques Derrida and the Legacies of Deconstruction*
Herlinde Pauer-Studer, ed., *Constructions of Practical Reason: Interviews on Moral and Political Philosophy*
Jean-Luc Marion, *Being Given That: Toward a Phenomenology of Givenness*
Theodor W. Adorno and Max Horkheimer, *Dialectic of Enlightenment*
Ian Balfour, *The Rhetoric of Romantic Prophecy*
Martin Stokhof, *World and Life as One: Ethics and Ontology in Wittgenstein's Early Thought*
Gianni Vattimo, *Nietzsche: An Introduction*
Jacques Derrida, *Negotiations: Interventions and Interviews, 1971–1998*, edited by Elizabeth Rottenberg
Brett Levinson, *The Ends of Literature: The Latin American "Boom" in the Neoliberal Marketplace*
Timothy J. Reiss, *Against Autonomy: Cultural Instruments, Mutualities, and the Fictive Imagination*
Hent de Vries and Samuel Weber, eds., *Religion and Media*
Niklas Luhmann, *Theories of Distinction: Re-Describing the Descriptions of Modernity*, edited and introduced by William Rasch
Johannes Fabian, *Anthropology with an Attitude: Critical Essays*
Michel Henry, *I Am the Truth: Toward a Philosophy of Christianity*
Gil Anidjar, *"Our Place in Al-Andalus": Kabbalah, Philosophy, Literature in Arab-Jewish Letters*
Hélène Cixous and Jacques Derrida, *Veils*
F. R. Ankersmit, *Historical Representation*
F. R. Ankersmit, *Political Representation*
Elissa Marder, *Dead Time: Temporal Disorders in the Wake of Modernity (Baudelaire and Flaubert)*
Reinhart Koselleck, *The Practice of Conceptual History: Timing History, Spacing Concepts*
Niklas Luhmann, *The Reality of the Mass Media*
Hubert Damisch, *A Theory of /Cloud/: Toward a History of Painting*
Jean-Luc Nancy, *The Speculative Remark: (One of Hegel's bon mots)*
Jean-François Lyotard, *Soundproof Room: Malraux's Anti-Aesthetics*

Jan Patočka, *Plato and Europe*
Hubert Damisch, *Skyline: The Narcissistic City*
Isabel Hoving, *In Praise of New Travelers: Reading Caribbean Migrant Women Writers*
Richard Rand, ed., *Futures: Of Jacques Derrida*
William Rasch, *Niklas Luhmann's Modernity: The Paradoxes of Differentiation*
Jacques Derrida and Anne Dufourmantelle, *Of Hospitality*
Jean-François Lyotard, *The Confession of Augustine*
Kaja Silverman, *World Spectators*
Samuel Weber, *Institution and Interpretation: Expanded Edition*
Jeffrey S. Librett, *The Rhetoric of Cultural Dialogue: Jews and Germans in the Epoch of Emancipation*
Ulrich Baer, *Remnants of Song: Trauma and the Experience of Modernity in Charles Baudelaire and Paul Celan*
Samuel C. Wheeler III, *Deconstruction as Analytic Philosophy*
David S. Ferris, *Silent Urns: Romanticism, Hellenism, Modernity*
Rodolphe Gasché, *Of Minimal Things: Studies on the Notion of Relation*
Sarah Winter, *Freud and the Institution of Psychoanalytic Knowledge*
Samuel Weber, *The Legend of Freud: Expanded Edition*
Aris Fioretos, ed., *The Solid Letter: Readings of Friedrich Hölderlin*
J. Hillis Miller / Manuel Asensi, *Black Holes / J. Hillis Miller; or, Boustrophedonic Reading*
Miryam Sas, *Fault Lines: Cultural Memory and Japanese Surrealism*
Peter Schwenger, *Fantasm and Fiction: On Textual Envisioning*
Didier Maleuvre, *Museum Memories: History, Technology, Art*
Jacques Derrida, *Monolingualism of the Other; or, The Prosthesis of Origin*
Andrew Baruch Wachtel, *Making a Nation, Breaking a Nation: Literature and Cultural Politics in Yugoslavia*
Niklas Luhmann, *Love as Passion: The Codification of Intimacy*
Mieke Bal, ed., *The Practice of Cultural Analysis: Exposing Interdisciplinary Interpretation*
Jacques Derrida and Gianni Vattimo, eds., *Religion*

The authorized representative in the EU for product safety and compliance is:
Mare Nostrum Group
B.V Doelen 72
4831 GR Breda
The Netherlands

www.ingramcontent.com/pod-product-compliance
Lightning Source LLC
Chambersburg PA
CBHW030540230426
43665CB00010B/971